ARKANA

CW00498918

THE MEANING OF FORGIVENESS

Kenneth Wapnick has a PhD in clinical psychology and has been working with *A Course in Miracles* since 1973. He was a close associate of Helen Schucman, the *Course*'s 'scribe', up until the time of her death. He teaches and lectures widely on the *Course*, as well as conducting a practice in pscyhotherapy. He is on the Board of the Foundation for Inner Peace, publishers of the *Course* in the USA, and is President and co-founder with his wife Gloria of the Foundation for *A Course in Miracles*, whose purpose is to further the understanding of the *Course* through publications, tapes, workshops and a Teaching and Healing Centre.

JESUS THE CHRIST

KENNETH WAPNICK

THE MEANING OF FORGIVENESS

THE MEETING PLACE OF
'A COURSE IN MIRACLES'
AND CHRISTIANITY

ARKANA

LONDON

First published in Great Britain in 1987 by ARKANA Paperbacks
ARKANA Paperbacks is an imprint of
Routledge & Kegan Paul Ltd
11 New Fetter Lane, London EC4P 4EE

Originally published in the USA as
'Forgiveness and Jesus'

Set in 10pt Bembo
by Columns of Reading
and printed in Great Britain
by The Guernsey Press Co. Ltd.,
Guernsey, Channel Islands.

British Library Cataloging in Publication Data
Wapnick, Kenneth
[Forgiveness and Jesus]. The meaning of
forgiveness : the meeting place of "A
Course in Miracles" and Christianity.
1. Forgiveness—Religious aspects—
Christianity
I. [Forgiveness and Jesus]   II. Title
284.4   BJ1476

ISBN 1-85063-074-7

In love and gratitude I dedicate this book to Helen Schucman and William Thetford, whose collaboration not only made A Course in Miracles *a reality, but whose example of true dedication and faithfulness to God's purpose, which they considered to be a "sacred trust," was the inspiration that made this book possible. I could never express fully enough in words the gift that their example and friendship have been for me this past decade. The Course says it best: "Love is the way I walk in gratitude."*

CONTENTS

FOREWORD

Thirteen years ago, my writing a book with this title would have been unthinkable. My marriage of five years had just broken up, with much unresolved bitterness and hurt. I was a psychologist, but with no real faith in psychology. However, with no real faith in anything else, I could only continue in my profession. I was twenty-eight years old and had no idea where my life was going. Something was wrong, but I did not know what it was. If I had looked back over those twenty-eight years, however, I might have discerned a pattern that would have clarified my situation and the direction my life was about to take.

I grew up in a Jewish home in Brooklyn, and though my parents were not truly religious there was a strong awareness of our Jewish identity. Not surprisingly, then, I was sent to a Yeshivah — a Hebrew parochial school — for my elementary education. I did not like it at all. I had many friends and did well in my English subjects, but resented learning Hebrew. For the most part, I did very poorly in that area. My parents did not force me to remain, but by the time I realized how much I disliked it I was almost near the end. I decided to complete the eight grades and then go to a public high school. When I finally left the Yeshivah, I wanted nothing more to do with the Jewish religion. Despite these negative feelings, however, the eight years had given me a solid foundation in all aspects of Judaism. We had studied the Torah — the first five books of the Old Testament —three times, and the remaining books at least once. I was well versed in all aspects of Jewish religious and cultural life, and could even think in Hebrew, not to mention read, write and speak it fluently. It was not for many years, though, that I would feel good about this education.

While a junior in high school, two developments occurred that shaped the course of my life. The first was discovering Freud. I had heard about psychoanalysis in school, and one day while in the psychology section of the library I picked up Calvin Hall's *A Freudian Primer*, a clear and succinct statement of basic psychoanalytic theory. Captivated by it,

I quickly began to devour everything I could find on the subject. I read many of Freud's major works, as well as those of the neo-Freudians. How much of it I really understood I don't know, but I did know I wanted to become a psychologist. I never questioned this decision until I was midway through my doctoral studies.

The second development was on a different level. My mother decided it would be a good idea if the family were exposed to classical music, and so she joined one of the classical record clubs. The introductory offer was the Toscanini recording of the nine Beethoven symphonies. It was love at first hearing for me, and it began a romance that was to continue for many, many years. Classical music, and especially Beethoven, opened up a world I had never known existed. It was not an outer world, but one within, beyond the normal range of my feelings and experiences. Over the years I felt myself increasingly drawn into this world, and music became the most important influence in my life. When I would hear the late music of Beethoven or the mature Mozart, I knew its depth was still beyond me, but it acted as a guide for an inner development I intuited but did not understand.

In my undergraduate years, I became distinctly aware of this inner and outer dimension. On the one hand, I was fascinated by the different psychological theories, understanding that each reflected some aspect of human behavior; on the other, I knew that none of the theories could address my experience of listening to music. These theories, in fact, seemed to have nothing to do with it. In my senior year, I attended a lecture by B. F. Skinner, the leading exponent of behaviorism and a man I greatly respected. Answering a question after his formal talk, he made the typical "Skinnerian" comment that if he were given an infant at birth, with total control over every aspect of that child's environment, he could make a Mozart. At that point in my life I did not believe in Heaven, but did know Mozart's music was not of this world and that environmental or psychological manipulation could never produce Mozart's sublimity. Strangely enough, however, despite my clear awareness of the duality between these inner and outer dimensions, I felt no conflict between them. I was quite comfortable following these two paths simultaneously.

This pattern continued into my second year of graduate school when, for the first time, I began to question what I was doing with my life. I was finding the study of psychology increasingly irrelevant to my real interest in music. However, I had no musical ability to speak of, and certainly was not interested in studying music from a theoretical point of view. Therefore, I finally resigned myself to finishing up my studies, but was now painfully aware of the inner tension between these two worlds.

The first serious attempt to integrate the two came in my dissertation, which began as a study of the spiritual dimension of Beethoven's music. However, it did not take me long to realize that this would never pass a doctoral committee. As I proceeded, I also realized that I had no real investment in the actual subject of the dissertation. My concern was only that its central idea remained; namely, that psychology tended to ignore or distort this inner dimension of human experience (this was in the 1960's). How I ended up with my ultimate subject, the 16th century mystic St. Teresa of Avila, would take another book. In retrospect, it was a most providential choice. Especially interesting to me was my strong positive identification with Teresa, at a time when I was not only not a Christian, but did not believe in God! However, even though I did not believe in Him, He certainly was around. Without God's help the dissertation could never have been completed and accepted. Thus, at the age of twenty-six, I had my Ph.D. in clinical psychology.

The next two years were difficult ones, as I struggled not very successfully to integrate these inner and outer worlds in my personal and professional life. The completion of the dissertation had strengthened my faith in this inner world, but that placed a strain on my external functioning. I went along as best I could, but my internal fear was still unknown to me. I knew only that "something" inside me needed protection, and that this concern must come before anyone or anything else. Unfortunately, it did. Two years later, in the summer of 1970, my wife and I separated (later divorced), and our one year old daughter remained with her. I moved to upstate New York and took a job in a state mental hospital.

Despite this upheaval, a marked change for the better began to occur in my life. A striking experience made it clear that this abstract inner world was far more personal than I had thought. I suddenly knew there was a God, and things began shifting into focus around this new Person in my life. I had never known such peace or happiness. There were difficult moments, to be sure, but I learned how even these could easily pass when turned over to God. Moreover, this acceptance of Him also brought with it an acceptance of Judaism. I felt God transcended the religious forms themselves, but for the first time I felt comfortable within them and grateful for the thorough Jewish education I had received.

Without any conscious awareness of what I was doing, since I was ignorant of such customs, my life became increasingly monastic in form. I lived within an ordered schedule which would have seemed ascetic to an outsider, but was pure joy for me. Nothing really mattered but God. Aside from my time at the hospital, I lived practically as a hermit. By the close of my first year I felt that music, having led me to God, had taken me as far as it could. It was no longer needed to fill the place in my life that He alone now filled.

Circumstances took a turn for the worse, however, as I found my living schedule increasingly more difficult to maintain. Thinking I was spiritually lax, I applied myself more diligently, and for a time was able to continue my basic life style. After a serious case of flu, however, I found it impossible to continue any form of spiritual activity or discipline. This state of internal disquiet remained for several months. Throughout it all, though, I never lost my faith in God. I knew that all I needed was to hold His hand and somehow He would get me through. I had read enough of the mystical literature to recognize I was going through a form of the "Dark Night of the Soul," a spiritual crisis that often foreshadows and accompanies a significant change in one's life. I had no idea what that meant specifically, which was probably good. If I had known what God had in mind for me, I would have run to hide under the bed and stayed there.

Finally, some light broke through my darkness. A series of steps led me to the books of Thomas Merton, the Trappist monk who, after a startling religious conversion, entered the Abbey of Gethsemani in Kentucky. Astonished to find that there were people actually living a life totally dedicated to God, I arranged to spend five days at this monastery later that summer. The fact that these monks were Christian never occurred to me as a problem. I knew they loved God as I did; everything else seemed unimportant.

Things began moving more rapidly now. Despite my lack of concern with Christianity, I did think it would be helpful to have some knowledge of the Catholic Church before visiting the monastery, especially since Merton had written so much about his priesthood. Therefore, I attended early morning Mass regularly in July. Much to my surprise, I had the same feelings I once had when listening to Beethoven. I knew these experiences were of God, but who would have thought I would have them in a Catholic Church?

At the end of the month, I did something I had delayed for some time. I gave away all that I owned and took a furnished room on the hospital grounds, hoping that divesting myself of possessions would magically bring me peace. Although that was not to be, I did feel good about my next step, and eagerly awaited my trip to Merton's Trappist monastery in the middle of August.

When I arrived at the monastery, I had the strangest feeling that I had come home, hardly something a Jewish boy from Brooklyn would expect to feel. I was so caught up in the monks' life that during the following morning's Mass, a special day of Mary, I decided that God wanted me to become a Catholic. Strongly associated with this was my desire to become a monk. I was not concerned by my lack of interest in either Jesus or the Church. All that mattered was my certainty that this was God's Will. I talked with some monks and this strengthened my decision. On returning to the hospital, I spoke to the Catholic chaplain and soon thereafter was baptized a Catholic.

I now felt it was time to leave my job and spend some time alone. My plan was to wait the required year, and then enter the Abbey of Gethsemani as a monk. It all seemed so clear. However, I thought I should first go to Israel, for reasons that were not all that clear. Trusting what I felt was God's direction, I left and soon found myself in the heart of the Old City of Jerusalem, unexpectedly feeling I was in the holiest place on earth. Though not yet fully identified as a Christian, I nonetheless felt something very special about the Christian holy places. Curiously enough, I also felt no less a Jew. Most importantly, I was at peace for the first time in months.

Although I was not anticipating this, I should have guessed my next stop: the Trappist monastery of Latroun, outside of Jerusalem. Thinking to spend only a week, I spent three and a half months, a time that solidified my desire to become a monk, as well as providing the opportunity to consolidate all that had happened in the preceding year. It took some catching up.

After Latroun, I spent several weeks in a more primitive monastic community called Lavra Netofa, atop a mountain overlooking the northern end of the Sea of Galilee. Content there, I postponed my immediate plans to enter the Trappists.

By the beginning of May, I thought it time I came back to the States for a brief visit, before settling into this monastic mountaintop. I was returning to repair injured relationships, especially with my family, see old friends and patients, and to look up a certain book on spiritual development that had been mentioned to me before I left. I did accomplish these things, never imagining their ramifications in my life. The summer of 1973 proved significant for three major reasons.

The first was a most necessary correction to my own personal theory of spirituality. Until this time, I believed that only by being alone could I find God. My way to Him was through the monastic life, and the more solitary the better. From the moment I left Israel, however, everything turned upside down. From a quiet, isolated existence, I found myself traveling a great deal, hardly ever alone. To my great surprise, for the first time in my life I found God to be as present when I was with people, living a "worldly" schedule, as I did when I was by myself. This was a revelation and freed me from a dependency on the monastic regimen. I realized I could be at peace anywhere, as long as I was where God desired me.

Secondly, I finally saw the book on "spiritual development," which was called *A Course in Miracles*[1]. It was the very thing for which I had unknowingly searched, for it resolved a seemingly insoluble problem. While I was never happier than when I was in the monastery, there was a thought that had always gnawed at me. I knew that becoming a psychologist had been God's idea and not my own, and that it was only through His help that I had completed school. I knew, too, that I valued my work with people and found it rewarding. Remaining a monk, however, would have meant ignoring this part of my life. That did not seem right to me, but I also did not see how psychology could be meaningfully reconciled with spirituality. The Course provided the answer, as I will discuss below, and so I once again changed my plans, deciding to remain in the United States. The monastery would be a nice place to visit, but was no longer to be my home.

Finally, came the most significant event of all. I had been a rather peculiar Christian. I found great nourishment and solace at the Christian holy places, participating in many of the religious practices and living the monastic rule which was decidedly Christian. Throughout it all, however, Jesus remained a non-entity for me. I consciously spent very little time, if any, thinking about him. Yet, during the past year or so, I had become increasingly aware of an even more personal and direct presence in my life, guiding and comforting me, providing helpful answers to my specific questions. I always identified this presence with God and never thought too much about it, other than feeling grateful for its gentleness and love. Imagine my great surprise, then, when during a visit with my Trappist friends in Kentucky that summer, I

[1]*Foundation for Inner Peace, P.O. Box 635, Tiburon, CA 94920.*

realized for the first time that this presence had a name, and its name was Jesus.

That moment of realization was truly the happiest and most joyful of my life. I suddenly knew that Jesus was more than a symbol or historical figure who lived once and then no more. He was a very real person, alive within me. I knew with a certainty that has never left, that not only was Jesus there, but that he would always be there. With that awareness, a chapter of thirty-one years came to a close. It had been a period of running away from Jesus — not recognizing who he was in my life— at the same time he was leading me to him. Now that we had at last met, we could begin our new life together and my preparation for the next stage in my journey to God.

That stage specifically involved *A Course in Miracles:* learning what it said and, even more importantly, seeking to implement its teachings on forgiveness in my personal and professional life. The Course is a set of three books, channeled from Jesus, written down over a seven year period beginning in the mid 1960's. It consists of a text, which sets forth the concepts on which the Course's thought system is based. These ideas provide the theoretical framework for the workbook, a series of three hundred and sixty-five lessons which are the practical application of the Course's principles. The manual for teachers, written in question and answer form, addresses some of the more likely questions a student might ask.

In our age of psychology and renewed interest in spirituality, the Course provides a unique blend of both worlds. It integrates the insights of psychology — particularly those of psychoanalysis — with the timeless truths of spirituality. The Course's central teaching is that the way to remember God is by undoing our guilt through forgiving others and therefore ourselves. In the healing of our relationships, our relationship with God, seemingly ruptured by the sin of separation, can be healed.

Despite the universal appeal of its message, the Course's teachings are presented within a Christian framework, and one of the more frequently asked questions regarding the Course is why this is so, with Jesus' identity as the source of the material so explicitly manifest. This has posed problems for many of the Course's students and would-be students. This group has included not only Jews who grew up midst Christian anti-semitism, but large numbers of Christians for whom Jesus has become a strong, anti-religious symbol. The answer to this question is found in the *modus operandi* of the Holy Spirit, who corrects our errors in the forms in which they appear, for forgiveness can only heal in the form in which the unforgiveness was expressed. By joining us in the world of our mistakes, the Holy Spirit gently corrects our illusions and leads us beyond them to the truth.

To even the most casual observer, it is clear that the most dominant element throughout two thousand years of Western history has been Christianity, and this influence has found its way into every major aspect of our society. Our years are numbered from the presumed birth of Jesus, and not a person, regardless of his or her religion, has failed to be influenced by Jesus and the religions that took his name. It is also apparent that Christianity has not been very Christian. Nietzsche remarked that "in truth, there was only *one* Christian, and he died on the cross," while Chesterton noted that the problem with Christianity is that "it has been found difficult and left untried."

One need not be a keen student of history, therefore, to realize that Christianity's gifts to the world have been two-edged. On the one hand, it preserved for centuries the memory and example of Jesus — the purest expression we have known of the love of God — including his gospel of forgiveness, as well as benefitting mankind with its many cultural and ethical contributions. On the other hand, Christianity has been a religion of sacrifice, guilt, persecution, murder and elitism, with Jesus its primary symbol — he whose gospel was only love, forgiveness, peace and unity. As the Course states: "Some bitter idols have been made of him who would be only brother to the world" (manual, p. 84). The development of Christianity can be seen in part as the history of a people who, though believing in Jesus and his message, often unwittingly brought tragedy instead of comfort and salvation to the world. Instead of uniting all people under God as one family, it has divided and subdivided this family. Before we can fully accept Jesus' radical message of forgiveness, which we shall discuss in Parts I and II of this book, the errors of the past must be undone. Within this context, it can be said that one of the goals of *A Course in Miracles* is to correct these mistakes of separation that entered into traditional Christian teachings, distorting Jesus' central message of God's love for *all* people, and our need to forgive each other as the means of restoring this love to our awareness.

Those who begin the Course expecting to find — for better or for worse — the Christianity they had learned and practiced, or the Christianity that seemed to condone bigotry and persecution, will be very much surprised. They will find many of the words they were familiar with — atonement, salvation, forgiveness of sins, Christ, Son of God, etc. — but with different meanings or connotations. The crucifixion remains the central event in Jesus' life, yet the Course's interpretation is 180 degrees from the traditional teaching that Jesus suffered and died for our sins. The opening sections in Chapters 3 and 6 in the Course specifically address this issue, which is taken up in Chapters 8 and 9 in this book.

In the Course, Jesus states: "All your past except its beauty is gone, and nothing is left but a blessing. I have saved all your kindnesses and every loving thought you ever had. I have purified them of the errors that hid their light, and kept them for you in their own perfect radiance" (text, p. 76). We can extend this same principle to the Course's purification of Christianity's errors while at the same time it retains its kindnesses and loving thoughts. In this sense, we can see *A Course in Miracles* as an extensive commentary on the Sermon on the Mount, perhaps the clearest distillation of what Jesus' teachings must have been, and whose principles of forgiveness are so perfectly exemplified in his own life. The Course helps us understand what these principles are, why Jesus made them the cornerstone of his gospel, and why he chose the crucifixion as the form in which he taught that our sins are forgiven.

Before we can transcend the separatisms of religion and know our oneness in God, the religions of the world must be purified of their errors. *A Course in Miracles* has been given to the world as one means of such purification. This book, therefore, seeks to elaborate on this purpose of the Course by presenting many of the teachings of Christianity in the light of the principles that the Course sets forth. The book is in four parts. The first discusses these principles, focusing on the dynamics of the ego and its undoing through forgiveness, including a discussion of the application of these principles to specific problems and issues. This presentation is made within a psychological and spiritual context, though not specific to any one religious faith. The second part relates the principles of forgiveness to the New Testament teachings, including the importance of Jesus' own life, death and resurrection, and the misunderstandings of his message. It is hoped that this part of the book will be of interest to Christians and non-Christians alike, serving to make the person and teachings of Jesus even more relevant to us in the modern age in which we live. The third part discusses the meaning of apostleship, and what it means to be in the world but not of it. The final part of the book focuses on the person of Jesus, and the importance he holds in our lives today.

ACKNOWLEDGMENTS

I am grateful to many people who read and commented on early forms of this manuscript. These included William Thetford, Doris Yokelson, Srs. Miriam Francis Perlewitz and Joan Metzner. Their comments and suggestions were most helpful in the book's evolution. I am especially grateful to Thomas Thompson, who faithfully read through the completed manuscript with a critical eye; to Anita Pierleoni and Evelyn Smith who graciously typed it; to Grace Longo, who assisted in the proof-reading and compilation of the Scriptural Index; and to my wife Gloria, whose astute suggestions and loving dedication to maintaining the purity of Jesus' message helped to shape the final version.

I would like to acknowledge my indebtedness to the insights of Joachim Jeremias, most specifically as found in *The Parables of Jesus*, SCM Press, Ltd., London. Although I have not quoted directly from Prof. Jeremias' work, much of my discussion in Part II, especially as related to the parables of Jesus, is based upon his remarkable and inspiring scholarship. Responsibility for the parallels to *A Course in Miracles*, however, remains my own.

The frontispiece portrait of "Jesus the Christ" is by Howard Chandler Christy, a famous American portrait painter who, shortly before his death, was granted his life's wish of having a vision of Jesus, which he then painted. I am grateful to Dr. Michael Marchetta and his wife Patience for graciously providing a slide of a print of the original picture, from which the book's frontispiece was made. To date I have been unable to locate the original portrait.

NOTE TO REVISED EDITION

Since the first printing of this book, Gloria and I were finally able to locate and see the original painting, which is owned by Abingdon Press and is stored at the United Methodist Publishing House in Nashville, Tennessee. The painting dates from 1944, about eight years before Christy's death. Though it is unclear whether it was his "life's wish" to have a vision of Jesus, the recollection of the retired President and Publisher of United Methodist was that Christy had had a dream of Jesus, which he then painted. An American flyer who had just returned from overseas served as the model for the portrait.

A 19" x 25" full color print of the original painting is available for $10; 8" x 10" for $4.50. Order from: The Universariun Foundation, Inc.; P.O. Box 890; Taylor, AZ 85939.

PART I: PRINCIPLES OF "A COURSE IN MIRACLES"

INTRODUCTION

At first glance, psychology and spirituality would seem to make unlikely bedfellows. For the first fifty years of this century, since the time of Freud's first published writings, psychology and religion have not been very friendly enemies. Religion, and rightly so, was suspicious of psychology's strong tendency to reduce *all* human behavior and experience to unconscious sexual forces (psychoanalysis), or to dismiss any experience as fundamentally irrelevant if it did not obey certain empirically validated laws and could not itself be observed and measured (behaviorism). Religionists were often quick to dismiss a psychology that reflected the values of a materialistic and secular culture, seeing it as the work of the devil and designed to explain away their faith or even destroy it.

This mistrustful and even hostile relationship began to shift dramatically during the 1960's, from both sides. In psychology, the seeds of change that were sown in many post-war writers began to bear fruit in the emergence of what Maslow termed the "Third Force" (to distinguish it from psychoanalysis and behaviorism). This grouping encompassed theorists like Jung, Rogers, and the existential and humanistic psychologists. The focus shifted to a more respectful view of our creative and spiritual strivings, placing greater emphasis on the present moment and evolving future as contrasted to seeing people imprisoned in the chains of their past. In fact, a "fourth force" has recently been described — transpersonal psychology —which seeks to explore the Self that is beyond our personal self through meditation, biofeedback training, drug experimentation, etc. As a result, humanistic and transpersonal psychologists have looked increasingly to spirituality as a guiding force for their investigations. Interestingly enough, to a great extent these endeavors have focused more on the east than the west, using techniques and teachers (gurus) from predominantly Hindu or Buddhist orientations, not to mention secular ones, as opposed to those from our own Judaeo-Christian heritage.

Accompanying this notable change in the psychological

attitude towards religious experience has been a similar shift on the part of religious institutions, as seen particularly in the Catholic Church since Vatican II. In the incredibly short period of time that followed that great Council, the doors closed to change burst open. As the newer forms of psychology were gaining popularity, the Church's desire to become more accessible to the secular world and receptive to the needs of its members directed it to its former adversary. This was seen most especially in the area of interpersonal relationships, where psychological insights and techniques were of great value.

Despite this rapprochement, however, the fact remains that psychology and spirituality *are* different. They emphasize different levels of experience because their foundations rest on mutually exclusive premises. Yet it is in that difference that psychology's value to spirituality is found. Psychology can teach us nothing about the spiritual life, but it *can* teach us a great deal about our personal self, what we call the "ego,"[1] which interferes with our relationship with God.

It is ironic that Freud's brilliant analysis of the psyche's functioning can be used to enhance one's spiritual growth. Throughout his life, Freud relentlessly pursued the idea that all religious experience and belief were neurotic at best and psychotic at worst, being *nothing but* projections of repressed infantile conflicts. His own theory, however, would teach us that one never strives so hard *against* something unless one were correspondingly attracted to it, even if that attraction remained out of awareness. One might conclude that Freud's whole theoretical system was designed, on one level, to defend against the "threat" he felt from his own powerful spirituality. Thus, he strove to believe that the material world was the only reality, and so his thought system became the veil behind which the life of the spirit lay hidden. Given a different purpose, however, Freud's systematized description of the dynamics of the ego can serve as a

[1]*Throughout the book, "ego" will be used as synonymous with our false self, somewhat similiar to Jung's concepts of "persona" and "shadow." It thus differs from the conventional psychoanalytic usage, where the ego is but one aspect of the tri-partite psyche. In the terminology adopted here, the ego would be roughly equivalent to this psyche, different from our spiritual Self which lies beyond it.*

powerful tool to release ourselves from the imprisonment of guilt and fear, the ego's major weapons in its war against God. Moreover, it is fair to say that without Freud there would not have been *A Course in Miracles*. Therefore, though not able to help us understand the God we seek, psychology may be extremely helpful in removing the barriers that interfere with our movement towards Him. It can become an important means that God uses to lead us closer to the ultimate truth about who we really are and who He, our Creator, is.

Chapter 1

THE DYNAMICS OF THE EGO

The World of Guilt: Two Levels

Although psychologists may differ in their understanding of its etiology, dynamics or descriptive terms, practically all would agree that the central life issue confronting people is the problem of guilt. Associated with our experience of ourselves as physical and psychological beings, guilt may be variously described as self-hatred and self-doubt, a gnawing awareness of inferiority and insecurity, feelings of incompletion, unfulfillment, lack, and a belief in one's personal failure before oneself, others and God.

Each of us is more than familiar with feeling guilty over things in our past. The history of our individual lives can be seen, from this point of view, to be a litany to our guilt over what we have done or not done, said or not said, thought or not thought. We feel guilty because we picked on a younger sibling, were caught stealing candy from the neighborhood store, cut school to go fishing or watch a baseball game, or were punished by the teacher for talking in class or not doing homework. As adults we feel guilty for being unkind to someone in need, having lost our temper, cheating on income taxes, not being faithful to the commandments, failing to perform prescribed religious rituals, or for harboring sexual feelings towards people forbidden by standards of morality.

The list is endless, yet despite the pain such memories and experiences leave in their wake, they are merely the tip of the iceberg. These specific instances for which we feel guilty reflect a much deeper and more generalized experience of unworthiness and inadequacy. Just as the greater bulk of the iceberg lies beneath the surface of the sea, so does this experience of guilt lie beneath the surface line that divides our conscious from our unconscious minds. It is a feeling so deeply-rooted that we believe there is no way we could be free of it; for not even God Himself would have the power or desire to redeem us from this permanent burden of guilt.

Where does the guilt come from? The Course's explanation for the ultimate origin of our guilt provides a larger metaphysical context for the psychological principles we are discussing, without which the basic meaning of guilt and its undoing through forgiveness could not be understood. It therefore warrants discussion before we continue.

Guilt arises from sin, which the Course defines at one point as lack of love (text, p. 9), the post-separation condition. Sin is the *belief* that we can and have indeed separated ourselves from our Creator, who *is* love. In this sense, the Course's view would be equivalent to the Judaeo-Christian understanding of original sin, when the thought of separation crept into the mind of God's Son. It is the seeming reality of the separation which makes the ego or false self that stands in opposition to the Self which God created one with Him. Guilt tells us we have sinned, and therefore it establishes sin's reality. The ego, which *is* this belief in a separated Self, now protects itself by projecting this original thought of separation, giving rise to a world of form that seems to exist apart from the split mind that thought it. As the Course states:

> *You do not realize the magnitude of that one error* [*of separation*]. *It was so vast and so completely incredible that from it a world of total unreality had to emerge. What else could come of it? . . .* [*The world*] *was the first projection of error outward. The world arose to hide it* [*the error of separation*], *and became the screen on which it was projected and drawn between you and the truth (text, p. 348).*

This world of separation is a world of bodies, which become literally the embodiments of the ego, symbolizing the sin of separation or attack on God for which we feel guilty. It is for this reason the Course states that "the world was made as an attack on God" (workbook, p. 403). In reality, therefore, the material world is as inherently illusory as the thought of separation that gave it birth. The Course teaches that ideas do not leave their source. Our experience to the contrary, the world exists only as an idea in our split mind, which is not the Mind that God created. Therefore, the separated world, too, cannot have been created by God, and does not truly exist.

Furthermore, the world of separation is a world of scarcity, conflict, suffering and death, in distinct contrast to God's world of abundance, peace and eternal life. Ours is a world of opposites, contrast and change; Heaven is unified and changeless. The Course elaborates:

> *The world you see is the delusional system of those made mad by guilt. Look carefully at this world, and you will realize that this is so. For this world is the symbol of punishment, and all the laws that seem to govern it are the laws of death. Children are born into it through pain and in pain. Their growth is attended by suffering, and they learn of sorrow and separation and death. Their minds seem to be trapped in their brain, and its powers to decline if their bodies are hurt. They seem to love, yet they desert and are deserted. They appear to lose what they love, perhaps the most insane belief of all. And their bodies wither and gasp and are laid in the ground, and are no more. Not one of them but has thought that God is cruel (text, p. 220).*

Even what brings us pleasure in this world is not what it seems: "While you believe it [the body] can give you pleasure, you will also believe that it can bring you pain" (text, p. 384). Objects of pleasure will bring us pain for two principal reasons: their absence, once we have become dependent on them, will be experienced as lack and deprivation, and therefore painful; secondly, when we experience anything in the material world as being a source of pleasure, believing its presence is essential to our well-being, we are giving it a power and reality it does not truly have, denying the power and reality that God or spirit *does* have. By using the world as a substitute for the role God alone should have in our lives, our belief in the separation from God is reinforced, and it is this that gave rise to the world of suffering and pain in the first place. As the Course says: "All real pleasure comes from doing God's Will" (text, p. 12). We shall return to this issue when we discuss special relationships.

We can observe this same principle of pleasure equaling pain in the world of nature. What we see and admire as beauty can also wreak havoc and catastrophe. The warmth of the sun that sustains life gives off scorching heat that can kill. The gentle rain nourishing our soil, when in excess, leads to floods that ravage towns and villages. Rain's prolonged absence, on the other hand, causes droughts that deprive us of the sustenance its presence has provided.

We admire the beauties and wondrous delicacies of nature. Yet within this same world we perceive competition and destructiveness. Majestic trees are felled by swarms of ants or termites. At the same time their branches arch to the heavens in verdant bloom, trees' roots strangle neighboring roots seeking *their* rightful soil. Animals prey upon each other, stalking the wilds to capitalize on another's vulnerability or carelessness. Tennessee Williams has given us a searing portrait of this underside to nature in his play, "Suddenly Last Summer." It is a description of a beach in the Galapagos Islands where:

> *the great sea-turtles crawl up out of the sea for their annual egg-laying. . . . Once a year the female of the sea-turtle crawls up out of the equatorial sea onto the blazing sand-beach of a volcanic island to dig a pit in the sand and deposit her eggs there. It's a long and dreadful thing, the depositing of the eggs in the sand-pits, and when it's finished the exhausted female turtle crawls back to the sea half-dead. She never sees her offspring. . . .* [*Meanwhile*] *the sky* [*is*] *in motion, too. . . . Full of flesh-eating birds and the noise of the birds, the horrible savage cries of the —carnivorous birds . . . as the just hatched sea-turtles scrambled out of the sand-pits and started their race to the sea . . . to escape the flesh-eating birds that made the sky almost as black as the beach! And the sand all alive, as the hatched sea-turtles made their dash for the sea, while the*

> *birds hovered and swooped to attack and hovered and — swooped to attack! They were diving down on the hatched sea-turtles, turning them over to expose their soft undersides, tearing the undersides open and rending and eating their flesh. . . . Only a hundredth of one per cent of their number would escape to the sea.*[1]

This ambivalence in the world of nature reflects our experience of this world, leading the Course to state that "no love in this world is without this ambivalence . . ." (text, p. 55).

The Course, therefore, can be understood on two levels, each reflecting a different emphasis in how we approach the world and the body.[2] The first level embraces this larger metaphysical context we have been describing. Here, the world is seen as illusory, having no existence beyond the mind that thought it. The guilt that arises from this mistaken belief is shared by all people and is inherent to living in a body, the symbol of this ego belief. All our personal experiences of sin, guilt and fear find their root in this deepest layer of our unconscious, buried beneath the layers of defense the ego has used to protect itself.

The second level relates to this world where we believe we are. Here, the world and body, though illusory, are neutral ("My body is a wholly neutral thing," workbook, p. 435), and can serve either the ego's purpose or God's. This level is the principal focus of this book, for it is here that forgiveness is directly applicable. By forgiving the layers of guilt in our personal lives, we are able finally to undo the original error of guilt upon which rests not only our personal world of pain and suffering, but the whole phenomenal world as well.

Sin, Guilt and Fear

We return now to the world of guilt which is part of our personal experience. Accompanying these guilt feelings of abject failure and self-deprecation are those of being utterly

[1] *New Directions, New York, 1958, pp. 19f.*
[2] *See my* Glossary-Index for "A Course in Miracles," *Foundation for "A Course in Miracles," New York, 1982, pp. 2-4.*

helpless in a world that threatens this weakened and damaged image of our self. We can appreciate this experience by looking at the beginnings of human life. Freud and the psychoanalysts have contributed greatly to our understanding of how far back in our lives these feelings of deprivation, bodily mutilation and worthlessness do actually go. In fact, the analyst Otto Rank placed great emphasis in his early work on the significance of the birth trauma in the etiology of all neurosis.

Until the moment of birth, the fetus has little or no awareness of itself as a separate being. It does not desire, since its basic physiological needs are instantly met. In many respects, life in the womb is similar to the state of paradise described in the second chapter of Genesis where Adam wanted for nothing, all having been given by God, reflecting what the Course refers to as the principle of abundance. In a state without lack there can be no sense of separation or "otherness." Scripture says of Adam and Eve before the Fall: they stood naked but "felt no shame in front of each other" (Gn 2:25). There was no shame (or guilt) for they had not yet committed the act of separation. This pre-separation state can be somewhat likened to the fetus' life, at one with its mother and at one with its world.

At birth all this is changed. In an action analogous to the expulsion from the Garden of Eden, the infant is suddenly expelled from its paradise into a world of separation. For the first time, it becomes painfully aware of having needs which are not immediately met, and sometimes are not met at all. This traumatic experience of separation, which guilt encompasses, leaves us feeling vulnerable and inadequate to meet our needs. The terror this induces remains with us, on some level, throughout our life. The real source of the "birth trauma," however, lies in its reminder of the original separation, which is the root of all guilt and fear.

Our bodies, which come to symbolize this state of separation, thus also symbolize the guilt of our sinfulness, and this results in the shame associated with our person and with certain bodily functions. One sees in our culture the strong reactions against this shame in the attempts to deny our self-disgust by making the body attractive. The huge success of the cosmetic industry is the result of this reaction. When we identify with our physical selves, the pain our bodies inevitably undergo thus unconsciously becomes the punishment we believe is deserved for our sinfulness. A vicious circle is established: the body's fragility witnesses to our sinfulness, which causes us to identify with the body even more strongly as we feel the need to protect it or make it attractive.

The normal developmental process, from birth to death, consists of learning to cope with the harsh realities of a separated life in a world experienced as hostile and threatening. We all more or less adjust to it, but it is an adjustment to a situation that at its core is one of terror lest our defenses break down, thrusting us back upon our feelings of helpless inadequacy.

Each of us evolves our own particular form of defensive adaptation to the world, learning to survive by taking various precautionary steps to ensure our physical and psychological safety and comfort. Such survival concerns are inevitable once we identify with this separated self of the ego, and they form the central theme of the ego's world.

Guilt, then, is an all-pervasive sense of alienation, isolation and helplessness that remains with us from the moment of birth to our death. It reminds us that we are helpless and vulnerable creatures who walk in terror midst a world that threatens to attack and even annihilate us at any moment. Guilt therefore includes not only those things we have done or said that we believe were wrong ("I feel guilty because I did such-and-such"), but an all-pervasive sense of *being* wrong. Thus, the antecedent condition of guilt is the belief there is something inherently unfit or sinful about us, a state for which we must always feel guilty and which the ego tells us can never be undone.

Once we feel guilty, it is equally impossible not to feel deserving of punishment for what we have done wrong, and to fear the form this punishment will take. All fear has its origin in guilt over the separation. Believing we have attacked our Creator by opposing Him, we must also believe that He is justified in attacking us in return. Guilt demands no less than this punishment at the hands of an avenging Father.

The dynamic is summarized this way in the Course:

> *[The thought of] separation from God . . . states, in the clearest form possible, that the mind which believes it has a separate will that can oppose the Will of God, also believes it can succeed. That this can hardly be a fact is obvious. Yet that it can be believed as fact is equally obvious. And herein lies the birthplace of guilt. Who usurps the place of God and takes it for himself now has a deadly "enemy." And he must stand alone in his protection, and make himself a shield to keep him safe from fury that can never be abated, and vengeance that can never be satisfied (manual, p. 43).*

The key to understanding this otherwise inexplicable passage lies in the concept of the unconscious which carries on a nightmarish life, seemingly independent of our conscious experience. Our fear, therefore, regardless of its seeming source in the world, begins with this unconscious belief in sin which demands that punishment will be forthcoming *because* we deserve it, whether the punishing agent is experienced as a parent, teacher, superior, or even God Himself. On the more impersonal level, the punishing agent can be the government, religious institutions, or world conditions in general. None of this has to do with external reality as it is but with our perceptions of it, and may or may not be reinforced by other people or circumstances. There is no way to avoid this fear once guilt has been accepted into our minds. The belief in our guilt unconsciously leads us to expect reprisal, and so we walk this earth in constant fear, believing that tragedy or catastrophe stalks our every step.

In summary, we may understand this dynamic of sin, guilt and fear as a unity. The belief in our inherent wrongness or *sinfulness* leads to our experience of *guilt* over who we are; and this leads us to *fear* the punishment we believe we deserve and will receive. This unholy trinity is truly a psychological hell and constitutes the ego. It is the separated self with which we identify, and consequently on which we base our beliefs, judgments, and perceptions. The world that arises from this self is a world of terror from which there seems to be no escape.

This relationship among sin, guilt and fear is clearly depicted in the third chapter of Genesis. We have already discussed the paradisal existence in the Garden prior to the Fall, where there was no experience of separation between creation and Creator. No needs existed and there was only the peace and joy of being in God's kingdom, united with all creation.

In the Fall, Adam and Eve sinned against God by disobeying His command not to eat of the tree of the knowledge of good and evil. Immediately upon eating the fruit of the forbidden tree, "the eyes of both of them were opened and they realized they were naked. So they sewed fig leaves together to make themselves loincloths" (Gn 3:7). They realized they had done something wrong and were ashamed. Following this, "they hid from . . . God among the trees of the garden" (Gn 3:8), since they feared what He might do in retaliation for their sin.

Thus, our answer to the oneness of God's creation is the birth of the separated ego, the dream of sin and guilt that culminates in the fear of what God would do in punishment for our sin. And indeed, the Genesis story continues the ego's dream by describing the punishment which God does inflict upon Adam and Eve, that through their disobedience to God in eating from the forbidden fruit, affirming a will separated from their Creator's, there came into being a life of suffering, pain and death:

> *Because you have done this . . . I will multiply your pains in childbearing; you shall give birth to your children in pain. . . . Because you . . . ate from the tree of which I had forbidden you to eat, accursed be the soil because of you. With suffering shall you get your food from it every day of your life. . . . With sweat on your brow shall you eat your bread, until you return to the soil as you were taken from it. For dust you are and to dust you shall return (Gn 3:14, 16, 17, 19).*

Through the action of his separate will— the ego— the creature whom God created in His own image and likeness (Gn 1:26), which being of spirit could never die (Ws 2:23), seemed to lose its likeness to the Creator and forfeit its immortality. Our true life in God— that original and eternal state of oneness with Him and with all creation— disappeared from our experience. Its place was taken by the world of the ego— the symbol of the separation— and its characteristics of guilt, fear, attack and pain. This is the world we made, and it is manifest in the very first incident described in Genesis after the expulsion from the Garden. The story of Cain and Abel (Chapter 4) is a tragedy of deprivation, jealousy, anger and ultimately murder; the exact opposite of the world of abundance, love and eternal life that God created, our true inheritance as Heaven's children.

Denial and Projection

The ego's existence is based on guilt and fear since they reinforce the sin of separation, and it must maintain them if it will continue to be. Therefore, it must ensure that we do not get too close to guilt, for then we would begin to question the ultimate reality of our separation from God. The ego teaches that the guilt would make us fearful and, indeed, the closer we come to the guilt in ourselves, the greater is our fear. The ego interprets this for us as the fear of God: that God will strike us dead because of our sinfulness. In Exodus, God tells His servant Moses that he cannot look upon His face, "for man cannot see me and live" (Ex 33:20), reflecting the ego's fear. We may speak similarly of our guilt, which is so horrifying that we believe we would be struck dead if we ever looked upon it. Always confusing God's Voice with its own, the ego would have us believe such avoidance is a divine imperative which we must obey, otherwise God Himself would punish us or, spared that fate, we would disappear into the oblivion of our own nothingness.

Therefore, according to the ego, it is best we keep our distance and never approach this basic guilt, always needing to defend against it. What the ego does not tell us is that the fear is its own. As we approach the guilt, we are also approaching the One who stands behind it, and it is this Divine Presence the ego fears. As the Course states: "Thoughts of God are unacceptable to the ego, because they clearly point to the nonexistence of the ego itself" (text p. 59). Yet there must be some solution to this problem of guilt, otherwise the fear and anxiety it generates would be too overwhelming for us to bear. And the ego does provide us with an answer. Despite its dependence on guilt for its existence, the ego offers us a means whereby we *seem* to be free of it and protected from the terror it induces in us. If the ego did not provide us with this assurance, we would never give it our allegiance. As the Course describes the ego's tactics:

> *The ego always tries to preserve conflict* [*guilt*]. *It is very ingenious in devising ways that seem to diminish conflict, because it does not want you to find conflict so intolerable that you will insist on giving it up. The ego therefore tries to persuade you that it can free you of conflict, lest you give the ego up and free yourself (text p. 120).*

In the midst of the terror over expected retaliation for our sins, reinforced by overwhelming guilt, the ego calls to us, saying: "Turn to me and I will free you from this terrible burden of your guilty self. Your fear will disappear and you will find safety and peace." Since the ego has already excluded God from the role of savior by virtue of our fear of Him, in desperation we have no recourse except to turn to the ego for help and to accept its version of salvation.

To help us deal with the overwhelming experience of our guilt, the ego employs two basic dynamics: denial or repression,[1] and projection. These dynamics are what Freud called defense mechanisms—the psychological devices we use to defend against the dangers we perceive—and is perhaps the area where he made his greatest contribution.

The ego's first response to our guilt is to deny it is even there. "Push it out of awareness," it tells us, "and then it won't bother you." Our guilt is so horrifying, therefore, we try simply to blot it from awareness, pretending that it did not exist. The popular saying "to sweep something under the carpet" expresses this principle of denial. If something is upsetting and we do not choose to deal with it in a way that would effectively resolve the problem, we dispose of it in

[1]*As the Course only uses the word "denial," we shall maintain that usage, although its meaning in the Course is virtually synonymous with repression.*

ostrich-like fashion by pretending it is not there. The maladaptive nature of this way of dealing with problems is quite clear, since the problem does not magically disappear simply because we have chosen not to look at it.

We should never underestimate the power of denial, however, for it can cause us to overlook the very obvious. A woman guilty over a certain expenditure may search endlessly for the bill which is right under her nose; a man zealously pursuing his career may totally overlook the effect of his psychological and physical absence on his wife and children whom he loves; religious fanatics have often failed to recognize the glaring inconsistency of persecuting or waging "holy wars" against those who disagreed with them, all done in the name of a God of love and peace.

Despite this power, denial will not suffice as a defense since somewhere we are painfully aware that the problem is still with us. Again the ego comes to our rescue, and this time with a solution that from its point of view works remarkably well. This tactic, known as projection, constitutes the most effective weapon in the ego's arsenal. If denial does not get rid of the guilt, the ego counsels, our next step is clear. Let us be rid of the guilt entirely by taking the problem from ourselves and placing it in someone or in something else. We literally, then, hurl the problem away from us. In this manner, not only has the guilt been pushed out of awareness, it has been placed outside us as well. And so, the ego convinces us, we have satisfactorily dealt with the problem. Our guilt is no longer experienced as being ours but has been projected onto agents outside of ourselves, who thus become the guilty parties. *They* are now responsibile for the terrible things that befall us, for which *they* must be punished. All the while, we innocently sneak out of the back door, free from all conscious sense of guilt or wrongdoing.

Thus, the ego's defense against our undesired guilt, once it has made it real in our minds, is a two-stage process: we deny the problem and then project it onto others, seeing it there rather than in ourselves. In three discrete passages, the Course describes the process in this way:

> *Defenses are not unintentional, nor are they made without awareness. They are secret, magic wands*

> *you wave when truth appears to threaten what you would believe. They seem to be unconscious but because of the rapidity with which you choose to use them. In that second, even less, in which the choice is made, you recognize exactly what you would attempt to do, and then proceed to think that it is done . . . [This] plan requires that you must forget you made it, so it seems to be external to your own intent; a happening beyond your state of mind . . . (workbook p. 250).*
>
> *[In this way] the ego seeks to "resolve" its problems, not at their source, but where they were not made. And thus it seeks to guarantee there will be no solution (text, pp. 331f).*
>
> *By doing this unconsciously, you try to keep the fact that you attacked yourself [by identifying with the ego] out of awareness, and thus imagine that you have made yourself safe (text, p. 89).*

To the ego, the specific object or form of the projection is irrelevant. Its only concern is that the person or situation chosen serve its purpose of being a repository for the projected guilt. This will always remain the ego's sole purpose: to convince us it has gotten rid of the guilt, while in reality it has merely pushed it underground where it is "safely" protected by denial and projection, no longer accessible to the threat of being raised to question and thus undone.

The ego's projection of guilt has two principal forms: special hate and special love relationships. The basic dynamics remain the same in both, yet the forms of expression are quite different. It should be noted that although we can and often do form special relationships with objects or situations — e.g., work, religious, social or political institutions, various forms of addiction — the most important of the ego's projections involve people, and this will be the focus of our discussion here.

Special Hate Relationships

In the special hate relationship, the responsibility for one's own misery and unhappiness is shifted to another. Under the ego's guidance we are taught to say: "It is not I who am guilty or the cause of my unhappy situation, but you who have done these terrible things to me." An "if only" orientation is thus established: if only my parents had been different, if only my spouse were more understanding, if only the government or Church were more liberal (or conservative) — if only something outside myself were changed, then I would be happy. This ego tactic nicely serves its goal of shifting the problem to where it can never be resolved: outside of us. As the workbook states:

> *The ego's plan for salvation centers around holding grievances. It maintains that, if someone else spoke or acted differently, if some external circumstance or event were changed, you would be saved. Thus, the source of salvation is constantly perceived as outside yourself. Each grievance you hold is a declaration, and an assertion in which you believe, that says, "If this were different, I would be saved" (workbook, p. 120).*

Once the person or situation has been selected who meets the requirements of the projection, it becomes imperative to demonstrate to ourselves and others this "guilty one." This is done through our anger which is an attempt to justify the projection of our guilt.

> *Anger always involves projection of separation, which must ultimately be accepted as one's own responsibility, rather than being blamed on others. Anger cannot occur unless you believe that you have been attacked, that your attack is justified in return, and that you are in no way responsible for it (text, p. 84).*

Since the ego's plan is to maintain our belief in the projection in order to be "free" of guilt, it will stop at nothing to reinforce the choice of the guilty party. All manner of evidence — real or imagined — is gathered for this purpose. Our anger — totally justified in our mind —says to the person: "Look at the terrible things you have done to me, how through your own doing I have suffered. Look at your sins and feel guilty . . . for that is how I am made free of my own."

Chapter 16 in Leviticus gives an almost literal description of the projection of guilt, a procedure which placed the word "scapegoat" in our vocabulary. On the Day of Atonement (Yom Kippur), the purification of the children of Israel was to be accomplished through two ritual acts: the intercession of the high priest who performed certain ritualistic sacrifices in the sanctuary, followed by the selection of a goat, on which "Aaron [the priest] must lay his hands on its head and confess all the faults of the sons of Israel . . . and the goat will bear all their faults away with it and into a desert place" (Lv 16:21f). The sins of the people have thus been transferred to (projected onto) the goat who is driven away, symbolically acting out the ego's maladaptive method of absolving us from our sins.

Familiar examples of this process abound in our everyday experience: the person who is chewed out by his boss and made to feel inferior and inadequate returns home in the evening and yells at his children, accusing them of the very faults found in himself; the great baseball star who after striking out in a critical moment returns to the bench and angrily kicks the water cooler in self-disgust; the lazy student who did not study fails the final exam and rails at her teacher for unfairly giving such a difficult test. In the story of Adam and Eve, when God confronts the two sinners with what they have done, Adam places the blame on Eve, who in turn transfers it to the serpent (Gn 3:12f).

Historically, we see the same dynamic in the lives of dictators and oppressors, who seek to compensate for their own perceived inadequacies and inferiorities by persecuting and even seeking to destroy those judged to be inferior. People who unconsciously believe they are damned have often sought to damn others, even in God's name. Finally, many countries pursuing imperialistic policies will justify their own actions by accusing other nations of doing the exact same thing, even forming alliances with other imperialist countries to strengthen their anti-imperialistic position.

However, while the ego is telling us that anger and attack will rid us of our guilt, it silently has the last laugh. Projection, while seeming to deliver us from guilt, in reality reinforces it. Placing guilt onto others, in whatever form it takes, must always involve attack. Somewhere inside us, the ego's words to the contrary, we know we are attacking falsely, for the true problem does not lie in others but only in ourselves. "Yet projection will always hurt you. It reinforces your belief in your own split mind, and its only purpose is to keep the separation going. It is solely a device of the ego to make you feel different from your brothers and separated from them" (text, p. 89). While on one level it is true that we are all affected by the world around us, it is also true that we are responsible for our own reactions *to* the world and to what happens to us. As the Course asks us to say to ourselves:

> *I am responsible for what I see.*
> *I choose the feelings I experience, and I decide upon the goal I would achieve.*
> *And everything that seems to happen to me*
> *I ask for, and receive as I have asked*
> *(text, p. 418).*

Our guilt, rather than being transferred to someone else, merely becomes strengthened due to our unfair attacks on another. This sets into motion a most vicious cycle of guilt-attack. The guiltier we feel, the greater will be our need to deny and project it out by attack; the more we attack, the guiltier we will feel. And the cycle continues. This seemingly unending process is antithetical to the popular saying. It is not love that makes the world go round but guilt.

This cycle of guilt and attack uncovers the ego's fundamental purpose, which it seeks always to conceal from us. The ego's plan for our "salvation" is first to convince us of our guilt, and then provide a means of escaping from it. Its true goal, however, is to retain guilt, for that alone sustains our belief in the ego, the symbol of the separation from God which is the foundation of the ego's very existence.

The ego's "secret plan" is what is responsible for the almost universal phenomenon found throughout history, not to mention in the personal lives of practically everyone: the tremendous investment in anger, leading to the need for a We–They orientation wherein someone must be found to fit the role of "villain," which we then justify by our variable standards of morality. Herein lies the great attraction of prejudice and discrimination. It is the reason we join in large public outcries condemning those who commit certain crimes, or judge public officials who are caught in illegal or unethical activities. In all these instances, we are really choosing to see and attack our unconscious sins in these scapegoats.

This same need to divide the world into black and white is what underlies the sense of relief, joy and triumph when we watch a movie where in the end the "good guys" win and the "bad guys" lose. It is also behind the tremendous over-identification we make with sports heroes, movie stars, or world and spiritual leaders, opposing them to their corresponding villains. It should be stated that while people obviously do not always do things they should, and others justifiably deserve our admiration, the focus here is on our *need* to see them that way, not the people in and of themselves. The 1980 winter Olympics provided Americans with a clear example of this process of identification. People who had no interest in hockey, and probably could not tell a puck from a basketball, a blue line from a red line, became instant enthusiasts as the newspapers reported the United States underdogs defeating the heavily favored Russian hockey team. Whether they were conscious of this or not, most Americans experienced this as good triumphing over evil.

In 1938, Americans had a similar experience, with some interesting twists. Racial discrimination was legally tolerated in this country, and prejudice against Negroes was clearly manifest. Yet all Americans, white and black, northern and southern, rallied around the black boxer Joe Louis (nicknamed the "Brown Bomber") — seventeen years before the historic Supreme Court desegregation decision! — as he pummeled the German Max Schmeling in a match that was headlined: "Joe Louis knocks out Hitler." Thus, a white racist paradoxically came to embrace the hated black against the German he hated even more. Prejudice makes strange bedfellows indeed. An even stranger twist was that the Nazi philosophy agreed with the racist position that Blacks were inferior. Here, however, the political prejudices outweighed the racial ones, and so the American racist ended up identifying with the American black against the German racist. Ironically, Schmeling himself never truly identified with Hitler's Nazism, and he and his wife had to speak continually to this issue after the war. The ego, however, is never concerned with facts, but merely its interpretation of the facts that suits its purpose.

Our ego's need to have an enemy is clearly seen in wartime, when we luxuriate and feel justified in hating this enemy. Countries rally around themselves, uniting as one people against the common opposition. A science-fiction story whose title and author I have forgotten illustrates this process.

The United States and Russia are a hair's breath away from nuclear war, and there seems no hope of averting the catastrophe that would destroy the whole world. Suddenly an even greater threat appears: an invasion from outer space seems imminent. Unless Earth acts immediately, its destruction would be certain. The two super-powers have no recourse but to join together, for only in their common effort can the invaders be overcome. They ultimately succeed and the planet is saved. The story has a surprise ending, however, for in reality there was no invasion at all. A greater Power, seeing the catastrophe about to befall Earth, created the illusion of the attack from outer space to unite the two enemies. It planned that, through their cooperation, they would learn mutual trust and come to know each other as friends.

The history of 20th century India reflects the same ego principle of joining against a common enemy, though unhappily with a different outcome. For decades, the Hindus and Moslems fought side by side against their shared enemy, Great Britain. When, under Gandhi's leadership, they finally succeeded in getting the British to leave in 1947, the Hindus and Moslems almost immediately began fighting with each other. Their egos demanded an enemy, and since it could no longer be the British they each served the other's need very well. As always within the ego's system, nothing had changed except the faces.

The perception of a We–They world reflects our own internal split, as the ego pits itself against our spiritual Self and God. This split is projected onto the world where we attack the "enemy" outside rather than see it in ourselves.

Though it is often couched in socially acceptable forms, our need to find scapegoats to hate is overwhelming. It is frightening to observe our rationalizations for anger. The history of religious and political persecution has provided ample witness to the hidden hate that has been concealed behind the language of love and peace. The explanation for such seemingly incomprehensible behavior lies not in the inherent evil or sinfulness of these people, but in their unawareness of the guilt that had been successfully denied and projected. We who live in a more psychologically sophisticated age should not be tempted to look smugly on these periods of horror with a "holier-than-thou" attitude, but rather should look at our own list of horrors – the nuclear arms race, the Holocaust, super-power conflict, discrimination, political persecutions and torture – and forgive ourselves for our illusions and mistakes.

Logically following from the guilt–attack cycle, and no less vicious in its outcome, is the culmination of the We-They mentality: the attack–defense cycle. This admirably serves the ego's purpose as it keeps the guilt securely intact beneath the battleground. We have seen how fear must necessarily follow guilt, as we unconsciously believe we are to be punished for our sins. Having projected our guilt onto others by attacking them and making attack real, we believe they will do the same to us, unconsciously believing that their attack is fully justified by our unfair actions. Expecting them to attack in kind, we will build defenses against what we seek to convince ourselves is a totally unjustified assault on our innocence. The more we defend our innocence, believing on another level that we are guilty, the more we reinforce our guilt, fanning the flames of this circle. When we find a partner in this ego insanity, then our guilt and fear reinforce each other's, and we continually attack in self-defense. It makes no difference whether the other party actually attacks or not. We unconsciously believe they will because our own guilt has made us vulnerable and fearful of retaliation. Thus, we remain on guard lest the enemy, seen to be outside, will assault us.

> *It is as if a circle held it fast, wherein another circle bound it and another one in that, until escape no*

> *longer can be hoped for nor obtained. Attack, defense; defense, attack, become the circles of the hours and the days that bind the mind in heavy bands of steel with iron overlaid, returning but to start again. There seems to be no break nor ending in the ever-tightening grip of the imprisonment upon the mind (workbook, p. 277).*

All the while the true enemy lies safely hidden within. As one of the characters in Walt Kelly's comic strip, "Pogo," exclaims: "We have met the enemy, and it is us'n."

The current nuclear arms build-up presents a glaring picture of how far this form of insanity can take us. The nations involved continually build up defensive systems, far beyond the realm of reason, out of fear of what other nations might do. The threats of attack reinforce other nations' fears who then must defend themselves, with the same effect. The result is a spiral of fear which seems to have no human resolution other than global destruction.

Special Love Relationships

There is probably no more insidious device in the ego's plan to save us from our guilt than special love, for it cleverly seems to be something it is not, concealing what it truly offers. There is usually no mistaking special hate relationships, but the hate concealed in special love is not easily seen, and so the guilt beneath the hate has a double protection. The Course states: "The special (love) relationship has the most imposing and deceptive frame of all the defenses the ego uses. Its thought system is offered here, surrounded by a frame so heavy and so elaborate that the picture is almost obliterated by its imposing structure" (text, p. 335).

We have seen that some of guilt's characteristics included a belief there is something lacking in us that could never be filled, an incompleteness that would remain forever beyond hope of wholeness. This is what the Course refers to as the scarcity principle. Guilt tells us that it is our justified fate to remain empty and vulnerable, at the mercy of a hostile and threatening world. As a result, we come to say to ourselves: "I can no longer tolerate how unworthy I feel. The pain of dealing with my utter failing in life is overwhelming, and the anxiety and terror it arouses is too great for me to bear."

This is the moment the ego has been waiting for. Having first convinced us of the truth of our guilt, it is now in the position to be our savior from it. Desperate in our terror, we eagerly grasp at the thin straws the ego holds out to us, and these straws inevitably come in the form of relationships. The ego says: "If this is how terrible you feel inside, without hope of your guilt ever being undone, let us find the answer outside." The Course states it thus: "No one who comes here but must still have hope, some lingering illusion, or some dream that there is something outside of himself that will bring happiness and peace to him" (text, p. 573).

Following the ego's direction, then, we embark on an endless search to find completion and satisfaction external to ourselves. The solace we cannot find in the inner morass of our sin, guilt and fear, we shall find in other people. The process follows this basic formula: "There are certain special needs or lacks I have that cannot be met within myself or by God, and without which I cannot find peace or happiness. But you, a special person with special characteristics and qualities, can meet my needs. In you I find my completion, and your love, support and approval prove to me I am worthwhile and not the wretched creature I believe myself to be."

It makes no difference to the ego who specifically fills this place in the formula. Those who fulfill this function of completion are those we love. And when we are able to reciprocate, fulfilling unmet special needs in them, we have the ego's version of "a marriage made in Heaven," the mutual sharing of needs that the world often mistakes for real love. As it is described in the Course: "The 'better' self the ego seeks is always one that is more special. And whoever seems to possess a special self is 'loved' for what can be taken from him. Where both partners see this special self in each other, the ego sees 'a union made in Heaven'" (text, p. 318). A closer look at these partnerships, however, shows them as they truly are: relationships made in hell. They are based not on love and genuine sharing but on sin and guilt, with fear being its primary motivation. They are a contract sealed in blood, however unconsciously the deal is made: "As long as you, my special love, continue to act so my needs are met and I can avoid my own guilt, I will love you and will reciprocate, helping you avoid your pain by fulfilling your special needs. But Heaven help you if you should change, or no longer fulfill your part in the agreement." It is this last sentence that belies the "love," and reveals the hate lurking underneath it, a projection of the hatred we feel for ourselves.

If, from the ego's point of view, the value we have given others is the capacity to shield us from our guilt, it becomes imperative for our peace of mind that they continue to fulfill that role. The smallest deviation from the arrangement threatens us with the breakthrough of the terror we have sought to conceal. We must do everything within our power that they return to their original position as protectors of our fear. This is done by the ego's weapon par excellence: manipulation through guilt. We attempt to make our special love partners guilty of no longer caring for us so they will stop their sinful actions, as we have judged them, and once again fulfill their role as saviors from our guilt. It now becomes their fault we feel so bad and stand in terror before this image of ourselves.

This is the basis for the jealousy and possessiveness that characterize special love relationships, and the meaning of the well-known saying: "Two's company; three's a crowd." Since we have placed our hopes for salvation on this one special person, attention devoted elsewhere is taken away from us. If love is shared we have less of it, and so this love must be jealously guarded and protected lest someone else's gain becomes our loss. The exclusive nature of special love contrasts with the sharing of real love, which is all-inclusive and needs no protection.

Thus, we see the special hate relationship revealed beneath the facade of love; the familiar projection of guilt. This shift from love to hate through manipulating guilt is well known as the "Jewish Mother syndrome," although its presence is hardly restricted to those of Jewish extraction or to mothers.

Feeling inadequate themselves, no longer receiving from each other the support and love they once enjoyed, parents often will turn to their children to meet their special needs, to give their lives the meaning and purpose they feel is lacking. Thus, they over-invest in their children who become, as it were, extensions of themselves, on whom they depend for their value and worth. If the children deviate from parental expectations, the parents' own inadequacies become exposed, which they must defend at any cost. The inevitable price paid is the imposition of guilt on the children, wherein is found the notoriety of the possessive parents' syndrome: "How could you do this to us? Is this the way to repay us for all the love we have given and the sacrifices we have made for you? Why can't you be as you once were — kind, thoughtful, selfless, sensitive, loving, caring and good?"

If the children return to the original "arrangement" of meeting their parents' needs, then the hate reverts to "love" and all remains as before. If the break is maintained, however, the bond will continue, but the cementing force will have shifted from love to hate, and the center of the parents' lives will be the ingratitude of their children. Similarly, their parents' insensitivity and lack of understanding become the childrens' substitutes for the special love they once received as reward for being "good." From the ego's point of view, then, nothing has really changed and it blesses both forms of specialness. The symbols of love trade off with those of hate, while the guilt underneath remains safe from exposure. When the imposition does not work — i.e., the person does not change — then the ego has no recourse than to throw the person overboard and find another. "Another can be found" (workbook, p. 319), the Course teaches, as the ego "embarks on an endless, unrewarding chain of special relationships" (text, p. 295). The rapidity with which love turns to hate when the honeymoon period ends can be even more clearly understood with two added factors of how special love reinforces guilt.

If the other person's meaning in a special love relationship is to shield us from our guilt, then that person inevitably will become a symbol of this self-hatred. Without this meaning, the ego would have no purpose for the relationship, and so we could not even think of this person without unconsciously associating our own inadequacy, incompleteness and special need. At the same time our conscious minds are thanking God for sending us this wonderful gift which means salvation to us, and we are filled with thoughts of peace, love and well-being when we are with or even think of this special person, our unconscious minds are silently reminding us of our guilt which established the need for this relationship. Thus, we see proof of the well-known psychological principle that dependency breeds contempt. We end up attacking and hating precisely those on whom we depend for help, for it is the contempt we have for ourselves that is called to mind in the other. Furthermore, our need for special love demands we keep constant vigilance lest the other stray from the "straight and narrow," at which point our love, as we have seen, quickly turns to hate. Our "beloved," then, ends up being nothing more than an added reinforcer of our guilt, rather than the deliverer from it. This illustrates the important principle stated in the Course: " . . . all defenses *do* what they would defend" (text, p. 334). Designed to protect us from our guilt and fear, defenses merely reinforce them, bringing about the very thing the ego tells us it is protecting us *from*.

Finally, there is perhaps the most basic source of guilt in these special relationships: using others to meet our own needs. The ego is totally indiscriminate and brutally insensitive to the welfare of those it uses to serve its purposes. From the view of the ego, our only interest in people is how they fulfill its hidden purpose of perpetuating guilt through projection. Our interest and involvement with others is not due to genuine concern for them as people, attracted by the light of Heaven that shines from them, but rather by their special qualities which match up with our own special needs. Once these qualities are gone and we have found, in Hamlet's phrase, "metal more attractive," we throw them overboard and move on to greener pastures. This misuse of others as instruments simply to meet our own needs cannot help but increase our guilt, impelling us still further to "protect" ourselves through additional special relationships. This is why the Course describes the special relationship as the home of guilt.

It is this "impersonal" quality that enables the symbols

of special hate and special love to alternate with such startling rapidity, as was seen, for example, at the close of World War II. The American ally, the Soviet Union, became the enemy in the Cold War that almost immediately followed, while the enemy, Japan, became a trusted ally, as did West Germany. Enemy soldiers have experienced this dynamic when circumstances suddenly place them together. Dropping their role of seeking to destroy each other, two men may suddenly find that they have more in common than otherwise. They are both afraid, angry, lonely and resentful, and in their shared situation they find the enemy has become their brother. When "tempted to attack a brother and perceive in him the symbol of your fear," the Course urges that we should remember the gift that is offered us, "and you will see him suddenly transformed from enemy to savior; from the devil into Christ" (workbook, p. 299).

This sudden shift was seen in an unusual way in the old Brooklyn Dodger baseball fans. For many Brooklynites, the center of their world was the Dodgers, and this special love relationship was intensified by the hatred felt for the rivals across the river, the New York Giants. These feelings ran very deep, so much so that once an argument in a bar over the respective merits of the two teams ended in one man fatally shooting the other. In the 1950's, the Giants had a pitcher, Sal Maglie, who was a particular nemesis to the Dodgers. Not only did he always seem to be at his best against them, but he pitched with a real vengeance. He was nicknamed the "Barber" because of the "close shaves" he gave opposing batters when he threw the ball dangerously close to their heads. His name in Brooklyn was anathema. Imagine the state of disbelief and confusion, then, when Maglie was traded to the Dodgers. The problem for Dodger fans was obvious. However, due to the ego's inherent lack of interest in the person, Brooklynites were able to make this shift from hate to love with startling ease. After a few days it was as if Maglie had always been a Dodger. When later in the pennant race he pitched a no-hitter, he was practically canonized a Brooklyn saint.

We can summarize the meaning of the special relationship in considering a glass jar, about one quarter filled with instant coffee grinds. The jar represents our self-concept, or how the ego views us, while the coffee symbolizes our guilt, which the ego has convinced us is our fundamental reality.

The ego teaches us to avoid this guilt at all costs, otherwise we would be overwhelmed and destroyed. Thus, we deny or repress our self-hatred, pushing the coffee to the jar's bottom which represents our unconscious. Once we have accepted the ego's ideas as true, we are committed to keeping our guilt denied and at the bottom of the jar. What maintains the success of our denial is a secure lid, which now becomes the function of our special relationships. As long as we are in specialness, the guilt we project onto others is "safely" buried in our minds. The special partners — whether hate or love — remain our lid as long as they play the game of guilt. When they do not, the lid on our jar begins to unscrew. The guilt rises in our awareness and we panic as the ego has taught us to. Still within the ego's system, we have no recourse but to have the lid be screwed on tight once again, manipulating the special partner through guilt. If this fails, we must throw the lid away, finding another who can now fulfill that function for us.

The Ego's Use of the Past

The ego attempts to justify its projections in special relationships by distorting perception, seeing people only in terms of the past and making them into what it wants them to be. Our experience to the contrary, perception is a relative phenomenon. It does not reflect a constant or absolute picture of the world around us — the seeming facts of the material universe — but rather perception is an *interpretation* of the world in which we live, which becomes, in effect, an unreal world. Thus the Course states: "Perception always involves some misuse of mind, because it brings the mind into areas of uncertainty" (text, p. 38). Moreover, "Perception is a continual process of accepting and rejecting, organizing and reorganizing, shifting and changing" (text, p. 41).

Physiological psychologists have demonstrated how our perceptions are distorted and limited by the very structure of our sensory apparatus. Dogs, for example, can hear sounds that remain inaudible to us. Our sense of smell is not nearly as developed as in other animals that must rely on this sense for survival. In vision, parallel lines will seem to meet at some distant point, as do the sea and sky at the horizon, the basic principles of geometry notwithstanding; and we all learn very early in our lives to correct for the literally upside-down image of the external world that is cast upon our retinas. More important for our purposes, however, are the psychological distortions we introduce into our perceptions. In this area, Freud was the first to show systematically that the world we experience is not the way it seems; that our perceptions and theoretical understanding of reality are affected and even drastically distorted by unresolved problems that are *not even within our awareness*. These hidden complexes are projected onto the world, acting as a filter through which we see. Thus, our perceptions often can reflect our unconscious needs and fears.

For example, people lost in a desert may, out of their need for water, imagine they see an oasis and may even think they hear the sound of running water. A frightened child in the dark may "see" ghosts or dragons attacking him. Finally, the presence of intense guilt may actually induce suffering people to believe that whispering voices are speaking about them, or that someone walking behind them is spying.

This basic process of our needs affecting our perceptions is at work all the time, both in normal, everyday situations as well as abnormal ones. We continually interpret the information brought us by our sensory organs, and these interpretations of necessity are based on past experience. Without the past, in fact, we could not perceive, for we would have no basis for organizing and understanding the multitudes of sensory stimuli that come to us. Without my past experience of a cup, for example, I would not know if it could hold my tea, let alone what it was. Furthermore, my need to drink would limit my perception to the cup's utilitarian function; a potter would look at the same object differently. Similarly, a bowl of fruit would appear one way to a hungry person, and quite another to a Cezanne, in whose vision it is transformed into a creative melange of color, shape and relationship. The classic Japanese movie "Rashomon" explored this area of perceptual distortions, wherein a rape and the husband's death are presented from the differing points of view of the rapist, wife, husband (through a medium), and a wood gatherer. It is as if one were observing a totally different event in each case.

The process of projection making perception is a basic law of the mind: what we see within determines what we see without. This process determines how we perceive the world and how we react to it. We first look inside then project onto the world what we have seen. While we cannot avoid projecting, the results will depend largely on the use we wish to make of it. Thus, the Course distinguishes between two types of "projection": One is called "extension," referring to extending the love of God that is accepted within. The other is an "inappropriate use of extension, or projection, [and] occurs when you believe that some emptiness or lack exists in you, and that you can fill it with your own ideas instead of truth" (text, p. 14). The ego's purpose is always to distort the present reality of a situation so as to project guilt or lack, and justify its attack. Since its goal is to maintain guilt, which has meaning only in terms of what *has* happened, it teaches us to overlook the present by approaching all situations from the perspective of the past, which contains our sins. The ego holds these sins against us through guilt, and it is thus protected from the correction that can only come in the present.

We can see how this operates in special relationships. In special hate relationships, the hated persons' past mistakes are used to justify our attack. All mistakes, however slight, are marshalled to the fore to build the case against them. Not one shred of evidence is overlooked by the ego to sustain the guilty verdict it has already made. In these relationships, people are unconsciously chosen because of their vulnerabilities so that their past can be used to justify the projection, overlooking whatever present reality there might be to change the verdict to not guilty. The Course refers to these special hate partners as "shadows of the past," which

> *represent the evil that you think was done to you. You bring them with you only that you may*

> *return evil for evil, hoping that their witness will enable you to think guiltily of another and not harm yourself. . . . The shadow figures always speak for vengeance. . . . This is why . . . whatever reminds you of your past grievances attracts you, and seems to go by the name of love, no matter how distorted the associations by which you arrive at the connection may be (text, p. 330).*

In special love relationships, it is our own sins of the past that are most remembered, that they may find absolution in someone else more holy than we. Needs that have not been met in the past but are still clung to are now capable of fulfillment in the love or concern of another. Thus, a man who still needs and wants a mother's love and protection is likely to be attracted to a woman who needs to mother and protect a man.

The ego's strong need to hold on to guilt, continually reinforcing it, is served by the principle known as "self-fulfilling prophecy." Here our worst fears, stemming from our guilt which "deservedly" merits attack and punishment, are often realized and brought about *by* fear, though we are unaware of the role we have played in the disastrous result. The ego has successfully "engineered" the outcome, while we believe it has been brought on by forces beyond our control. For example, an unfounded rumor that a certain bank is no longer solvent begins to spread. As a result, the depositors start to withdraw their money, eventually bringing about a real bank failure. A parent convinced that a child will not be able to function successfully in the world may continually protect and baby him, so much so that the son grows up to be a "Mama's boy," totally fearful of being on his own, lacking confidence in his ability to live as a "man."

Much the same process occurs when we perceive the present in terms of the past. Because people have responded in particular ways before, or situations have evolved along a certain well-defined pattern, we expect the same to occur in the present. In fact, our expectations can lead to behavior on our part that does bring this about. This is well illustrated by a story told by the popular comedian, Danny Thomas:

A man driving down a deserted country road late at

night gets a flat tire, and discovers to his horror that he does not have a jack. Lost in the middle of nowhere he is beside himself until he remembers having passed a farmhouse several miles back. He has no choice but to set out on foot to borrow a jack from the farmer. As he makes his way, not even sure how far he has to walk, he turns over and over in his mind what might happen: there may be no one home; the farmer does not have a jack; or worse still, the farmer may be so incensed at having himself and his family awakened in the middle of the night he will slam the door in the man's face. It is this last possibility the man latches onto. As he draws nearer the house, he has convinced himself of the farmer's refusal to help him. In turn, he himself becomes outraged at the farmer's lack of decency and human kindness, and by the time he reaches the front door has worked himself into a self-righteous fury at what he now believes will be the farmer's response. He knocks on the door, and after a few short minutes the farmer appears. Before he even has a chance to speak, the man screams in the farmer's face: "Keep your lousy jack!" And he storms off.

In the story, the man had projected his own fears of the situation onto the farmer, making them real in his own mind. By reacting to his projections as if they *were* real, they became real and brought on the very thing he dreaded most: not getting a jack. This dynamic is a common one, where we often cause the very situations that make us miserable and unhappy but are not aware of our part in the process.

While certain habit-patterns are obviously necessary for our adaptation to the physical universe — imagine, for example, having to check each step as we walk down a flight of stairs — they become maladaptive when, in relating to the world on a psychological level, we become rigid, fearful, and content to remain with "how things always were," reluctant to make changes in ourselves or to be open to the possibility of change in others. By this unwillingness to consider a shift in our perceptions, the past becomes projected into the future and the present is denied. Thus it is that our projections give us a distorted view of reality, and make it impossible to see ourselves or others as they truly are. We perceive, then, through the filter of our own needs and desires, making others into the images and likenesses we wish them to be.

That people assigned to the roles of special hate (the enemy) or special love (the savior-idol) are not what they seem is delightfully portrayed in the famous film, "The Wizard of Oz." The hated Wicked Witch of the West who fills Dorothy and her friends with such dread is nothing more than a bar of green soap, which melts once boiling water is poured on top of it. The great and wonderful Wizard, the object of awe and veneration, ends up to be a meek, little man in front of an amplifying system surrounded by all sorts of supernatural effects. The characters in Oz, of course, are part of Dorothy's dream. But so are the characters in our ego's dream. We people it with projected images of our own guilt and fear, and then forget we made them up. Thus, the objects of our special relationships assume a proportion they do not really have. When we are in the dream, however, we believe they are real and we act accordingly, moving the figures about like chess pieces to meet our needs at any particular time. Once we pour the waters of truth over their seeming reality, the illusory image or idol disappears "into the nothingness from which it came . . . "(manual, p. 32).

Summary

The ego's foundation is based on sin, guilt and fear. Our belief that we are inherently sinful, a state of separation and alienation that seems beyond correction from Heaven or earth, causes us to experience guilt over what we believe we have done and even more basically, who we believe we are. Due to this sense of basic wrongness and wrongdoing, we will fear the punishment we are sure is forthcoming as our just desserts. We are seemingly helpless in the face of the basic anxiety and terror that inevitably accompany the belief in our own guilt.

The ego offers us a way out of our dilemma, at the same time that it reinforces it. It convinces us that the way to be free from guilt is to project it onto others. We do this in two principal ways: either by making other people guilty for our sinfulness, a projection justified by our anger (special hate relationships), or by denying our incompleteness through finding completion in someone else, sustaining this arrangement by manipulating guilt (special love relationships). Both forms, however, do what they would defend against. Ostensibly seen as ways of avoiding fear by getting rid of our guilt, these special relationships actually reinforce it, and the resultant fear continues to drive the whole process further from awareness, making it impossible to undo. In this way, the ego maintains its hold over us.

Chapter 2

THE MEANING OF FORGIVENESS

The Holy Spirit

The defensive web the ego has woven around itself, with fear reinforcing fear, seems to make guilt forever safe from healing. It is so heavily concealed behind the ego's protective devices, of which the special relationship is the most highly developed, that it is virtually impossible to deal directly with our own guilt. Since we are the ones who made guilt, and then made a world which protects it by our identification with the world, we cannot be the ones to remove this guilt. We need help from outside the ego's system, much as a man sinking in quicksand needs someone on solid ground, outside the quicksand, to reach in and pull him out. This help is God, who sends His Holy Spirit into our world to lead us out of it.

At the instant the separation seemed to occur, God created the Holy Spirit, who is described as "the communication link between God the Father and His separated Sons" (text, p. 88). The Holy Spirit represents the principle of the Atonement, which undoes the ego by healing the belief in the reality of the separation. This is the error called sin, but which God knows never truly happened. "Ideas leave not their source" (text, p. 515): We are an idea in the Mind of God, and what comes from God can never leave Him. Through the Holy Spirit, placed in our separated minds by God, the connection with our Creator remains inviolate. If we remain joined with God through His Spirit, we cannot be separate from Him. Thus is the separation undone in the same instant it seemed to occur:

> *Yet separation is but empty space, enclosing nothing, doing nothing, and as unsubstantial as the empty place between the ripples that a ship has made in passing by. And covered just as fast, as water rushes in to close the gap, and as the waves in joining cover it. Where is the gap between the*

waves when they have joined, and covered up the space which seemed to keep them separate for a little while? (text, p. 554).

Therefore the Holy Spirit, the Voice for God, is the part of God that extends into the ego world. Joining with us there, He helps us forget the ego's lessons and remember God's single truth that we remain as He created us: one with Him and all creation. Forgiveness is the Holy Spirit's great teaching aid in bringing about this undoing, and is the substitute for the ego's use of relationships. "In crucifixion is redemption laid" (text, p. 518), the Course states, for in the very place of our sickness — the destructiveness of our special relationships — God has placed the seed of healing. This seed is forgiveness, blessed by the waters of love the Holy Spirit brings to us from God.

The Holy Spirit's Purpose of Relationships

The guilt we project onto others is the same guilt we nurture within ourselves. If we imagine ourselves as a movie projector, our guilt is the film continually running through the machinery of our mind. The people that move across this screen in front of us are seen filtered through this projected guilt. Those personal attributes we find the most objectionable we will see somewhere else and attack, rather than admit our true feelings about ourselves. For example, an overweight person may find obesity in others a source of real disgust; or a quick-tempered parent may become furious over reports of child abuse. However, it is not always the specific form of behavior in another with which we identify, but its underlying meaning. Thus, a woman enraged over her husband's drinking is not necessarily reacting to a latent tendency towards alcoholism in herself, but rather to her spouse's attempts to avoid certain personal problems through his drinking, which mirrors her defense of running away from problems, albeit in different forms. People who are withholding or self-centered in their relationships may become judgmental of those who advocate freer governmental spending to benefit the poor, seeing in them a condemnation of their own believed emotional miserliness.

Forgiveness of others, therefore, actually constitutes

forgiveness of ourselves, for it is our own guilt we see in them. We are not truly forgiving other people for what they have thought or done; we are forgiving ourselves for what *we* have thought or done. This process constitutes a reversal of projection by undoing the error of blaming others for our mistakes in thought or deed. Thus, if we had not first projected our guilt by judgment and attack, there would be no reason to forgive. Since projection must always follow guilt, the guiltless have nothing to forgive for they see no projected guilt or sin around them. God's forgiveness is really another way of expressing His unending love and mercy; a love, as the Course points out, that does not forgive since it has never condemned (workbook, p. 73). Our prayer asking God to forgive us is thus a prayer for ourselves to forgive; that we be open to accept the love of God which our guilt obstructs, becoming free to love others as He has loved us.

Typically, every human relationship in its inception is a special relationship, for the ego always speaks first and speaks of separation. Its sole purpose for all relationships, regardless of their form, is to project guilt. But what we have projected onto others remains within us: "Ideas leave not their source." Unlike the material things of this world, thoughts are not diminished by their sharing. This holds for thoughts of God as well as those of the ego. The Course teaches: "If you share a physical possession, you do divide its ownership. If you share an idea, however, you do not lessen it. All of it is still yours although all of it has been given away" (text, p. 67). The more love we extend to others the more we receive in return, for the Source of love has never left us: "Ideas leave not their source." In giving love we make love real for us, and thus remember it is within. The same principle holds for guilt and fear. The more we "give it away" the more we reinforce its presence in ourselves. Thus, the guilt we have projected onto others does not leave. As long as we sustain the projection, believing it to be real, we are maintaining its hold over us.

We have seen that we cannot be rid of our guilt by dealing with it directly or wishing it away, yet through the opportunities for forgiveness offered us in our relationships it can be undone. Because of its direct association with the ego, one is inclined to think of special relationships in a pejorative sense. However, these relationships become holy when their original purpose of preserving guilt is changed to forgiveness; when a person we hated or held grievances against becomes someone we forgive and love. As the Course says, in what could be taken as a definition of the miracle: "The holiest of all the spots on earth is where an ancient hatred has become a present love (text, p. 522)." Completing this process of forgiveness is the purpose of our special function:

> *Such is the Holy Spirit's kind perception of specialness; His use of what you made, to heal instead of harm. To each He gives a special function in salvation he alone can fill; a part for only him. Nor is the plan complete until he finds his special function, and fulfills the part assigned to him . . . . And by this act of special faithfulness to one perceived as other than himself, he learns the gift was given to himself, and so they must be one . . . . The specialness he chose to hurt himself did God appoint to be the means for his salvation, from the very instant that the choice was made. His special sin was made his special grace. His special hate became his special love (text, p. 493).*

"There are no accidents in salvation" (manual, p. 6), and all people drawn into our lives, the more intimate and the most casual, are part of the curriculum planned for undoing our guilt. Each of us is both teacher and pupil, for we all have come to learn the Holy Spirit's lesson of forgiveness. These lessons are taught in the classroom of our relationships, which are reinterpreted for us by our Teacher. Thus, "the pupil [and teacher] comes at the right time to the right place" (manual, p. 4). Each and every person we meet offers us the opportunity of choosing between projection or forgiveness, separation or union. "When you meet anyone, remember it is a holy encounter. . . . Whenever two Sons of God meet, they are given another chance at salvation" (text, p. 132). We find people coming into our lives who present us with the strongest temptation to project our own needs, to form either special hate or special love relationships. At the very same moment the ego sees its opportunity to project, the Holy Spirit speaks to us as well, gently urging that we look at this person through His eyes. We are asked to shift our perception from projecting the dictates of the ego —guilt—to extending the love and peace of God. By choosing to look differently at this person, forgiving what we have condemned by going beyond appearances to "the light that shines . . . in perfect constancy" (text, p. 622), we are making the same choice for ourselves. In this way, the unholiness of the special relationship is transformed by the Holy Spirit into a holy relationship, fulfilling our function of forgiveness which will free us from our guilt.

The Process of Forgiveness: Three Steps

The process of forgiveness essentially consists of three steps that lead us from our egos back to God.

1) The first entails the recognition that what we have attacked and judged against in another is indeed what we have condemned in ourselves. This is the first step in reversing the process of projection and undoing its effects. As long as we maintain the problem is not in us but in someone else, our attention will have been successfully diverted from the source of the problem. The ego fixes our attention away from the guilt and, by convincing us that it is not inside us, we devote our attention to correcting the problem where it is not. All projection has this as its aim: to be a distraction or smoke screen that we may never look within to where the problem truly is. Thus the Course states the ego's dictum: "Seek and do *not* find" (text, p. 208).

If we think of the coffee grinds in the special relationship jar as representing the belief in our own sinfulness or guilt, the ego's goal is to keep us from ever approaching them. We either confront, as we have seen, the terror of oblivion and nothingness, or else the awesome spectre of a wrathful God waiting to annihilate us. Thus, by denying the guilt, we hope magically to escape the anxiety it engenders. What the ego does not reveal, of course, is that beyond the guilt is the God who is always with us, and whose loving Presence dispels the ego's fearful world which is based on separation from Him. This love is the proof that the ego's premises are mistaken.

The ego, therefore, seeks always to keep us from approaching our guilt, and it offers many seductions, both in positive and negative forms, to distract us from becoming too close to it. Following the ego's guidance, we continually seek lids for the jar, and these searches constitute the various life problems and involvements — both large or small —that serve to keep us from the fundamental life problem of undoing the separation and returning to God. The Course elaborates on this ego ploy:

> *Everyone in this world seems to have his own special problems. Yet they are all the same, and must be recognized as one if the one solution that solves them all is to be accepted. Who can see that a problem has been solved if he thinks the problem is something else? . . . That is the position in which you find yourself now. . . . The temptation to regard problems as many is the temptation to keep the problem of separation unsolved. The world seems to present you with a vast number of problems, each requiring a different answer . . . [Yet] all this complexity is but a desperate attempt not to recognize the problem, and therefore not to let it be resolved (workbook, p. 139).*

As a prominent aspect of the ego's distraction attempts is the past, so an essential element in forgiveness must be releasing the past: to forgive and forget. The ego tenaciously holds on to past mistakes, using them against the attacked person, saying, "I will never let you forget what you did to me. May your sin remain forever before your eyes as a damning witness to your guilt."

By seeing only past sins, the ego overlooks the person's present reality where God is made manifest. It is impossible to forgive and *not* forget. Just as light and darkness cannot co-exist, neither can forgiveness and guilt. If forgiveness is to be real, the other's past must be forgotten. Regardless of the seeming justifications for it, holding on to what *has* happened can only be a defense against the peace and love that *is* happening now, but must remain hidden in the darkened shadows of the past.

The first step, therefore, questions the reality of the smokescreen so we may realize the problem is not elsewhere. The guilt is our own. We recognize it is not the other who needs to be changed, but ourselves. In this step we say: "The problem that I see is one I made up. It has no reality beyond my belief in it. It is my interpretation that has caused my loss of peace, and thus it is my interpretation that must be changed."

While this step does not resolve the problem of our guilt, it at least leads us closer to its resolution. By maintaining the problem is outside, and thus its solution as well, we are fulfilling the ego's purpose of keeping the problem from God's Answer, the Holy Spirit He placed within our mind to correct the mistaken thought of separation. By withdrawing our belief in the projection, we have taken the first step towards allowing God to speak to us from within, where He is. We sometimes see this process at work in dreams, as in the following example where an ego dream masked the message of the Holy Spirit.

A man dreamt he was back in college, taking a program he was close to failing. The dream concluded with a stern, older woman informing him that he was too far behind in his work. There was no recourse but that he would flunk out of school. The dream offered no solution and the man awoke, paralyzed with fear. It was suggested to him that perhaps there was a way out of the dream's problem; in fact, there might be another dream behind this one which would present a solution to him. Despite his fear and overriding sense of failure, he gave the idea some thought and began to meditate, trying to set aside his ego's way of looking at the situation. After a while, he fell into a twilight sleep in which he dreamt of a second woman, more kindly and understanding than the first, who presented a viable way he could meet the requirements of the course and go on to complete his education. By withdrawing his investment in the ego's dream he opened himself to the possibility of receiving the Holy Spirit's. This time he awoke feeling at peace, confident in himself once more.

Another example of the ego's use of distraction involved a man about to enter his analyst's office. For reasons of which he was totally unaware, he removed his shoe. Since feet are often seen in psychoanalysis as important sexual symbols, he and his analyst spent a great deal of time trying to understand the significance of his action. No explanation seemed to account for it, and it was not until much later the analyst realized her patient had unconsciously set up this shoe incident to distract their attention from a problem he was reluctant to discuss.

Bringing the problem to the answer is thus the burden of this first step. It is recognizing that our projected anger is a decision we had made to avoid our guilt by seeing it in someone else, and is now a decision we wish to change.

2) The second step entails our understanding that the guilt, too, represents a decision, and one that can now be changed. The shift is not something we can do by ourselves, but it must be something we want. This can be our choice.

Our guilt is not God's gift to us. It comes from a mistaken belief about who we are and who our Creator is. Its correction is the key step in our healing, and it ultimately rests on how we experience God and our relationship to Him. Guilt, as we have seen, cannot be separated from the belief that there is something inherently wrong with us and that nothing but punishment is deserved due to our reprehensible nature. From this constellation of sin, guilt and fear, experiencing God as a loving and forgiving Father is psychologically impossible. There is no way we can hold to this ego view of ourselves and at the same time feel assured of God's loving Presence in us. Love must wait behind the veils of guilt and hate, just as peace cannot be experienced where there is fear and conflict.

In this second step, we must begin to look at this relationship differently. Examining the underlying premises of the ego's thought system lets us see how impossible they are if God is truly a God of love. Mutually exclusive premises cannot be maintained without perpetual conflict. If we believe our identity is the ego, we must also believe that God is not love for He must punish us for our attack on Him. Love and forgiveness have no place in the ego's world.

The ego's system is heavily secured by this belief in the wrath of God, which may at any moment descend upon our guilty heads. In fact, most threatening of all to the ego is the idea that God does *not* condemn us, that He loves us with an everlasting love. To believe a God of love can change into a God of hate, and therefore fear, is to attribute to Him the ego's use of projection and attack. This insane idea constitutes the third law of chaos, which is described this way in the Course:

> *God . . . must accept his Son's belief in what he is, and hate him for it. See how the fear of God is reinforced by this. . . . Now it becomes impossible to turn to Him for help in misery. For now He has become the "enemy" Who caused it, to Whom appeal is useless. . . . Atonement thus becomes a myth, and vengeance, not forgiveness, is the Will of God (text, p. 456).*

God, through His Holy Spirit, reaches down to us in our world, but He hardly adopts our insane premises in the process. Thus, the ego's thought system demands that God be this vengeful and insane Father, and it can never forgive Him because he is not: "[Those involved in special relationships] hate the call that would awaken them, and they curse God because He did not make their dream reality" (text, p. 471). It is, therefore, not the forgiveness from God we need, but ours of Him. We must forgive Him for *not* seeking to punish us for our sins against Him. If God were indeed a punitive Father, our ego's premises would be true and its thought system validated. The fact that He is not undermines the ego entirely, and it is for this our ego can never forgive Him. The ego's belief in guilt is superseded by the reality of God's love, and it will have no part of this love if it can help it. The Course states we must "forgive [our] Father it was not His Will that [we] be crucified" (text, p. 471). Our egos must forgive God for loving us instead of vengefully seeking our punishment.

The 19th century composer Wagner has given us a powerful portrayal of the ego's difficulty with God's mercy. In Wagner's final opera, "Parsifal," the sinner-penitent,

Kundry, describes her own hellish odyssey which began with a life of sexual immorality in the time of Jesus. Standing beneath him at the cross, she looked up, sneered contemptuously at his torment, and laughed. Jesus mercifully looked down upon her and his eyes of forgiveness shone through her guilt, but her inability to accept it drove her into a frenzy. As a result, she wandered through the ages, endlessly compelled to repeat her life of sin, at the same time yearning for the repentance which finally comes through Parsifal, the Christ-figure who is not tempted by her seduction and sees beyond her ego to who she really is.

This second step thus questions our decision to be guilty, now that it has been brought to our awareness. We decide now to abandon our investment in the ego as our self and our creator, choosing to identify instead with our real Self, knowing that God is our loving Father. Here we say: "I have chosen wrongly about myself and now I wish to choose again. This time I choose with the Holy Spirit, and let Him make the decision of guiltlessness for me."

3) This opens the way for the third step, which is the work of the Holy Spirit. If we could undo our guilt by ourselves we would not have needed salvation in the first place. It is precisely because we are so enmeshed in our ego that the Holy Spirit enters our world of fear and guilt. It is a particularly tempting ego device to convince us that we can undo our guilt alone, without God's help. The Course urges:

> *You prepare your mind for it* [*undoing our guilt through the holy instant*] *only to the extent of recognizing that you want it above all else. It is not necessary that you do more; indeed, it is necessary that you realize that you cannot do more. Do not attempt to give the Holy Spirit what He does not ask, or you will add the ego to Him and confuse the two (text, pp. 354f).*

The Holy Spirit asks only for our little willingness, that He may join it with the unlimited power of God's Will.

> *Do not assume His function for Him. Give Him but what He asks, that you may learn how little is your part, and how great is His. . . . Never*

> *attempt to overlook your guilt before you ask the Holy Spirit's help. That is* His *function. Your part is only to offer Him a little willingness to let Him remove all fear and hatred, and to be forgiven (text, pp. 356f).*

Thus, the first two steps of forgiveness represent our decision to let the Holy Spirit do His healing work in us. The third step is His. There is a prayer the Course urges us to use whenever we are not joyous, and it contains within it the three steps we are describing:

> *I must have decided wrongly, because I am not at peace.*
> *I made the decision myself, but I can also decide otherwise.*
> *I want to decide otherwise, because I want to be at peace.*
> *I do not feel guilty, because the Holy Spirit will undo all the consequences of my wrong decision if I will let Him.*
> *I choose to let Him, by allowing Him to decide for God for me (text, p. 83)*

Our one responsibility is in deciding it is His life we wish and not the ego's, for the Holy Spirit can take away our guilt only when we have withdrawn our investment in it. This is why the Course states that *"the sole responsibility of the miracle worker is to accept the Atonement for himself"* (text, p. 22), meaning to accept the unreality of our guilt through forgiveness.

In summary, then, the decision for God is a decision to look on our special relationships, to forgive rather than condemn, and to see that nothing has been done to us because we, in fact, have done this to ourselves. "The secret of salvation is but this: That you are doing this unto yourself" (text, p. 545). We realize that we are not the victims of the world we see (workbook, p. 48), but rather of ourselves, and that we now can look at this differently. The first step forgives others; the second forgives ourselves. Thus, our investment in anger and guilt is undone and replaced by the love of God, the final step in our healing. As it is summarized in the Course: " . . . you are not trapped in the world you see, because its cause can be changed. This change requires, first, that the cause be identified and then [second] let go, so that [third] it can be replaced. The first two steps in this process require your cooperation. The final one does not" (workbook, p. 34).

False Forgiveness

Forgiveness is based on defenselessness, the awareness that because God is our rock we are invulnerable to the things of the world and therefore need no defenses against them. In fact, without such an awareness true forgiveness is impossible.

Psychologically speaking, we are not able to forgive while we believe something has been done to hurt us (or those loved ones with whom we identify). This belief inevitably follows our body identification, since only a body can be hurt. "Spirit is far beyond the need of your protection" (text, p. 51), the Course emphasizes. Forgiveness that follows from a perception of attack cannot truly forgive, for it seeks to pardon where it has seen wrongdoing or sin. It itself, then, becomes a subtle form of attack in the guise of a "holier-than-thou" attitude, taking this form: "You are a terrible person because of what you have done to hurt me, an innocent victim of your unjustified attack. But, in the goodness of my heart, I will forgive you anyway, praying that God have mercy on your sinful soul." There is obviously no love in such a statement.

The Course gives this description of false forgiveness:

> *Who has been injured by his brother, and could love and trust him still? He has attacked and will attack again. Protect him not, because your damaged body shows that you must be protected from him. To forgive may be an act of charity, but not his due. He may be pitied for his guilt, but not exonerated. . . . Forgiveness is not pity, which but seeks to pardon what it thinks to be the truth. Good cannot be returned for evil, for forgiveness does not first establish sin and then forgive it. Who can say and mean, "My brother, you have injured me, and yet, because I am the better of the*

> *two, I pardon you my hurt." His pardon and your hurt cannot exist together. One denies the other and must make it false. To witness sin and yet forgive it is a paradox . . . (text, p. 528).*

Such forgiveness excludes the forgiver from the healing power of forgiveness, for it is the other's sin that is the object, not one's own. This is one more example of the ego's deceptiveness, having us focus on the sins outside, so that we do not deal with the sins we believe are inside:

> *Thus, is forgiveness basically unsound. . . . The sin that you forgive is not your own. Someone apart from you committed it. And if you then are gracious unto him by giving him what he does not deserve, the gift is no more yours than was his sin . . . (workbook, p. 222).*
>
> *Forgiveness cannot be for one and not the other. . . . [It] is not real unless it brings a healing to your brother and yourself (text, pp. 528f).*

Cause and Effect

The healing power of forgiveness is best understood in the context of the law of cause and effect. This law is fundamental to the functioning of the world, and has two basic principles:

1) The relationship between cause and effect is indivisible as well as interdependent. A cause without an effect is an impossibility, by definition, as is its converse: there can be no effect without a cause. Paraphrasing the Course, we see that a cause is made a cause by its effect (text, p. 550); if there is no effect there can be no cause, and vice versa.

2) If something exists it must be a cause, since all being affects the universe on some level. In physics, this principle is stated as: every action must have a reaction. Our thoughts, too, have effects. As the Course teaches: "I have no neutral thoughts" (workbook, p. 26).

Summarizing these two principles, then, we conclude that if something is shown to have no effects it cannot be a cause, and therefore does not exist. The law of cause and effect operates in Heaven as well as in this world, as seen in Table 1.

TABLE 1

	CAUSE ⟷ EFFECT
HEAVEN	God ⟷ creation (Father) ⟷ (Son)
WORLD	sin ⟷ { suffering, sickness, death }

In Heaven, God is the First Cause, and creation, His Son, is His Effect. Although God is not dependent on His creation for His own existence, He is dependent on it for His role as Creator or Father. What establishes the fatherhood (cause) of a man is his children (effect) — ". . . the Father *is* a Father by His Son" (text, p. 550) — just as a child becomes a child because of its parents.

In the ego's world of separation, we observe the same relationship, although its content is exactly the opposite. In Chapter 1, we saw how "God's" punishment of suffering and death was inflicted on Adam and Eve as the consequence (effect) of their sin (cause) against Him. Adam's sin was therefore the *cause* of this suffering, which is the lot of every person born into this world.

Since sin is the cause of suffering, which is its effect, it can only be undone (or forgiven) by demonstrating there is no suffering. If sin has no effect it cannot be a cause (principle #1), and if it is not a cause, it does not exist (principle #2). As the Course says: "What has no effect does not exist, and to the Holy Spirit the effects of error are nonexistent. By steadily and consistently cancelling out all its effects, everywhere and in all respects, He teaches that the ego does not exist and proves it" (text, pp. 157f). On the other hand, we prove sin's reality by witnessing to the reality of its effect. If I suffer, I am pointing an accusing finger at the one I believe has caused my suffering.

> *For no one in whom true forgiveness rests can suffer. He holds not the proof of sin before his brother's eyes. . . . You must attest his sins have no effect on you to demonstrate they are not real. How else could he be guiltless? And how could his innocence be justified unless his sins have no effect to warrant guilt? (text, pp. 528f).*

Defensiveness vs. Defenselessness

Let us examine a practical example of this principle of cause and effect. Imagine you speak harshly to me. There are two ways I can react: according to the ego or the Holy Spirit. In the ego's system, I believe that I am self-made rather than God-created. Thus, I must believe in the entire thought system outlined in the preceding chapter. It is one of the characteristics of the ego that its thought system is cohesive and consistent. Each principle logically follows from the preceding one, and therefore each ego tenet depends on all the others. If one is proved false, the entire system must crumble. Any student of logic knows that a thought system may be totally logical and yet totally wrong. If you begin with a false premise, then the entire system will be false, even though it may logically hold together. So it is with the ego. It begins with the premise that the separation from God has actually occurred, and that the ego itself has succeeded in usurping God's place as Creator. From this single belief, an entire thought system comes into being which includes the reality of sin, guilt, fear, attack, pain and death.

Therefore, at the moment I am insulted and believe I am an ego, separated from my Creator, I must also believe that I am guilty and vulnerable, deserving of the punishment my guilt has taught is coming to me. Whether I am conscious of this expectation or not, it still remains within me. My ego will be constantly vigilant, seeking to prove how guilty I am by interpreting events as threatening. Thus, when you insult me, my ego understands this as an attack that I deserve, regardless of its lack of justification in the eyes of the world. Consequently, I shall feel hurt by your remarks and will take them personally. The attack will have reinforced my guilt, reinforcing the belief that I am an ego.

My ego, however, does not stop here. Now that the guilt has been reinforced, the next step is for me to deny my responsibility for it by projecting it out. My conscious thought becomes that I do *not* deserve the attack that my unconscious self knows I *do* deserve. By projecting my guilt back onto you, it now appears that you have unjustly treated me, the innocent victim of your unfair attack: "I am the thing you made of me, and as you look on me, you stand condemned because of what I am" (text, p. 611). Once I perceive attack, I am bound by the ego's laws to respond in a defensive way, feeling perfectly justified in becoming angry. This anger can be expressed either by nursing my wounds in sulky silence saying, in paraphrase of the Course: Behold me, my brother, at your hands I suffer (text, p. 526); or else I can attack directly, accusing you of treating me unfairly.

Either type of defensive response accomplishes two things, both very appealing to the ego. By telling you how you have hurt me, I am demonstrating that your sin against me has had an effect, and therefore you should feel sinful. Since you will already feel guilty for attacking me (since attack always leads to increased guilt), my defensiveness will reinforce this. But it does the same for me. My need to attack you could only result from my belief that I am an ego (since only an ego can seek to defend itself and attack). My very need to defend myself confirms my vulnerability and guilt, otherwise there is no need to be defensive. Moreover, my attacking in return, regardless of my attempts to justify this to myself or others — trying to hurt you for what I unconsciously believe I have done to myself — will make me even guiltier. Thus, my attack strengthens the shared belief in the reality of our sinfulness as children of the ego.

Your call from fear is met by my own, perpetuating this mistake and maintaining the ego's hold over both of us. Sin has again been proven to be real, for its effects have been witnessed to by both of us.

The problem lies not in what *you* have said to me, but what *I* have said to myself prior to your remarks. For me, your harsh words would have had no effect. If I am wearing a blue suit, for example, and am criticized for wearing such an unbecoming color as brown, the remark would not bother me since I know what I am wearing. If I *were* wearing brown, however, and were unsure of its appropriateness for me, my reaction might be much different, defending my choice of color or attacking you for your lack of taste.

But there is another possibility that is open to me. I can begin with the Holy Spirit's premise that I am a child of God, loved by my Creator and secure in His love and in His protection. Thus, I know, in the words of two workbook lessons, that "there is nothing to fear," for "I am sustained by the Love of God" (workbook, pp. 77, 79). Identifying with the Holy Spirit's thought system rather than the ego's, I will have no guilt to project onto you, nor any guilt that will demand my punishment. Thus am I free to share the Holy Spirit's perception of the situation, rather than my ego's.

To the Holy Spirit, "there is but one interpretation of motivation that makes any sense. . . . Every loving thought is true. Everything else is an appeal for healing and help, regardless of the form it takes" (text, p. 200). He sees nothing else in all the universe. The foundation for this perception is the Johannine statement cited so frequently in the Course: "Perfect love casts out fear" (1 Jn 4:18). If people are filled with the peace of God, aware that God's love is always with them, not only would they experience no fear, but there would be no guilt or need to attack. It would be impossible to seek ever to hurt anyone else. St. Augustine taught: "Love and do what you will." When love is in our hearts, all that we do radiates this love, and our will and God's are experienced as one. Thus, those who do attack cannot be filled with God's peace. Believing that the ego and not God is their Father, these people experience themselves as alienated from Him and from all people. Their attack, then, originates in this belief, representing the magical attempt to deny their own guilt and terror by projecting it onto others. In this insane thinking, they believe their protection rests in attack. This is summarized in the Course in this way:

> [*The Holy Spirit has taught how*] . . . *to perceive attack as a call for love. We have already learned that fear and attack are inevitably associated. If only attack produces fear, and if you see attack as the call for help that it is, the unreality of fear must dawn on you. For fear is a call for love, in unconscious recognition of what has been denied (text, p. 202).*

Thus, following the Holy Spirit's judgment, I am guided to see your seeming attack as a call for the love that you do not believe you deserve. This is true forgiveness, which reflects the miracle's shift in perception, a different way of looking at what has been done. This does not deny that on the ego level a person has sought to hurt another, but it teaches that there is another way of perceiving the action. We look beyond the external behavior to its true motivation. My true forgiveness, mediated through my defenselessness, shows that you are forgiven for what you have *not* done to me. On the deepest level, nothing *has* been done. My invulnerability witnesses to your innocence, just as my vulnerability attested to your guilt. Thus, my defenselessness undoes the cause which was your sin, for I have shown you that it has had no effects.

Shakespeare has given a poignant example of this principle in *King Lear*. Certainly, few literary characters would have been more justified to be hurt and angry than Cordelia, whom Lear rejected; yet she was the only one of his three daughters who loved him. Her simple honesty gained her Lear's towering rage and vengeance, leading to tragedy for both of them. It is only near the play's end that Lear recognizes his mistake, and humbly speaks to his daughter:

> *Be your tears wet? Yes, faith, I pray, weep not:*
> *If you have poison for me, I will drink it.*
> *I know you do not love me; for your sisters*

Have, as I do remember, done me wrong:
You have some cause, they have not (IV, vii).

Cordelia softly responds: "No cause, no cause," telling her father he has no need to ask forgiveness. Her love for him has remained, unbroken by his actions against her. From her innocence and defenselessness, she extends to him the love that true forgiveness reflects. In that forgiveness, offered and accepted, father and daughter are reconciled and at least find peace before they die.

By following the Holy Spirit's judgment, I am now also free to hear His Voice say that your call is for the same love I am seeking, and that in forgiving you for what you have not done to me, I am forgiving myself for the sins I have not truly committed as well. I would hear my Teacher remind me that the way to remember God is to "perceive the healing of your brother as the healing of yourself" (text, p. 203).

Thus, if you attack me and I respond without attack, I am reinforcing a different lesson for both of us. By showing you that your attack on me has no effect — i.e., I am not angry, hurt or defensive — I demonstrate that you need not feel guilty over what you have done. Your insult has not caused me to suffer pain (which my counter-attack would affirm), but rather it is seen as a call for help to which I am responding. To deny the same need in myself would be to exclude myself from healing, seeing you and me as separate. This reinforces the very error of separation my offer of forgiveness would be healing. "The holiness of your relationship forgives you and your brother, undoing the effects of what you both believed and saw. And with their going is the need for sin gone with them" (text, p. 435).

Therefore, my defenselessness not only proves your innocence, it reinforces the belief in my own. If I need no defense, it is because there is no guilt to be defended against. The love I extend to you can only come from a place of love in myself. By giving it to you, answering your call for love by extending love, I am answering my own call too, receiving the love I believe I lack. Thus is the Holy Spirit's purpose for the encounter — our joint healing — fulfilled through my forgiveness.

Opportunities for Forgiveness

The Course states: "Certain it is that all distress does not appear to be but unforgiveness" (workbook, p. 357), since it is our guilt that prevents God's love from healing our perceived hurts and wounds. The solution to problems must, therefore, lie in forgiveness which undoes guilt. Whenever we are depressed or upset and pray for the Holy Spirit's help, His response to our prayer will come through a relationship that needs healing. The manner in which our guilt is experienced will be matched in the opportunity for forgiveness presented to us. In each and every encounter, the Holy Spirit gently speaks to us in our need, saying: "Choose once again. In this person you are given to see your holiness or unholiness, for what you see in the other reflects what you see in yourself. Together you remain prisoners of fear, or together you leave your house of darkness and walk hand in hand into the light that forgiveness brings. Turn to Me, who has joined with you, and let Me help you make the one choice that will bring you peace."

We see such an opportunity in the following example. Frank felt guilty all his life for a basic insensitivity to others which was concealed behind a superficial orientation of friendliness and concern. Deep within, however, he found people to be a nuisance and a bother, and wished only that they would keep out of his way. One day, while waiting at a subway station, he observed a man shove his way through a crowd, ultimately pushing a young girl who was in his way onto the tracks. For many months, Frank was enraged and filled with a violent hatred toward the man that went beyond the natural reaction of a person witnessing such an event. When he finally was able to make the connection between the man's actions and his own unconscious desires, he could forgive both himself and the man, and return to a more balanced view of the incident. It did not matter that the form of the "sin" was different: Frank would never have acted out the unconscious thought in such a violent way. The underlying meaning of the thought — to push people out of one's way — was shared by both men. Thus, Frank came to understand that the Holy Spirit had provided this opportunity to help him forgive an aspect of himself he could never face before. It was no accident he had been standing in the station at that moment.

By going out to another in forgiveness, we are joining the Holy Spirit, whose only purpose in relationships is forgiveness. In our union, the ego's belief in separation is undone. Guilt disappears since its roots lie in the attack that separation from others and God engenders. The forgiveness we offer to another and to ourselves will also be the answer to the prayer of those we forgive, for all healing is reciprocal. If we honestly seek the Holy Spirit's goal of truth, we must also accept His purpose of forgiveness for the unhealed relationships of our lives to find this truth.

The Course asks us: "You recognize you want the goal. Are you not also willing to accept the means? . . . A purpose is attained by means, and if you want a purpose you must be willing to want the means as well. How can one be sincere and say, 'I want this above all else, and yet I do not want to learn the means to get it'?" (text, p. 410). Acceptance of the means of forgiveness ensures that the love of God will extend through us, bringing us the peace we desire above all else.

In another example, we see how a situation filled with hurt and anger became the means of bringing peace to both people involved. One of the major lessons in forgiveness that Cecelia had to learn in her life was that she was not the victim of others, even in situations where the world would have supported such a belief. This following incident very specifically addressed this issue for her.

Cecelia had had a long and harried teaching day, and left school forgetting to place the next day's lesson plan on her department chairman's desk, as was required of all teachers. Unexpected family illness kept her home from school the following day, and upon her return she found a scathing letter from her chairman in her mailbox, accusing her of upsetting the department, not to mention the entire school, because of her negligence regarding the lesson plan. Not only that, he was placing a copy of this letter in her permanent file, which is always consulted for promotions, etc.

Cecelia felt very hurt, for the letter reinforced a long history of temptations to see herself as victimized and unfairly treated. She had been teaching for over fifteen years, always conscientious in her work and generous with her time in assisting the department. Her relations with her chairman, moreover, had always been good. She could not understand the letter at all, and was very tempted to storm into his office and let him have a piece of her angry mind. All she could do to protest the injustice filled her thoughts, until she suddenly remembered that there was another way to look at this. Able to take a few short moments by herself before her first class, Cecelia called out to God for help, and very clearly understood that she was to go to her chairman and apologize. Her immediate response was increased anger, feeling it was *his* place to apologize to her, not the other way around. However, she could not deny the Holy Spirit, and before she knew it, was in front of her chairman, hearing herself tell him how sorry she was for any problem and inconvenience she had caused.

Her chairman, very much the strong, "macho" type, grew red in the face and almost meekly apologized to Cecelia for having written the letter. He explained that he had had a very bad morning the previous day, beset with many personal and school-related problems, and had unknowingly taken it out on her. He was immediately removing the letter from the file, and considered the whole matter closed and forgotten.

Tempted at first to see herself as the victim and her chairman as the victimizer, and tempted to reinforce the attack-defense cycle that had begun in both of them, Cecelia was able to change her mind. Through her defenselessness, she enabled her chairman to forgive himself for "victimizing" her, at the same time she could forgive herself for being the victim once again. Their special hate relationship had become holy, and Cecelia had taken a significant step forward in releasing herself totally from this problem.

"Love is the way I walk in gratitude" (workbook, p. 362), the Course teaches, for we are asked to offer thanks for every opportunity given to choose again. The very people who present us with the greatest problems, the biggest "pains in the neck" of our lives, are the very people for whom we should feel the most grateful. The greater our ego reaction — anger, hurt or fear — the more deeply repressed has been the projected guilt, the greater the chunk of the iceberg that has been surfaced. Without these opportunities, this guilt would lie unknown and thus uncorrected.

> *It is insane to offer thanks because of suffering. But it is equally insane to fail in gratitude to One Who offers you the certain means whereby all pain is healed, and suffering replaced with laughter and with happiness. . . . We thank our Father for one thing alone; that we are separate from no living thing, and therefore one with Him (workbook, p. 362).*

Tempted to perceive separation by one we called an enemy, we now see him anew as our brother, afraid as we are afraid, alone as we are alone, calling for help as we call for help. Joined now in love and gratitude, we walk together forgiveness' way to God.

Therefore, in any given situation where attack seems to be occurring, we are presented with one of two perceptual alternatives. Either we see the person as sinful, evil and deserving of punishment, or we see the attacker as desperately calling for help: the call of one who believes in a vengeful God, and whose attack is in reality a plea for the mercy and love he or she feels is undeserved.

There is no other perceptual choice open to us, and our response will directly follow from how we have seen the action. If we perceive attack, we have no recourse but to defend ourselves in some way. If, on the other hand, we perceive the same action as a call for love, what response could we give but love? "Where there is love, your brother must give it to you because of what it is. But where there is a call for love, you must give it because of what you are" (text, p. 275).

It is here we see the importance of the concept discussed in the first chapter: projection makes perception. How we perceive this situation of attack and injury will depend on how we see ourselves. If we believe we are separated from God and that His love and strength do not protect us, we, too, will feel vulnerable and afraid, sharing the belief of the attacker. Our own identification with the ego and the body leads to a perception of the world as threatening and hostile, and the world's projected fear — its expressions of anger and attack — reinforces our belief that we be justly punished for our sins.

If, however, we identify with our spiritual Self, with the strength and protection of God that is our true reality and foundation, we will know we are invulnerable. We will recognize we have no needs that God has not already met, and therefore we need not seek for anything outside ourselves. This principle of abundance contrasts with the ego's principle of scarcity, that what we lack can be found in another. Believing in our abundance, we know that nothing in the world can rob us of the peace, joy and happiness that comes from knowing God is with us. Many people throughout history were able to undergo seemingly cruel deaths, totally at peace with their assassins, because they knew their God had not left them comfortless, even if their physical lives were taken from them. They knew their real identity was not this physical self, but the Self that rests indestructibly in God for all eternity. From such awareness and certainty, only peace is possible. Knowing love is in us, we look out and see love in others or the call for it. It is from this perception that forgiveness becomes the living expression of God's love here on earth.

Chapter 3

FORGIVENESS OF INJUSTICE
The Problems of Anger, Sickness and Suffering

Reversal of Cause and Effect

Now that we have established the principles of the ego — the projection of guilt in special relationships — and its correction through forgiveness, we can turn our attention to specific expressions of these principles in what the world considers its major problems.

The fifth lesson in the workbook states: "I am never upset for the reason I think" (workbook, p. 8). Through the dynamic of projection, the ego continually seeks to have us believe our problems are outside us in the world of the body — our own or others'. Thus we believe that what upsets us are problems perceived as external to us, beyond our control, for which we must find solutions. As long as we believe in the ego's seductive smokescreens, the true source of the problem — our misthoughts — forever remains beyond recognition and therefore beyond correction. As we have seen, this is the ego's fundamental purpose in all situations: to obscure the belief in the reality of the separation that alone upsets us.

The belief in separation constitutes a decision we make to hear the voice of the ego, rather than the Voice for God. From this decision arises two distinct ways of looking at the world. The ego's eyes *see* problems, differing forms of the special relationship. Central to this perception is the belief in injustice, seeing the world as divided into victims and victimizers, the former being the innocent objects of the sinful actions or thoughts of the latter. All beliefs in anger, sickness, and suffering are beliefs that justify this perception.

The vision of the Holy Spirit, on the other hand, transforms our problems into learning opportunities, the special functions through which we practice our lessons of forgiveness. Expressions of anger — towards others or ourselves — become transformed through His loving perception into calls for help, which His love gently answers through our forgiveness, healing the suffering injustice that once seemed so real. Thus do special or unholy relationships become holy. Table 2 summarizes these two ways of seeing.

TABLE 2

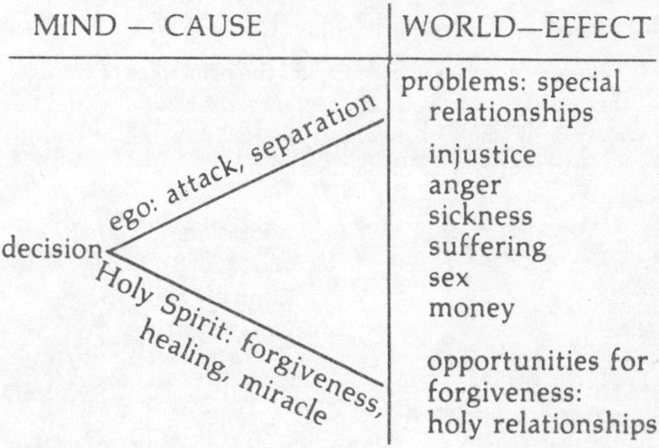

Thus, our real problem is that we have chosen to *see* a problem, since it is a question of perception, not the situation itself. What we see and experience reflects what we have chosen to see and experience. This choice, as we have seen, is limited to love or fear. As the Course explains, we first choose the messages we wish to receive, and then send out messengers of love or fear, the Holy Spirit or the ego, to bring back what we have asked for. "Relationships in this world are the result of how the world is seen. And this depends on which emotion was called on to send its messengers to look upon it, and return with word of what they saw" (text, p. 382).

Problems appear in this world because of the ego's success at reversing cause and effect, a dynamic we now explore. The only true cause in this world is the mind, as we discussed in Chapter 1, and all aspects of the material world are the mind's effect. There can be no exceptions to this principle, for the mind is the only creative agent. This is so even when it is "miscreating," or making illusions. Miscreation, or the distortion of God's creative power, is analogous to placing a prism in front of a light. The light that has passed through the prism is broken up and changed, yet is still derived from the pure light which is the only source. Thus, the phenomenal world is nothing more than the manifestation of these broken rays of light of our mind, appearing to us in a physical form. Modern physics tells us these forms of matter are but expressions of energy or thought, for physicists have recognized that there is no true distinction between subject and object, our thoughts and what we perceive outside ourselves. They are all one: "Ideas leave not their source."

We have already examined the ego's basic tactic of making smokescreens to conceal the problem's real source in the mind. The process works in this manner: the ego begins by denying the causal connection between the mind and body, thus denying that the cause of all distress is in the mind that believes in separation. All defenses "seem to be unconscious but because of the rapidity with which you choose to use them" (workbook, p. 250). Once this connection between cause and effect is denied or forgotten, the ego reverses them, projecting the role of cause onto its effect. Now it appears that the *effect* is now the *cause*, while the *cause* now seems to be the *effect:* "Effect and cause are split off [denial], and then reversed [projection], so that effect becomes a cause; the cause, effect" (text, p. 552).

The world of separation has become the cause of the mind's suffering. An external agent is experienced as "a happening beyond your state of mind, an outcome with a real effect on you, instead of one effected by yourself" (workbook, p. 250). Now, of course, no problem can ever be solved or healed, for the magical remedies are sought outside yourself. Indeed, we should never "underestimate the power of denial." This entire world rests on the idea that we have forgotten we made it up. We are all extremely capable, on an individual ego level as well as the larger collective ego we all share, of not recognizing the most obvious, let alone the subtle causes of our distress. As we see in Table 2, *cause* only lies in the mind, while *effects* are in the world.

Among the most tempting of the world's problems that the ego would make real are three specific forms of injustice: anger, sickness and suffering. These will be the focus of this chapter. Two other major problems — sex and money — will be discussed in Chapters 4 and 5 respectively.

The Problem of Anger

As any psychotherapist knows, anger, or the special hate relationship, is one of the central problems confronting most people. Its widespread interest today, not only in psychological but religious circles as well, warrants special discussion as one of the ego's most important weapons in its war against God.

For the first fifty years of this century, the psychological approach to feelings or emotions was dominated largely by Freud and the psychoanalysts, who emphasized analysis and sublimation, rather than expression, as the solution to the problem. It is helpful to remember that the soil that gave birth to psychoanalysis was Victorian Vienna of the late 19th century, and Freud's theoretical approach was very much in keeping with the mores of his time which looked negatively on the expression of feelings. Therefore, although Freud would have encouraged the analysis of feelings rather than their repression, the result often was the latter.

Part of the Third Force reaction against psychoanalysis, discussed in the introduction to Part I, included interest in T-groups, encounter groups, sensitivity training, marathon experiences, etc. These turned Freudian conservatism upside down, and swung the pendulum of dealing with emotions to the other extreme. No longer bound to repress or sublimate feelings, followers of this movement were encouraged to express what they felt, and break through the suppressive influence of society. Couples having marital problems, for example, were urged to "fight it out" and, indeed, expressing one's feelings became the panacea for almost all our ills, including the prevention of psychosomatic disturbances.

A similar pattern occurred within many religious circles. For centuries, as an example, Christians were urged to "turn the other cheek" when confronted by an anger-inducing situation, and almost literally to sit on their feelings rather than commit the "sin" of self-expression. But the significant innovations of the post-Vatican II Catholic Church as well as other Christian churches, including the Pentecostal and Charismatic movements, created an atmosphere of liberation similar to psychology's. Undoing several centuries of constraint, church members were now urged to become more in touch with their feelings and to express them.

From the standpoint of the ego, the situation could not have worked out more to its advantage for, given the two alternatives — repression or expression — it cannot lose. Either way, anger has been made into the problem that must be solved, and the *true* problem — the underlying guilt — is hidden effectively behind the ego's smokescreen. Based upon this, anger is seen as if it were a quantifiable mass of energy, a basic human emotion that requires an outlet either through sublimation (the Freudian ideal) or direct expression. However, anger is not a basic human emotion at all. The Course teaches that "you have but two emotions, and one you made and one was given you" (text, p. 232): love, given us by God; and fear, the ego's substitute for God's love. Emotions such as joy, happiness, peace and contentment are expressions of love; while feelings of disappointment, frustration, anxiety, jealousy, despair, depression and anger, are derived from fear. We have already seen how anger results from the projection of guilt, set into motion by our fear of it. The basic problem, therefore, is not anger but the guilt that it conceals. As long as the anger is given primary attention, the guilt goes unnoticed and the ego's diversionary tactics of seek but do not find will have been successful. As was shown in the diagram, anger belongs on the right side of Table 2, the effect of the real problem: our decision to be guilty.

A practical question now remains: What do we do with our angry feelings if we are not to repress our express them? People who espouse the "cause" of expressing anger frequently cite the postive experience of "getting it out of my system": "It felt so good to express my anger," or "I felt so freed of my inhibitions." The actual source of the good feeling, however, is the magical belief that at last one is released from the terrible burden of guilt by having transferred it to another. That is why the Course asks: "In honesty, is it not harder for you to say 'I love' than 'I hate'?"(text, p. 226).

As long as these experiences of anger seem to be positive, their truly destructive nature will be concealed. It is not long after an angry outburst that a person becomes overwhelmed with guilt over his attack, and depression or a "psychological hangover" becomes inevitable. Depression is frequently described as unexpressed rage, but even more to the point is the guilt that is protected, for it is this guilt that depression masks. Encouraging the expression of anger merely reinforces the hidden build-up of guilt, and thus it acts at our expense, not to mention the expense of those whom we have attacked. The following example highlights this dynamic.

John was very angry at his good friend, Bob, both members of a religious community. One day, Bob asked John if he would mind staying in the house to entertain a friend while he, Bob, kept an important appointment elsewhere. Ordinarily, John would have been delighted to help out, but this time he resented the perceived intrusion on his time and saw a wonderful opportunity for "getting even" with his friend. He told Bob he could not help him because he was sick and had to stay in bed. In fact, he remained home from teaching school that day to emphasize this, even though he was feeling fine. Bob became suspicious, and that evening angrily accused John of feigning illness. John, in turn, self-righteously protested his innocence, becoming increasingly incensed that his friend would doubt his word. Their argument continued into the following morning, and climaxed in John's writing Bob a lengthy letter accusing him of projecting his own guilt, as well as highlighting the details of his illness. The letter had the desired effect, and a contrite Bob "realized his error" and came to John begging his forgiveness. For a brief period, John was elated over his success. But within a matter of hours he was horrified with what he had done and became filled with guilt. From the heights of triumph he plunged to the depths of depression, feeling ten times guiltier than before.

When people are encouraged to be honest with each other and "tell it like it is," and then proceed to unload a barrage of venomous invectives on another in the name of truth, they are hardly being honest or helpful. Yet, when we are angry, it is essential that we do not deny or push away our feelings, for this merely intensifies them and reinforces the presence of what is now the "enemy." If the internal pressure is too great and anger must be expressed, at least the recognition, if only to oneself, that the anger is not what it seems will suffice. Better still, perhaps, would be a statement like this to the other, which would do justice to the feelings, at the same time honestly stating the problem: "I am furious because of what you did, but I know my anger is not really directed at you, but at myself. At the moment I cannot help what I feel; please do not take it personally." If the anger cannot be contained, at least such an attitude minimizes the guilt and allows for the possibility of moving beyond it. This recognition is enough to invite the Holy Spirit's help, for it expresses the little willingness He needs to take away our guilt.

This process of acknowledging our mistakes is something referred to as "healthy guilt" or "owning up to your mistakes." A shift in perception is what is really meant, a turning away from the ego back to God, representing what traditionally was referred to as repentance or conversion. It is seeing our mistakes for what they are, eager to have their effects be corrected and desiring not to repeat them again. Holding on to the mistakes through rationalization or self-justification merely retains the underlying guilt and prevents its undoing through forgiveness.

There can be a positive result of expressing anger at this point as well. If one has spent a lifetime fearing one's anger, unconsciously believing that its expression will either destroy the world or oneself, there can be value in expressing these feelings and seeing that, indeed, nothing happens. To be afraid of something is to give it a reality it does not have. Thus "getting the anger out of one's system," usually without physical expression, and seeing one can do it without disastrous effects — i.e., objects of our wrath survive, as we do — can be a helpful stepping-stone along the path of transcending the anger entirely. However, the overall goal of moving beyond the projection of guilt to the guilt itself must remain the purpose, even if not consciously realized at the time.

A danger here is obvious. The temptation merely to shift the problem from one extreme to the other is very great. Moving from repression to expression is a common experience in the world, carrying with it the illusion of freedom. We have seen this principle at work many times throughout history when oppressed people finally come to power and, in the name of liberation and justice, begin to oppress those who had oppressed them. All that happens, of course, is that the same errors of separation and projection are reproduced, and the seeds of the next revolution are sown even before the blood shed from the current one has dried. It is only in recognizing that the problem is not somewhere else but within us that true liberation can be achieved, for all solutions aimed at resolving the pseudo-problem will fail and themselves act as a deterrent to any healing.

Thus, the first step in dealing with one's anger may entail learning not to be afraid of it. But this must be followed by recognizing that the anger is not the problem at all. Somewhere inside us, even as the anger seems to mount, we must be willing to step back and look at it differently. At these moments our prayer should be: "Father, I cannot help becoming angry at what I think this person has done to me. But please help me look at the situation as You do, recognizing that to attack another is to attack myself. And why should I attack Your child and prevent Your love from reaching me?"

The desire to attack precludes our accepting the Will of a God of peace, but desiring God's help prepares us to accept His Will for us in any situation. Asking to see peace allows us to receive it through the guidance of the One who speaks for peace, and teaches us to find its source within ourselves.

The Meaning of Sickness

Sickness remains one of the ego's most compelling witnesses in its case against God. It effectively serves the ego's purpose of directing our attention to *effect* and not *cause*, making the body seem real, autonomous to the mind and therefore beyond our control.

Let us begin with a working definition: sickness is a conflict in the mind that is displaced onto the body. Regardless of the many seeming conflicts that beset us, in reality there is one: that between the ego and God. In truth, no such conflict exists, for God does not even recognize the existence of what is inherently illusory. To the ego, however, the war against God is very real, and as long as we identify with this thought system, we shall identify with the belief that our mind is a battlefield. This basic conflict rests on the belief in separation, of which our guilt continually reminds us. Sickness, therefore, is the projection of this guilt, the same dynamic we observed in anger where the guilt in our minds is projected onto other people's bodies. In sickness this guilt is projected onto our own. To the ego, it makes no difference whom the object of its projection is, as long as someone can serve to distract us from the real home of guilt in our minds.

This projection of guilt can be understood in three ways. First, by attacking ourselves the ego seeks to expiate our sinfulness, expressing our unconscious bargain with God to punish ourselves, rather than having God punish us. As the Course states: " . . . illness is a form of magic. It might be better to say that it is a form of magical solution. The ego believes that by punishing itself it will mitigate the punishment of God" (text, p. 78). Our suffering body, with which we identify, becomes the price we pay for our sin, hoping that this will satisfy the angry Father we believe we attacked in our separation from Him. Since defences do what they would defend, this ego device merely reinforces our guilt, "appeasing" the god we made, perhaps, but hardly appeasing the ego whose desire for guilt is insatiable.

Secondly, it is not enough that *we* be attacked, for the ego continues its ongoing search for scapegoats. In one of the more powerful sections of *A Course in Miracles*, we read:

> *Whenever you consent to suffer pain, to be deprived, unfairly treated or in need of anything, you but accuse your brother of attack upon God's Son.*

> *You hold a picture of your crucifixion before his eyes, that he may see his sins are writ in Heaven in your blood and death, and go before him, closing off the gate and damning him to hell. . . . A sick and suffering you but represents your brother's guilt; the witness that you send lest he forget the injuries he gave, from which you swear he never will escape. This sick and sorry picture you accept, if only it can serve to punish him. The sick are merciless to everyone, and in contagion do they seek to kill. Death seems an easy price, if they can say, "Behold me, brother, at your hand I die." For sickness is the witness to his guilt, and death would prove his errors must be sins. Sickness is but a "little" death, a form of vengeance not yet total. Yet it speaks with certainty for what it represents (text, pp. 525f).*

The ego's need to project guilt is thus doubly served: it first projects the guilt onto our own body, making us sick as punishment for our "sins." Then it seeks to project the responsibility for this suffering onto another. In back of every form of physical distress lies the name of one we judge as responsible for it. It does not matter who the person is, nor if he or she is even alive. Usually this accusation is unconscious, but occasionally we are aware of a secret pleasure derived from accusing someone else of our sickness: "Because of what you have done to me, I now am sick."

The third use the ego has for sickness is as "a defense against the truth." As the workbook states:

> *Sickness is a decision. It is not a thing that happens to you, quite unsought, which makes you weak and brings you suffering. It is a choice you make, a plan you lay, when for an instant truth arises in your own deluded mind, and all your world appears to totter and prepare to fall. Now are you sick, that truth may go away and threaten your establishments no more (workbook, p. 251).*

Truth is spirit, our true identity and only reality. As we

proceed along the spiritual path, increasingly recognizing that this world's only meaning lies in helping us remember our true Home, the ego will attack this truth by reinforcing our physical identity. One of its most powerful means of accomplishing this is to make us sick. If we are in pain, we make the body real; if the body is real, spirit cannot be. Thus is the ego safe from truth's "attack."

Sickness, then, is purposive. It is "a method, conceived in madness, for placing God's Son on his Father's throne" (manual, p. 16). It reinforces the belief in separation, which first gave rise to the guilt that underlies the decision to be sick. The ego's vicious circle of guilt and attack thus is maintained. Someone, for example, who feels called upon by the Holy Spirit to speak His words of truth may suddenly develop a case of laryngitis, or even more serious throat ailments, as part of the ego's attempt to punish him for his "sin" of speaking the truth against it. A woman afraid "to take the next step" along the spiritual path may trip and break her ankle, or develop phlebitis or other foot ailments. Although symptoms need not always be as obvious as in these examples, if one searched to discover the meaning of any specific symptom, one would find that its form mirrored the specific type of unforgiveness that lies buried in the ego's mind. Such insight, however, does not heal, for forgiveness must first be chosen in place of guilt. Spending endless hours in pursuit of such insight can nicely serve the ego's diversionary tactics of "Seek and do not find." It is the *content* of guilt behind the *form* that is essential.

Therefore, we can see that sickness is no different from any form in the world that reflects the ego purpose. We have already discussed that the physical world is nothing but the projection of the underlying thought of separation. Thus, the body merely carries out the wishes of the mind, having no power within itself. As the Course states: "Only the mind is capable of error. The body can act wrongly only when it is responding to misthought" (text, p. 148). Our difficulty in accepting this simple truth witnesses to our close identification with the ego's thought system that equates us with the body. We believe the body is autonomous, vulnerable to forces outside itself and capable of being "healed" by other outside forces. Within the laws of the ego's world our bodies *are* vulnerable, and the laws of sickness as well as the laws of medicine *do* hold. Yet they hold because we believe in them, not because they are true.

There is a famous story that illustrates this point. Samuel Johnson, the 18th century British man of letters, was walking with Bishop Berkeley, the philosophical idealist. They were debating Berkeley's belief that the material world was illusory, and to make his point Dr. Johnson kicked his foot against a tree, exclaiming in pain: "So much for an illusion!" What Johnson failed to realize, however, was that his foot was as much a part of the illusory world as the tree. It merely did what his mind told it to do. Being within the ego's world, his body was subject to its laws and thus felt pain. It is only when we choose the miracle, and can say and truly believe that "I am under no laws but God's (workbook, p. 132) that the effects of the ego's laws disappear: "Miracles reawaken the awareness that the spirit, not the body, is the altar of truth. This is the recognition that leads to the healing power of the miracle" (text, p. 2).

Sickness can be understood, therefore, as a problem of the mind (the left side of Table 2) and not the body (the right side). It is an *interpretation* about the body stating that the separation from God is a fact. Since it takes two people to witness to the separation, it must also take two people to make a sickness: one who believes he is sick, and another who supports that belief. "No mind is sick until another mind agrees that they are separate. And thus it is their joint decision to be sick" (text, p. 553). If you develop physical symptoms and I share your belief that you are sick, then I am as sick as you, for I am sharing the belief in separation that *is* the sickness. Healing is now necessary for both of us.

The difficulty in accepting such a seemingly outlandish view of sickness is ameliorated when we are able to break our association between sickness and the physical or psychological body. Sickness here is redefined as existing only in the mind that believes in separation, totally independent of the form that belief may be manifest in. This is the crucial distinction between the two sides of the diagram in Table 2. This difference in how sickness is seen is reflected in the views of healing that the definition of sickness generates.

False vs. True Healing: Magic vs. the Miracle

Since sickness is a problem of guilt in the mind, healing must be of the mind as well, for problems can be undone only at their source. False healing, therefore, is directed at healing a problem where it is not; on the right side of Table 2, rather than the left. Magic is another name for this error, which reflects the belief that since it is the body that is sick, it is the body that needs healing. Such interventions, however, can never heal, since the unforgiveness that is the cause of the sickness is left untouched.

Believing that magic has healing properties falls nicely into the ego's trap of having us first seek solutions where they cannot be found, and then having us believe we have indeed found them. "All material means that you accept as remedies for bodily ills are restatements of magic principles" (text, p. 20). This would include not only traditional forms of medical treatment such as drugs, surgery and rest, but also many of the New Age techniques of acupuncture, massage, special diets, vitamins, exercise, aura manipulation, laying on of hands, repetition of certain prayers or rituals, forms of breathing and meditation, etc. All of these focus on the body in some way or another.

This does not mean, however, "that the use of such agents for corrective purposes is evil" (text, p. 20), or that they should not be used. If a person's fear level is too great to abandon the ego's investment in guilt, seeking healing through the love of the Holy Spirit would merely reinforce the underlying fear of this love. This would hardly be helpful. "In this case it may be wise to utilize a compromise approach to mind and body, in which something from the outside is temporarily given healing belief. . . . Physical medications are forms of 'spells,' but if you are afraid to use the mind to heal, you should not attempt to do so" (text, pp. 20f).

As we all have experienced, magic *does* work at its own level. An aspirin, for example, can alleviate the tension and pain of a headache; an operation can remove or repair an injured organ and bring relief. Although it is not a mistake to use such agents, it *is* a mistake to ascribe healing properties to them, for they do not remove the causes that brought on the symptom. To believe that magic heals closes off the power of the miracle to undo the guilt that *is* the cause of sickness, "protecting" the guilt from healing by refusing to recognize its existence. Further, the belief in magic subtly reinforces the guilt over the separation by placing the focus on the body. Having denied the power of the mind to make the sickness (which is the sickness), magic denies the mind its power to heal itself. Thus is guilt as well as sickness retained in the mind. The only true healing agent, on the other hand, is joining with another in forgiveness: looking beyond the symptoms that make the body real in our shared experience to the light of spirit that shines in this person and ourselves as one.

Just as it is impossible not to form special relationships in this world, so is it impossible not to develop physical symptoms from time to time. As long as guilt is present in us it will have to be projected, and our bodies are favorite targets of the ego. The last thing in the world that would be of help during a sickness, or when we get angry, is to feel guilty, for the ego is out to "get us twice." It first attacks by making us sick, and then "steps on our faces," as it were, by making us guilty for becoming sick. People working with *A Course in Miracles* frequently become tempted in this regard. Having been taught that all "sickness is a defense against the truth," they then become upset when they develop colds, headaches, not to mention seemingly more serious symptoms; or else they unwittingly reinforce other people's guilt over *their* symptoms. No healing can ever result from such an attitude.

What *is* helpful when sickness appears to strike is to see it as our "call for help," a red flag pointing to a hidden cornerstone we were not aware of before, now clearly seen on the body's screen onto which we have projected our guilt. Thus, for example, if one is suffering from a bad headache and cannot sleep, and unable to undo the error of the mind that caused the pain, it can hardly be a mistake to take a pain-killer, leaving for a less fearful time asking for the Holy Spirit's help. When we *are* able to turn to Him, we ask to become aware of those we hold grievances against, that we may forgive them. These attacks establish a gap wherein were planted the seeds of sickness. Utilizing magic as a *healing* agent prevents us from recognizing the causal connection between the symptoms and our unforgiveness.

The Course emphasizes how the Holy Spirit uses all the world's forms to bring about His healing. The forms which were made to separate and hurt can be utilized by Him to join and heal. "They become but means by which you can understand, but which you recognize is not the unity where true communication can be found" (workbook, p. 337). The following example illustrates how medicine, though not healing in itself, became an instrument of healing and forgiveness.

Mary developed a growth on her thyroid, which she was not able to reduce through her usual meditations, even though she was vaguely aware of the specific unforgiveness that the symptom expressed. The unconscious investment in "punishing" the other party was too great to allow her to be healed. Finally, after a few months, she decided to consult a surgeon who recommended surgery to remove the growth. What made the choice of surgeon particularly interesting was an experience Mary had shortly before meeting him. She had seen "flashbacks" of past lives where she was being persecuted and killed by religious authorities for her spiritual beliefs and teachings. In one of these, a man in a black hood was chopping off her head with an axe. In the course of her conversation with her surgeon-to-be, he made a joke about how some people say that he slits their throats. At that moment the room disappeared for Mary, including the doctor's face which was replaced by the black-hooded executioner's. She realized her former adversary was now her surgeon; yet she felt no fear or anger, only trust. In placing her life in his hands she was, in effect, forgiving him and herself, the "victimizer" and the "victim." Where once this person had *taken* her life by cutting her throat, now he would *save* it by cutting her throat. It was the same experience in form, despite the differing circumstances, but the content now had a different purpose. Usually very apprehensive about doctors and hospitals, Mary went through the surgery with relatively little anxiety.

Of additional interest was that the problem of unforgiveness that Mary was working on prior to the appearance of the growth represented the same issue of being condemned, in the name of God, for her spiritual beliefs and practices. She was learning that, paraphrasing the words of the workbook, she was not the persecuted victim of the world she saw (workbook, p. 48). Though the unforgiveness remained after the successful surgery, Mary now felt strengthened through the resolution of her symptom problem to work on forgiving the person who currently represented the real problem of forgiving her "persecutors."

The only means of help that Mary could have accepted at first was medical intervention, which was the form of help the surgeon could offer as well — for his salvation as well as hers. By their joining together in this act of trust and forgiveness, the Holy Spirit had been invited in to heal and to bless. It certainly is not always the case that a person has the moment of recognition that Mary experienced, but this recognition or insight is not needed for salvation's purpose. The joining suffices, for "God's Teacher speaks to any two who join together for learning purposes. The relationship is holy because of that purpose, and God has promised to send His Spirit into any holy relationship" (manual, p. 5). It does not matter, moreover, if one or even both people share the belief in magic; their coming together is enough to undo the belief in separate interests that is the source of every sickness.

What heals, therefore, is not the particular form of medical magic that seems to alleviate the pain, but the joining of two people in the name of the One who heals. This restores the true cause-effect relationship, which promotes healing. It

> *is the first step in giving back to cause the function of causation, not effect. . . .* [*It*] *returns the cause of fear to you who made it. . . . Thus is the body healed by miracles because they show the*

> *mind made sickness, and employed the body to be victim, or effect of what it made. The miracle is useless if you learn but that the body can be healed, for this is not the lesson it was sent to teach. The lesson is the mind was sick that thought the body could be sick; projecting out its guilt caused nothing, and had no effect (text, pp. 552f).*

Thus does forgiveness heal, for it joins where the ego had separated. The seeds of sickness are replaced by the seeds of the miracle, which unites and heals in the one love of God, in whom are all dreams of sickness and pain ended.

One of my first therapy experiences after I began working with the Course afforded me with a powerful example of the relationship between healing and forgiveness. I had seen Sister Annette for about two months. She was fifty years old and had been in religious life almost thirty years. She was also one of the angriest people I had ever worked with, filled with a silent hatred toward those in authority that would have destroyed mountains. Over the first few sessions, Sister Annette was able to begin questioning some of her attitudes toward her Order and her desire for revenge. She no longer seemed quite as committed to the retaliative steps she had contemplated. Or so I thought. Then one day Annette walked into the office with her face coldly exhibiting the "wrath of God." Her convent coordinator had done something she judged as being beyond forgiveness, and Sister Annette was hell bent on war, absolutely closed to any suggestions she do otherwise.

That same morning I had come down with a very bad cold and felt miserable. Not all my prayers and meditation were able to shift this, and I sat before Annette feeling utterly helpless and discouraged. I knew that if she left me as she had come in, she would be making an irrevocable mistake she would regret the rest of her life. Yet nothing I said could budge her, and my growing frustration only made my cold worse. The more frustrated I became, the more real I made Annette's angry symptoms and, correspondingly, my own as well. Obviously, I was projecting my unforgiveness of myself onto Annette, seeing in her stubborn clinging to her anger the mirror of my stubborn clinging to my cold, not to mention my own failure as a therapist. Separation through our symptoms became reinforced, and healing through joining retreated still further behind clouds of guilt and anger.

What added to my difficulty was the belief that Annette had been sent to me from God, and as she was in serious trouble it was my responsibility to help her. And I was obviously failing. About midway through the session, my desperation led me finally to remember that I was not the Therapist, and that I certainly could not be more concerned for Annette than Jesus was. Even as I was talking and listening to her, in another part of my mind I began to pray for help, asking Jesus to provide the words that would heal her anger and fear, and restore to her awareness the love that was her true identity.

The response was immediate, and I suddenly became available to the help that was there — for me. A warm surge of energy rose up from my chest, through my lungs, nose and throat, and I could feel my cold being healed and my head clearing up. At the same time I began to speak. I don't recall what I said, and doubt if it were anything too different from what I had said previously. Only now I was different. I no longer saw Annette as separate from me, a patient in trouble whom I, as therapist, had to help. She now was my sister, and by joining with her I was joining with Jesus. I had become the patient as well, and together we received healing from the forgiving love of God. By the end of the session, her softened face reflected the shift from anger and fear to forgiveness and love, as my well-being reflected the same shift in myself. I had learned my lesson that day, to be relearned many times thereafter.

In summary, then, just as forgiveness undoes the ego's plan for justifying anger, so too does healing reverse the ego's plan to make sickness real. As sickness is only in the mind and not the body, it cannot be the body that needs healing. Healing must occur in the place where it is needed, in the mind that conceived of the insane idea of separation. As in forgiveness, healing restores the problem to where it truly is: "All sickness comes from separation. When the separation is denied, it goes" (text, p. 514). This occurs through "uniting with a brother's mind [which] prevents the cause of sickness and perceived effects. Healing is the effect of minds that join, as sickness comes from minds that separate" (text, p. 553).

Our function on earth, the Course reminds us, is to heal. As we heal *we* are healed. These opportunities often take the form of being presented with another's sickness. The form of sickness we observe in another and make real by our reactions of anxiety, guilt or concern will mirror the form of unforgiveness in ourselves that needs healing. The ego's plan for "salvation" is replaced by the Holy Spirit's as we are asked to "accept the Atonement for ourselves." We accept the Atonement when we do not "give support to someone's dream of sickness" (text, p. 555), not sharing his or her dream to separate. This undoes our belief in the reality of separation and guilt by shifting our perception of another's sickness to a call for help and unity.

The Course teaches that "no one is sick if someone else accepts his union with him. His desire to be a sick and separated mind cannot remain without a witness or a cause. And both are gone if someone wills to be united with him" (text, p. 557). Thus do physician (or therapist) and patient, teacher and pupil, friend and friend come together in a holy instant, witnessing to the truth of healing and denying the ego's witness to the illusion of separation. This, then, "is all the Healer of God's Son requires. He will place the seeds of healing where the seeds of sickness were. And there will be no loss, but only gain" (text, p. 557).

The Meaning of Injustice and Suffering

We have seen how all anger is an attempt to have others change so that we do not; to stop their behavior that *we* have judged as undesirable; to make them feel guilty enough over their action not to repeat it; and to teach the lesson of ego identification we wish them to learn with us. We can recognize this motivation in ourselves most clearly in those actions that are directly hostile, both in individual cases as well as those social and international situations where innocent people are seen to be oppressed and persecuted. No one would deny the need to intervene so that injustice is corrected and people do not suffer, but we must first define what injustice and suffering are, and who the real intervening agent would be in a situation that is calling for help. This is the focus of the following three sections.

If we perceive someone unjustly treating another, whether the other be ourselves, loved ones, or people living in a foreign country, we cannot avoid believing the perpetrator of injustice is bad and deserving of punishment. The lesson we are teaching, then, is that people should not hurt others because it makes *us* angry, and we do not approve of it or them. These actions are "evil," and therefore so are the ones committing them. If people wish to be "good," they must cease what they are doing, for our approval of them depends on their behavior; not only our approval but God's, whom we believe we represent. Therefore, once the perception of injustice is made, no alternative can follow but that of a judgment that subtly sets up the conditions of "love":either people behave in accordance with our values, or they are denied salvation and cast out of God's kingdom. This is another example of what the Course terms the arrogance of the ego, presuming to know God's Will and taking upon itself the right to carry it out.

If, on the other hand, we perceive acts of injustice as being frightened calls for help, following the judgment of the Holy Spirit discussed above, we can no longer see the agent of this injustice as evil or sinful. The lesson we wish to teach, therefore, is that this person is loved by God and deserves this love, regardless of his or her actions. There can be no other lesson we would teach, for there is no other lesson we would learn. A person who feels the love of God would want only to demonstrate this love to those who do not know it. This does not mean we necessarily approve of the actions of the "victimizer," but merely that we expand the circle of help to include among those who suffer the ones who seem to be bringing it about. A perception that excludes them comes from an unconscious need to find a scapegoat so that our own guilt can be projected.

One of the most powerful witnesses to this process of forgiveness was the two Ten Boom sisters, Corrie and Betsie, during their internment in a German concentration camp, told in Corrie's inspiring book, *The Hiding Place.* Confronted by the ostensible brutality of the German soldiers and the pitiful sufferings of those around them, the sisters came to the realization that if they were to be true to their Christian faith they must forgive their Nazi tormenters, seeing them as their brothers and the same as those who were suffering. This was not an easy task they set for themselves, and the book describes their struggles to demonstrate truly what the love of God meant. Once, after observing a guard whipping a feeble-minded girl who was soiling herself, Corrie whispered to Betsie:

> *"What can we do for these people? Afterward I mean. Can't we make a home for them and care for them and love them?"*
>
> *"Corrie, I pray every day that we will be allowed to do this! To show them that love is greater!"*
>
> *"And it wasn't until I was gathering twigs later in the morning," Corrie writes, "that I realized that I had been thinking of the feeble-minded, and Betsie of their persecutors."*[1]

At the close of the war, the surviving sister, Corrie, returned to her native Holland and established recovery homes, not only for the displaced refugees, but for the psychologically displaced Germans as well.

We must begin, then, with our own attitude before we can discuss appropriate action for, as the Course teaches, all behavior flows from our thoughts. Central to this issue is our understanding of suffering. It is one of the more convincing illusions of the world that suffering is the effect of what has been done to us; that our pain is the result of causes beyond our control. Thus, it reflects the same error of cause-effect reversal we saw in sickness. "The body suffers just in order that the mind will fail to see it is a victim of itself. The body's

[1]*Corrie Ten Boom,* The Hiding Place, *Bantam Books, New York, 1971, pp. 209f.*

suffering is a mask the mind holds up to hide what really suffers"(workbook, p. 132). As the Course explains further: "Suffering is an emphasis upon all that the world has done to injure you. . . . Like to a dream of punishment, in which the dreamer is unconscious of what brought on the attack against himself, he sees himself attacked unjustly and by something not himself. He is the victim of this 'something else,' a thing outside himself, for which he has no reason to be held responsible" (text, p. 539).

Suffering is the direct result of believing in the reality of the body, for only a body (physical or psychological) can suffer pain. Since the body is equated with the separation, pain serves the ego's purpose of denying the reality of God and His creation. "Pain is a sign illusions reign in place of truth. It demonstrates God is denied, confused with fear, perceived as mad, and seen as traitor to Himself. If God is real, there is no pain. If pain is real, there is no God" (workbook, p. 351).

This is not to deny that people experience physical and psychological pain or that one should not minister to others at the level of their experienced need: a starving person should be fed, for example; a naked one clothed; medication offered those with physical or psychological pain, etc. But beyond this level of pain, another level is present as well. Our true pain comes from our mistaken interpretation of reality, not from what that reality is. It comes from the belief that we are children of the ego and this separated world of form, not children of God and His Heaven. Thus, we cannot suffer at anyone's hands but our own, since we alone are responsible for our beliefs. Our mistaken belief about ourselves, not the external agent onto which we have projected the cause, is the source of our pain, which disappears when our minds are healed. As the Course emphasizes: "It is your thoughts alone that cause you pain. Nothing external to your mind can hurt or injure you in any way. There is no cause beyond yourself that can reach down and bring oppression. No one but yourself affects you. There is nothing in the world that has the power to make you ill or sad, or weak or frail" (workbook, p. 351).

Suffering is the *effect* of the belief in separation, which is the *cause*. Thus, whenever we choose to identify the cause of our suffering as external to us — be it another's attack, the cruel vagaries of fate, the injustices done to us in the past, or the attacks on our bodies we call sickness — we are falling into the ego's trap of denying the true cause of our problems — the ego itself — by hiding it behind the projected causes of the world.

Any true solution to a problem, regardless of the problem's form, must undo the cause found in our mistaken mind. Healing, whether individual or social, however holy it may seem, that does not have as its ultimate aim the reawakening of the spiritual Self will eventually fail. It will not heal because the guilt of the separation will remain. It has sought to correct the effect but not the cause.

Therefore, when we react to suffering — ours or another's — as reality, we are merely reinforcing the basic error of the separation that gave rise to the suffering in the first place. It is an example of what the Course would term false empathy, joining with another's weakness rather than uniting with his strength. "To empathize does not mean to join in suffering, for that is what you must *refuse* to understand. That is the ego's interpretation of empathy, and is always used to form a special relationship in which the suffering is shared. . . . The ego always empathizes to weaken, and to weaken is always to attack" (text, p. 307). It is uniting with someone's form of ego darkness, rather than with the light of spirit that always shines. Rather we should practice true empathy: identifying with another's richness and strength — the light of Heaven — rather than with one's poverty and weakness — the darkness of the ego.

Therefore, it is not injustice, evil or sin that is the problem we wish to correct. It is the error of separation. If we believe in the reality of suffering, we must believe that someone or something has brought it about, and that this someone must be punished for his crime or wrongdoing. Thus the world outside — of good and evil — mirrors the world we believe is inside us — separated and conflicted.

It has been said that if there is a crucified, there must be

Both these, live 'inside'

a crucifier. If there is suffering, there must be both a victim *and* a victimizer. Once this perception is established, the inherent unity of the Sonship of God is destroyed, love is seen as divided, and fear, guilt and separation become the distorted reality of God's kingdom. We cannot forgive what we have first made real. If we perceive suffering as real, we cannot truly forgive its perpetrators. Once this perception of suffering is accorded reality, divisions are set up between victim and persecutor, justice and injustice, oppressed and oppressor. Forgiveness, love and justice have become impossible.

True Justice

Justice based upon separation and division cannot be the justice of Heaven, which sees all people as one. "There is a kind of justice in salvation of which the world knows nothing. To the world, justice and vengeance are the same, for sinners see justice only as their punishment, perhaps sustained by someone else, but not escaped" (text, p. 497f).

But what about the obvious injustice that exists around us: the oppression, poverty, suffering and abuse that have become such a part of our world? To help the needy and afflicted has always been central to our Judaeo-Christian ethic. As Isaiah wrote, paralleled in Matthew 25: "[God wants] to break unjust fetters and undo the thongs of the yoke, to let the oppressed go free, and break every yoke, to share . . . bread with the hungry, and shelter the homeless poor, to clothe the many . . . [seen] to be naked . . . " (Is 58:6f). No one could deny the validity of this ethic, or brush aside the spiritual necessity of helping another in distress. Yet the Course tells us that one who learns its lessons "laughs . . . at pain and loss, at sickness and at grief, at poverty, starvation and at death" (workbook, p. 346). The seeming conflict between these two statements is resolved when we recognize that this laughter is not derisive, nor is it based on indifference to the plight of others. Rather, it is a "gentle laughter," born of the vision that the suffering is not what it seems, for when we understand the dynamics of fear and guilt we are able to redefine the dimensions of poverty and oppression. We recognize that the world's afflictions are not really material or external (the right side of Table 2), but are internal (the left side). Moreover, they are afflictions we all share as children of the ego. All people are impoverished who lack inner peace, the interior awareness of God's presence and of their identity as His children: "The poor are merely those who have invested wrongly, and they are poor indeed! . . . For poverty is lack, and there is but one lack since there is but one need" (text, p. 205). Who among us is exempt from this mistaken investment in the ego's thought system?

As we have seen in the preceding chapter, people would not seek to hurt, oppress, victimize, persecute or even murder, unless inside themselves they felt impoverished, guilty and vulnerable. Their outer acts of violence and injustice are the projections of their own interior fear and guilt, the attempts to deny their guilt by perceiving outside agents doing to them the injustice of separation they unconsciously believe they have perpetrated on themselves, on others and on God.

For this reason, the face of true justice must look on all people as the same and recognize that each of the myriad forms of fear conceals the same meaning. The arms of justice extend to embrace each one in forgiveness and in pardon — not for the seemingly terrible things that were done, but to undo the fear and guilt that underlie them. The rock on which salvation rests, according to the Course, is the idea that "no one can lose for anyone to gain. And everyone *must* gain, if anyone would be a gainer. . . . No one can suffer for the Will of God to be fulfilled" (text, pp. 496f). Justice does not punish one so that another might feel justified, for justifying one against the other merely reinforces the belief in separation that was the original problem. Because it knows both parties will lose, justice cannot take away from one so that another may gain. Love has no price, and there can be no sacrifice in Heaven's plan for salvation. "You who believe that sacrifice is love must learn that sacrifice is separation from love" (text, pp. 304f). Punishment in any form is the attempt to project guilt onto another, and to shift responsibility for our unhappiness onto someone or something external to ourselves. A loving God would never treat His children this way.

Practicing True Justice

Once our thoughts are aligned with the healing thoughts of the Holy Spirit, sharing His perception of the situation, we can address the more practical questions of what we are to do in the face of attack, injustice and suffering. The answer will always be based upon a desire to help *all* those concerned. The focus is not on *what* we do, but *why*. It is fundamentally a question of motivation.

For example, imagine we are walking down a street and are suddenly confronted by a crazed man with a knife pointed at our throat. Based on our own state of mind, we can either act to stop him defenselessly out of love, or defensively in fear. Turning the other cheek does not mean we passively let our own throats be cut, silently blessing our assassin as he murders us. Nor does it mean trying to kill him before he kills us, feeling the justice of Heaven is directing our hands. Most definitely we should take steps to stop the would-be murderer, not only to prevent reinforcing our belief in pain, but also to prevent his making a mistake for which he would pay through guilt. Regardless of his actions, he remains our brother. Guilt demands punishment, as we have seen, and the ego would always have us seek this punishment outside ourselves, disguising the real source of punishment which is our self-inflicted guilt. Thus, we must continually be aware of our attempts to project responsibility for the "injustice" of our guilt onto other people or situations in the world, regardless of their appearance. Independent of circumstances, we *are* in control of our peace of mind, as seen in the following example.

Several years ago, I was awakened in the middle of the night by the sudden realization there was someone standing in my room. After the momentary shock, I remembered "there is nothing to fear" (workbook, p. 77), and calmly asked my uninvited guest: "What can I do for you?" The situation was not obscure, however. It was clear that the man was on drugs and desperately needed money for his next fix; burglars rarely enter occupied apartments. He threateningly held his hand in his jacket as if he had a gun, to punctuate his demand. My defenselessness seemed to change the atmosphere in the room, however, and the man soon began apologizing for having broken in and disturbing my sleep. I gave him whatever money I had in my wallet, and the man paused as he took it and then returned a couple of dollars, saying: "This is *all* your money; I can't leave you with nothing." And he went on apologizing. I assured him it was all right, and urged him to do what he had to do. As I ushered the man to the hall, waiting with him for the elevator, I said: "God bless you." His final words as he disappeared into the elevator were: "Please pray for me." I assured him I would, although I knew that this holy encounter had *been* the prayer. No injustice had been done, for there had been no real loss. The amount of money was small "price" indeed for the blessing of forgiveness that had been given and received as one.

Similarly, many missionaries — religious or lay — who are sent into third world countries which suffer under oppressive governments have the difficult lesson of working for the end of "injustice," yet doing so out of love for all people involved, "oppressed" and "oppressor" alike. To undo injustice by acting unjustly through a belief in separation is merely to reinforce the basic "injustice" which *is* separation. These missioners must work in the face of great temptation to identify with the oppressed *against* the oppressor, recognizing that this temptation represents the projection of the split inside themselves.

Our response to injustice, therefore, is one of love and concern, not fear or desire for revenge. We "protect" ourselves, not to punish or because we are frightened, but because we wish to help all who are present in the situation. We have heard our "assailants" call and seek to answer; our attitude of non-attack teaches they are loved even as they sought to hate. The judgment we make in this situation, therefore, is not based on condemnation but on a desire to help, seeing in the others' attack their need for love. Self-protection in this context becomes more than a defense against attack. It has become a loving response to a call for love that we share. It should be added that we need not feel this love totally. To be completely without fear would involve a level of sanctity few if any of us have attained. If our love were that perfect, we would not need Heaven's aid. Thus, our simple desire to see the situation differently, despite our fear, is enough to allow the Holy Spirit to work through us.

Setting limits on people's attempts to destroy social and/or personal boundaries is often the most loving act we can do. There is perhaps no more terrifying experience than believing that the world cannot contain us, that we, in fact, are omnipotent and beyond the power of personal or governmental authorities. Such experience in our personal world reinforces the fundamental ego belief that, by virtue of our separation from God, we are in charge of the universe. Since we have usurped His place, He is now powerless against us. This belief inevitably leads to our terrifying fear of what will be done to us in retaliation for what we believe we have done. This experience of terror is clearly manifest in seriously disturbed people, whose very disturbance has often resulted, on one level, from their lack of trust in others to control, comfort and love them. The following example is illustrative of the application of structure which is not punitive but loving.

Jimmy was a hyperactive six-year-old who was unable to establish any limits to his behavior. He finally had to be placed in a special school, where through an individualized, structured program he began internalizing this control. This minimized his anxiety so that he could begin to sit still, trusting he was protected and that his fear was not shared by others. In time, Jimmy was able to return to the classroom and under the firm and loving discipline of his teacher continued to grow. However, his teacher unexpectedly had to leave the school and was replaced by a relatively inexperienced woman who had never worked with children like Jimmy. It did not take long for Jimmy to catch on, and his old behavior began to return. The climax came one morning when Jimmy acted up and as a punishment was asked to stand in the corner of the room. Responding to the teacher's latent insecurity, his own began to mount. By performing little annoyances he began testing his teacher's inability to contain him. Her own fear made it impossible to respond constructively, and Jimmy's anxiety grew until finally he bolted from the room, his flight desperately crying out that he be stopped. At this point in their relationship it was the teacher who needed help, for it was her difficulty that was exacerbating Jimmy's. She then became the "pupil," and as she was able to impose limits out of love and not fear, Jimmy's self-control returned and his progress was able to continue.

To experience suffering, then, can be part of a transforming experience for us, whether the suffering is our own or seen elsewhere. It can never be God's Will that any of his children suffers pain, but it *is* His Will that we learn from it, once we have chosen to make pain real for ourselves. Following the same principle we have observed before, when suffering is turned over to the Holy Spirit it can provide us with the opportunity of learning His lesson: since peace lies forever invulnerable to anything outside of it, God's child can *not* truly suffer. What we label as suffering we have made real in our minds. This is where correction is needed.

Painful opportunities, trials on whatever level, are merely chances for us to practice forgiveness:

> *Trials are but lessons that you failed to learn presented once again, so where you made a faulty choice before you now can make a better one, and thus escape all pain that what you chose before has brought to you (text, p. 620).*
>
> *This single lesson learned [undoing projection] will set you free from suffering, whatever form it takes. The Holy Spirit will repeat this one inclusive lesson of deliverance until it has been learned, regardless of the form of suffering that brings you pain. Whatever hurt you bring to Him He will make answer with this very simple truth. For this one answer takes away the cause of every form of sorrow and of pain (text, p. 545).*

This answer is forgiveness, the basis of true justice. It is based not upon pain or hurt, but upon the perception that there is nothing to forgive. The sinner's sins have been shown never to have happened, because they have been transformed in our awareness from sins into mistakes to be corrected. Without the projection of guilt there *is* no guilt, and so there can be no desire to punish. Guiltless, we seek to prevent acts of oppression or violence in the world, not to punish or "protect" but to heal all people: the oppressed, the oppressor and ourselves. All embody the effects of the same mistake: the belief that there *can* be inflicted suffering in the world. We involve ourselves in programs of alleviating pain in the world so that *all* of us can be free from the pain of our belief in separation.

How the undoing of this pain is brought about is beyond our capacity to understand. As the Course says of the holy relationship: " . . . your understanding is not necessary. All that was necessary was merely the *wish* to understand" (text, p. 353). By undoing our own belief in separation through joining with another in forgiveness, the Holy Spirit is able to heal our minds and all minds through ours. "And as you let yourself be healed, you see all those around you or who cross your mind, or whom you touch or those who seem to have no contact with you, healed along with you" (workbook, p. 255). When we are healed, the workbook lesson says, we are not healed alone.

Unless our goal is to help every person involved in the mistake, we will be responding to the projection of our own guilt and still looking out on a world of separate interests. Such perception can only come from a prior belief about ourselves. If we believe we are separated, we will see a world of separation — of people with opposing characteristics of good and evil, love and hate, those to be supported and those to be opposed, those to be judged and those to be overcome. True healing and correction thus become impos sible.

The Role of the Holy Spirit

Once we have defined the problem as injustice, it is inevitable we will believe we are the ones who can solve it.

Once again we can see the ego subtly reinforcing itself, reproducing the original error of believing we can and have usurped the role of God. A common fallacy is believing that we are the ones who teach lessons, who correct the mistakes of others.

> *To the ego it is kind and right and good to point out errors and "correct" them. This makes perfect sense to the ego, which is unaware of what errors are and what correction is. Errors are of the ego, and correction of errors lies in the relinquishment of the ego. . . . When you react at all to errors, you are not listening to the Holy Spirit. He has merely disregarded them, and if you attend to them you are not hearing Him. If you do not hear Him, you are listening to your ego and making as little sense as the brother whose errors you perceive. This cannot be correction. . . . You cannot correct yourself. Is it possible, then, for you to correct another? . . . Any attempt you make to correct a brother means that you believe correction by you is possible, and this can only be the arrogance of the ego. Correction is of God, Who does not know of arrogance (text, pp. 155f).*

When one stops to consider what correction really involves, the impossibility of ever knowing what needs to be done becomes very clear.

> *In order to judge anything rightly, one would have to be fully aware of an inconceivably wide range of things: past, present and to come. One would have to recognize in advance all the effects of his judgments on everyone and everything involved in them in any way. And one would have to be certain there is no distortion in his perception, so that his judgment would be wholly fair to everyone on whom it rests now and in the future. Who is in a position to do this? Who except in grandiose fantasies would claim this for himself? . . . Wisdom is not judgment; it is the relinquishment of judgment. Make then but one*

> *more judgment. It is this: There is Someone with you Whose judgment is perfect. He does know all the facts: past, present and to come. He does know all the effects of His judgment on everyone and everything involved in any way. And He is wholly fair to everyone, for there is no distortion in His perception (manual pp. 26f).*

Thus, to think that we know what is right for ourselves and those who are close to us, let alone the whole world, is truly arrogant. Most of us are very skillful at deceiving ourselves on this point. It is easy to cloak our arrogance in terms of justice, love, freedom and spirituality. The temptation to do so must be fully recognized. We need only consider how much blood has been spilled in the name of God, love and peace to realize this is so. Only if we follow the guidance of the Holy Spirit can we be sure there is no attack and our response is loving, not only to others but to ourselves. In His way of solving a problem, in contrast to the ego's, no one can lose and everyone must gain. He does not "take from Peter to pay Paul." Love can only give; it never demands sacrifice or causes suffering or pain.

The power of love contrasted with force is expressed in the fairy tale of the sun and wind arguing over which was the stronger. Looking down to earth, they saw a man walking with his jacket on. They decided to settle their argument by seeing which of the two could get the man to remove his jacket. The wind went first and blew as hard as it could. But this merely caused the man to wrap his coat even more tightly around him. When the sun's turn came, it simply began to shine. The more it shone, the warmer the man felt, and within minutes he removed the jacket. The lesson is clear. To effect a change in others we need only let God's light shine. Applying pressure in any way merely causes others to increase their defensiveness. Our ego meets another ego and the results must always be counter-productive, often bringing about the very things we do not want.

Thus, we return to the basic problem of how we can hear the Holy Spirit, that we may let His light shine through us. To do this we *must* let go of our guilt, which is not only an attack on ourselves, but an assault on God by attempting to deny his Presence and make His Voice forever inaudible. As long as guilt continues its static noise in our minds, we can never hear the Voice that speaks for our guiltlessness and that of all our brothers and sisters. Not only does guilt hide our true Self, it makes it impossible to see the light of that Self in others. As attack is nothing more than projected guilt, attack in any form will conceal the Holy Spirit in a cloud of guilt. But deciding to see attack as a call for help expresses the desire to hear His Voice, that we may be shown the vision of forgiveness that will forgive us our guilt. Thus, a desperate intruder is offering us an opportunity to meet attack with love, and thereby learn the very lesson we are teaching.

In fact, any time we are confronted by a situation that makes us impatient, annoyed or angry, it is a clear sign that we have forgotten our lesson and have once again been tempted by the ego. To become aware of how well we may have generalized the Holy Spirit's lessons we need only turn on the evening news and observe our reactions to the inevitable reports of rape, murder, injustice, oppression, catastrophes, etc. Our reactions will be a good indicator of the degree of unforgiveness that still remains locked in our mind. That half an hour spent with the ego's world can become a powerful classroom that the Holy Spirit can use to heal our minds.

Regardless of what another has asked of us, or seems to be doing to us or others, we must turn to the Holy Spirit for help that we may look at the situation differently:

> *"Forgive, and you will see this differently." These are the words the Holy Spirit speaks in all your tribulations, all your pain, all suffering regardless of its form. . . . There is a way to look on everything that lets it be to you another step to Him, and to salvation of the world. To all that speaks of terror, answer thus: "I will forgive, and this will disappear" (workbook, pp. 357-59).*

In asking for healing we are made open to the only Source of healing there is. In responding to another's call for love we are asking God to respond to ours. "He will teach you how to see yourself without condemnation, by learning how to look on everything without it. Condemnation will then not be real to you, and all your errors will be forgiven" (text, p. 156). In this way the one love of our Father is brought to all His children by the one Person who knows what that love is, and how it can best be taught to those who have forgotten it.

Chapter 4

THE MEANING OF LOVE AND SEXUALITY

Chapter 1 described the ego's version of love in special relationships. Understanding the Holy Spirit's purpose in relationships, we can now discuss His meaning of love as well as the role of sexuality.

It can be said that due to the ego's profound distortions of relationships, unambivalent love, as we have seen, is impossible in this world. Only an "advanced teacher of God" would be able to relate to others independent of ego-projections. Despite our human frailties, however, the love of God can be reflected in our lives. The scriptural commandment that we love our neighbor is really a commandment to forgive, for it is through forgiveness that our guilt is undone and we are better able to love one another as God loves us. It is in the context of forgiveness that we find love's meaning.

C. G. Jung once observed that every problem over the age of thirty-five was a spiritual problem. The number is obviously an arbitrary one. The dividing line between the two stages in our lives usually ranges from our late twenties to somewhere in our thirties, although there are many exceptions on both ends. The first half of our life is spent in developing the tools of survival, learning to cope with the physical, psychological and social world, and can be thought of as a period of preparation. This period is natural in our human lives. Not to develop a personal identity or sense of self (ego) leads to psychosis and, in extreme cases, autism. It is the paradox of our human lives that we must spend this first part of our lives in developing an ego, which we must then unlearn in the second part.

This second stage involves implementing these abilities and skills, answering the question: which master do we follow, God or the ego? This is the real meaning of the "mid-life crisis." For this reason Jung spoke of the spiritual nature of problems during this period. If we follow our ego we deny our spiritual function, seeing the purpose of our life only in terms of meeting the unfulfilled security needs of the past, projected into the future. One problem after another presents itself, a process which ultimately can be traced to this denial of our true Self. When, on the other hand, we place our lives in God's service, all problems are seen as opportunities for remembering our true identity in Him. As there are specific developmental times for walking, talking, reasoning, etc., there is a developmental readiness for spiritual learning. True spiritual maturity is not possible until we come of age. Many of the relationships in the first part of our lives are the building blocks through which we will later learn the lessons of forgiveness that will lead us back to God.

Forgiveness and Love: The Holy Relationship

In all relationships we see the Holy Spirit at work, helping us with the lessons that teach that true peace is found only in the living God within us, and never in another. The obstacle to experiencing peace is guilt. This guilt, though abstract and all-pervasive, is expressed in specific ways for each of us. It is within these forms that guilt must be unlearned; our special functions discussed in Chapter 2. We choose God in the very situations we would be most tempted to choose the ego. The purpose of all relationships, therefore, is to help us make this choice, and it is not by chance that we are born into particular families, nor whom we marry or who our friends are. Each relationship can be part of the Holy Spirit's Atonement plan for us, if we let it.

1. Parents and Children

The most basic of all love relationships is that between parent and child. Because we have been the most dependent on our parents, this special relationship holds the greatest potential for learning forgiveness. Freud was quite correct in emphasizing the importance of our feelings towards our mother and father. The successful resolution of the Oedipus Complex, the prototype for all special love and hate relationships, is really an exercise in forgiveness. We must learn to forgive the parent of the opposite sex for not being our savior, possession of whom, our unconscious believed, would always make us content and happy. At the same time, we forgive the parent of the same sex for not being our enemy, the special hate rival for the affections of our special love parent.

No one's parents are perfect. They, too, had parents who struggled with ego problems, which inevitably were projected onto their children. In this sense, the "sins" of the fathers *are* visited unto succeeding generations. It has frequently been observed, for example, that abused children frequently become abusing parents when they grow up. None of us was treated as perfectly in our childhood as we believed we deserved, or received all the material and psychological things we needed. It is thus very difficult to avoid the ego's "if only" formulation discussed earlier: If only my parents had treated me differently, if only my parents had more money, if only my parents had remained together, if only my parents . . . I would be happier today. True forgiveness recognizes that our childhood situations were part of the Holy Spirit's plan to teach us forgiveness in the forms necessary for our learning. They are the curriculum through which we learn that salvation does not rest in the "good" circumstances of our lives, any more than misery and suffering rest in the "bad" ones. In the Holy Spirit's eyes they are the same, sharing the same purpose of forgiving the past that we may remember God in the present.

As children we are almost totally dependent on our own parents, not only for our material needs but for our own self-image. We grow to see ourselves largely as our parents or parenting figures have seen us, and there is little we can do about this when we are young. If we are rejected by our parents, for example, feelings of unworthiness and self-blame are inevitable; if over-protected, the belief that we are inadequate to be on our own is reinforced. On the other hand, to be loved and accepted will help us develop a strong sense of personal identity and self-worth. Still, in the second stage of life we must transcend this personal self and find our true Self in God.

As adults, knowing ourselves as children of our Father in Heaven, we need no longer be as dependent on others for our physical and psychological well-being. To continue to remain dependent represents a decision. Freud showed how the past affects the present, that the patterns of childhood are repeated in adult life. If we see ourselves as others have seen us, we are inevitably bound by what has happened in the past. The child will be father of the man. The basic problem, however, does not lie with the past, but in the present where we make the decisive choice to live in the present or the past.

The distinction is a critical one, for seeing the past as the prime determiner of our self concept keeps us imprisoned as innocent victims of a cruel world and of events that cannot be changed. There can be no hope in such a position. However, to see ourselves free to choose allows us to identify with more than our ego, and places full responsibility for this identification on our power of decision. It is true that on one level children are not responsible for what happens to them, but it is also true that as adults we are no longer bound by what our parents did or did not do. They are not responsible for our present unhappiness, for real happiness is not dependent on the things or persons of this world. Only if this were so could it be possible for us to be deprived of it.

The recognition that our real parent is God and we depend only on Him, or that as parents we are really God's instruments and not His substitute, is the basis of real love between parents and children. Parental overconcern or overprotectiveness is not love, but an expression of fear, lack of faith, and the parents' need to have their children become what they need them to be. This leads to frustration, anger and a desire to prevent the children — grown or otherwise — from learning their own particular lessons in the Holy Spirit's classroom. Similarly, loving one's parents out of duty or obligation can only lead to resentment and guilt. We know whether we are instruments of God's love or the ego's fear by the peace that results in ourselves and in our parents or children.

It is therefore in parents and children forgiving each other for what they have not done that the Holy Spirit's lessons are learned. Each will have looked on the other, no longer to fulfill certain needs through specific roles, but as brother and sister whom God has joined to walk forgiveness' path together. Without this step in changing an unholy relationship into a holy one, no one can truly identify as a child of God. The guilt that specialness holds fast prevents this recognition of our Father's love for us.

Consider a girl whose parents were poor and emotionally ungiving. Having been deprived of the love she always craved, she learned to identify material gifts with emotional ones, substituting in her mind material possessions for love. As an adult, she demands of others – spouse, friends, superiors – that they demonstrate their affection by tangible gifts. Remaining at the core, however, is the basic unforgiveness of her parents, not to mention God, for never giving what she needed, and of herself for having these needs in the first place. Each relationship in her life, therefore, expresses this unconscious condemnation of her parents. She walks the world feeling empty and deprived, seeking to fill this need by the things of the world; happy when she receives them, unhappy when she does not. Forgiveness, then, would teach that what she truly wants she has, since a child of God has all that she needs. This reflects the principle of abundance, and underlies the statement in the Course that "the only meaningful prayer is for forgiveness, because those who have been forgiven have everything . . . [recognizing] what [they] already have" (text, p. 40).

As long as we believe there are needs that must be met because they were not met in the past, we are reinforcing our belief in scarcity. Following the law of projection, we will shift the responsibility for this belief onto others. Thus, we feel deprived of the happiness we believe would be ours, were it not for the terrible things that were done to us. However, following the ego's law, the more we project this guilt the more we reinforce the belief that we are limited and lacking, and therefore the worse we feel about ourselves. With this mind set, love for others is impossible, for only out of our belief in abundance, coming from God, can love be truly expressed.

However, as adults we are free to choose again. In forgiving others for *not* having deprived us, we are taking the first step of forgiveness in undoing the belief in scarcity which was the true problem. As we then change our mind about ourselves (the second step), substituting abundance for scarcity, our guilt is removed from us (the third step) and we are able finally to accept God's gift, sharing His love with those He has sent into our lives. Thus would we remember our Father in Heaven as we forgive our parents on earth.

2. Romantic Love

As people come into our lives, we are attracted to them for either of two reasons. To the ego, people are attractive for their capacity to be objects of projection (special love partners). We are attracted to their physical appearance, personality, financial status, etc. However, this attraction of special love, as we have seen, is nothing more than a thin veil over hate. Yet, there is another attraction as well. As our ego calls to its counterpart to join in an unholy alliance of guilt, the Holy Spirit calls in each of us that we join in a holy relationship of forgiveness. This is the true attraction which the ego continually seeks to obscure. The real "love at first sight" of which the poets sing is the Holy Spirit's love, calling from one person to another. It is the "attraction of love for love" (text, p. 219), calling to itself that it be joined as one, no longer kept separate. Each of us sees in the other God's opportunity to forgive our guilt and be made whole; not that we find completion in the other, as the ego would tell us, but that through forgiveness of our guilt (the belief in scarcity) our own wholeness is made manifest. It is the love this wholeness reflects that truly attracts us, in contrast to the attraction of guilt found in special relationships. "Falling in love," therefore, lies in recognizing the potential for seeing the light of Heaven in another, recognizing one's "chosen learning partner who presents him with unlimited opportunities for learning" (manual, p. 7). Looking past the darkness of our projected guilt undoes our own. In this joining in light we experience the Holy Spirit's blessing of love.

The experience of "growing in love" likewise has two interpretations. To the ego, it means two people increasingly meeting the other's needs, thus growing in dependency.

This constitutes the extension of the ego's "honeymoon period" described in Chapter 1, and strengthens the specialness the ego values so highly. To the Holy Spirit, the term reflects a growing in forgiveness. Each of us is joined in love to all people, for this is the reality of oneness given by God in our creation. "What God calls one will be forever one, not separate. His Kingdom is united; thus it was created, and thus will it ever be" (text, pp. 517f). We do not have the power nor the freedom to undo what God established as reality. However, we do have the freedom not to accept it. "Truth is beyond your ability to destroy, but entirely within your ability to accept" (text, p. 74). What obscures our awareness of love's presence in ourselves and our relationships is guilt. As two people continue to learn their lessons of forgiveness, their guilt correspondingly decreases: the less guilt present, the more love we can experience. It is this love that "grows" in a relationship. In reality, it is the decrease in guilt through forgiveness that allows the love that always was to dawn within our minds.

Love has only one Source and can have only one purpose, the fulfillment of itself. It is an endless circle that extends to embrace all God's children. While it is not possible to love each person in the same way or share a level of intimacy with everyone, it is possible to have no interferences to love's extension. Thus, no one is excluded. It is the undoing of these interferences that is the goal of all relationships, casual or lifelong.

In this context, we may understand marriage or any long-term friendship as the union of two whom the Holy Spirit has joined together, that each may overlook the many temptations to project, and find in the other the image of one's real Self. These temptations fall under the categories of the special love and special hate relationships already discussed. In these relationships, we use our partners to avoid our own guilt, making them into either savior or scapegoat. The following two examples illustrate the ego's distortions of love relationships to meet its ends.

A man who saw his mother as the answer to all his problems may try to transfer that role to his wife, as in the words of the popular song: "I want a girl just like the girl that married dear old Dad." Investing her with all the special attributes he envisions necessary for his happiness and well-being, he falls in love with her. In fact, however, it is a made-up image he loves, like Pygmalion, and not his wife as a person in her own right. If the Holy Spirit's purpose for their union is to be realized, the man must relinquish his investment in the image, forgiving his wife for being or *not* being like his mother and the savior of his dreams. By this process, he would come to accept their essential wholeness as God's children, allowing their relationship to become the temple of the Holy Spirit that the Course describes (text, pp. 406-09). Similarly, if his wife needed to be her husband's mother, she must forgive *him* for being or not being the "dutiful son" her ego demanded.

In another example, a woman with a strong investment in seeing herself unfairly treated may be attracted to a man who will mistreat her. Her need to see him this way will cause her to distort his actions in her mind, and preclude her recognizing his own ego needs and call for help. Thus, she may indulge in self-pity, continually bemoaning her cruel fate at being married to such a person. If her husband needs a mate onto whom he can project his own self-hatred, magically hoping to establish himself as superior and more powerful by abusing his wife, we find another example of the ego's "Heavenly marriage": the mutual meeting of needs wherein the proper hand fits into the proper glove. If, however, the wife is able to understand her investment in being mistreated by her husband, and thus forgive him for her own need to be punished, demanded by her guilt, she will see the situation differently. Choosing to see herself as guiltless in God's eyes, she will no longer look at her husband as an enemy, but as a friend and brother calling out for help. Similarly, her husband may take the step of recognizing her ego's need to project, thereby forgiving himself and his wife. This shift in perception begins the holy relationship, the Holy Spirit's answer to the special relationship.

Problems in relationships, therefore, are always projections of problems of guilt within each of the individuals involved. Rather than seeing the guilt within, the partners choose to see it in each other. The unconscious duplicity of these maneuvers prevents any real healing from occuring. The desire to terminate a relationship that has become strained can sometimes be a temptation *not* to learn the lessons of undoing guilt the Holy Spirit has provided. Our fear of the peace that forgiveness brings becomes too great, and we seem to have no recourse except to follow our ego and repeatedly seek comfort in special relationships.

This does not necessarily mean, however, that all relationships must remain permanent in form. A relationship may fall into the second category discussed earlier: "a more sustained relationship, in which, for a time, two people enter into a fairly intense teaching-learning situation and then appear to separate" (manual, p. 7). Thus, two people may have fulfilled all that was theirs to teach and learn at that time, or they may decide to go no further in their learning, only to complete those lessons later. Thus, a marriage can end in divorce, college friends may drift apart upon graduation, etc. It is not for us to judge these situations. The Holy Spirit does not evaluate according to form but purpose. If a mistake has been made, i.e., the guidance of the ego has been sought, He will correct it. If it is His will that has been followed, He will uphold it. We are asked only to do the best we can in trying to hear His Voice. If we have followed the Voice of truth, regardless of the form that may evolve for the relationship, the oneness of God's children will remain in our awareness: "Whom God has joined as one, the ego cannot put asunder" (text p. 332). Thus, the lessons in forgiveness will have been learned and peace will be the result. Projected guilt makes this peace impossible.

Therefore, no relationship can be healed without addressing this basic problem of guilt. However, it is not necessary that *both* parties choose to do this. Forgiveness is a process that occurs in one's mind, since that is where the thoughts of separation and guilt are found. All that is required is that one of the two asks for help to make the shift. It takes two to agree on separation, but only one healed mind to correct [undo] it: "Whoever is saner at the time the threat is perceived should remember how deep is his indebtedness to the other and how much gratitude is due him, and be glad that he can pay his debt by bringing happiness to both" (text, p. 358). When a couple has problems, it very often is one of the two who must take this first step. Whoever is closer to recognizing the true source of the conflict must be willing to shift from an attitude of fault-finding to forgiveness, seeing the partner's mistakes as calls for help. This can be done only by realizing that the help offered to this particular partner is the same help God offers to oneself. We recognize that our unhappiness is not attributable to external circumstances but to our disrupted relationship with God (the separation).

This healing is accepted at the instant it is offered: "Whenever a teacher of God has tried to be a channel for healing he has succeeded" (manual, p. 21). However, peoples' fear of healing or forgiveness may prevent them from consciously accepting this gift: "Healing will always stand aside when it would be seen as threat. The instant it is welcome it is there. Where healing has been given it will be received" (manual, p. 19). The Holy Spirit holds the gift of healing or forgiveness until the time when the fear has abated sufficiently for the gift to be accepted. Therefore, "no teacher of God should feel disappointed if he has offered healing and it does not appear to have been received. It is not up to him to judge when his gift should be accepted. Let him be certain it has been received, and trust that it will be accepted when it is recognized as a blessing and not a curse" (manual, p. 19). The person offering forgiveness is asked to have faith that its purpose has been accomplished. Despite the appearance of continuing problems, he or she trusts that the offering has been blessed by God, who guarantees that He will complete what has been begun. Now the relationship has been saved, for it has become a classroom where the Holy Spirit's lessons can be taught and learned. The sounds of warfare are changed to cries for help, and the battlefield transformed into a temple where two have come together to worship at the altar of forgiveness. Of such is love's kingdom on earth.

Sexuality and Celibacy

1. The Two Uses of Sexuality

The moral and religious strictures against sexuality go

back to the beginnings of civilization. These are understandable in terms of the almost universal associations between sex and aggression, and therefore between sex and guilt. Genesis teaches that Adam and Eve's first action after eating the forbidden fruit was to cover their nakedness with loincloths. Indeed, for some of the early Christian Fathers, notably St. Augustine, original sin was equated with concupiscence. This equation is inevitable for, with the exception of death or eating, there is no more heavily body-invested activity than sex. We have already seen how the ego transfers its "sin" onto the body, and it is but another step to focus this guilt specifically on sexuality.

On another level, we can see how guilt must inevitably follow using another's body as a means of satisfying our own needs, with little or no concern for the person *within* the body. In such a situation, which can serve as one of the prototypes for special relationships, we overlook the person within our own body as well. Because of this identification with the body, sex can admirably serve the ego's purpose of reinforcing guilt. Becoming a symbol of our sin, sex, like anger, can be a powerful weapon in the ego's arsenal: making up pseudo-problems to distract us from the problem in our mind (see Table 2). Problems of impotence or frigidity, concerns over sexual outlets or forms, promiscuity, struggles with celibacy, etc., are smokescreens set up by the ego to keep us from dealing with the deeper problems of guilt and our relationship with God that transcend sexuality altogether.

Thus, it is not uncommon that people on the verge of making an important life decision such as marriage or religious vows, or about to take any action reflecting commitment to God, may develop sudden "attacks" of sexuality in various forms: a young woman about to marry "discovers" she is a lesbian; a man soon to be ordained a priest finds himself obsessed with sexual desires for a particular woman. All that really happens in many of these instances is the ego's panic in the face of our decision to follow God's Will rather than its own, and its attempt to sabotage this decision. Treating these problems as serious in their own right is the perfect way to hold on to them, for fighting ego defenses merely makes them stronger. Once seen as harmless distractions they will disappear as easily as the sun burns away an early morning mist. What remains is the Will of God.

Some of the misconceptions about sex can be clarified in remembering the two levels discussed at the beginning of Chapter 1. On the first level, sex, being a body activity, is pure illusion. To pursue or to avoid sex is to give it a meaning it does not have. Our rationalizations and justifications to the contrary, sex cannot become the reality it never was, nor can it bring the peace and happiness that is beyond the capability of any illusion.

On the second level, sex is neither holy nor unholy. It is wholly neutral, waiting for the use the mind gives it. If we are following the Holy Spirit, the decision for sexual involvement with another does not meet our ego needs — be they physical or psychological, conscious or unconscious — but rather meets our real need of forgiveness. Each person sees in the other the learning opportunity offered by the Holy Spirit to forgive oneself and another. Thus they learn that sex is not sinful but, like any body function, can serve the Holy Spirit's purpose while we are learning in this world's classrooms. Properly focused, the sexual impulse becomes holy, for it becomes part of a relationship, chosen by Him, for us to learn and teach the love He would extend through our healed relationship. As in other forms of interpersonal functioning which can teach us to undo separate interests, so do sexual partners learn to share with each other, uniting in a common goal. In such a union there will be no fantasy, but thoughts of peace and love. Only here is real pleasure found. The Holy Spirit will have been invited in, and He remains to honor and bless. If one's personal needs begin to overshadow concern for others, it is a sign that we have returned to the ego for guidance. Now we should turn quickly to the Holy Spirit for help, shifting the sexual impulse back to its purpose of forgiveness. We must learn again that bodies are not for pleasure, domination or exclusion, but for teaching that we are joined together on a level beyond the body. By placing shared above personal interests, we can acknowledge our spiritual identity that unites us both as one.

To the ego, on the other hand, sex serves the purpose of making the body real in our experience, thereby reinforcing our belief in the reality of the separation. One of the prominent ways the ego "lures" us into this trap is by teaching that bodies *can* join with each other: our incompleteness due to the separation can be overcome by sexual union. This denies the Course's principle: "Minds are joined; bodies are not" (text, p. 359). Once convincing us that sex is desirable for reasons of union, attracting us to it by virtue of physical pleasure, the ego is now able to offer its real gift of guilt. Its underlying intentions in sex can be seen in the fantasies that often accompany sexual activity or impulses: these often include hostility, triumph, vengeance, self-debasement, or other forms of lack of love, all of which belie the ego's arguments on behalf of the "beauty" or "holiness" of sex.

One of the prevalent ego beliefs concerning sex is that it is a release of tension, a central tenet in Freud's theory. It is another form of the same mistake we observed earlier that held anger to be a basic human emotion, and therefore one whose energy had to be expressed or repressed. Tension does not come from the body, however, but results from the conflict in our minds between God and the ego. Its only true release comes when we choose the One, and let the other go. To shift this tension to sexual drives, seeking to resolve the problem on that level as the ego would have us do, merely reinforces the error of ego-body identification that is the ultimate source of the tension. Thus, this source is held still further apart from healing.

The basic issue, then, is not "To bed or not to bed," but which voice do we follow? Whenever we pursue the ego's goals, guilt will result in any one of its various forms, for its purpose will be to attack and separate. By choosing to follow the ego we have chosen to follow specialness. Thus, another becomes the object who can fulfill our special need. By seeing ourselves *needing* the fulfillment, we are self-demeaning as well. Guilt and hatred are the only rewards we shall reap, instead of the love the Holy Spirit's forgiveness brings.

2. Celibacy

Part of the ego's success in maintaining the illusion of

sexuality as a problem has come through its advocacy of celibacy in the spiritual life. Celibacy has been a prominent symbol of holiness in Christianity, as it has been in many world religions. Its manifest purpose was a life style in which all energies and thoughts were directed to God alone. By not having one special love object, celibates strove to have God be the sole recipient of their love; needing nothing outside to complete themselves, they would find the Source of completion within. Their goal was the spiritual marriage of which the mystics speak.

However, all too frequently celibacy has focused on the physical aspect of relationships, often mistaking the letter of the law for its spirit, form for content. Most recently, this error has taken the extreme form that one can lead a celibate religious life as long as any sexual encounter stops short of intercourse. This emphasis subtly shifts the problem from the mind to the body, where there can be no real resolution of the problem, the ego's ultimate goal. Once this shift is made, we are in the characteristic ego position of being placed between Scylla and Charybdis: damned if we do, and damned if we do not. If we indulge our sexual appetites we will feel guilty; if we abstain from sexual activity we will feel frustrated and resentful, often leading to repression of the guilt which remains hidden under a cloud of depression, prone to projection. Either way, the ego emerges triumphant.

Celibacy has also reinforced an arbitrary distinction between religious and the laity, insofar as a sexually chaste life was seen as "higher" or more spiritual than a non-celibate one. This distinction is blessed by the ego, as it underscores the separation that is its constant goal. Moreover, this conclusion of spiritual superiority is not necessarily valid. If one faithfully lives an abstaining life of consecrated celibacy but continually harbors sexual thoughts, guilt over such thoughts will remain and be just as disrupting as if the persons were sexually acting out the thoughts and fantasies. This is certainly not to condone promiscuity on the grounds that since it "does not matter anyway" you might as well enjoy yourself, but merely to emphasize that controlling one's actions is not sufficient to achieve real peace. As the

Course teaches: "It is pointless to believe that controlling the outcome of misthought can result in healing. . . . You must change your mind, not your behavior. . . . Correction belongs only at the level where change is possible. Change does not mean anything at the symptom level, where it cannot work" (text, p. 25). Controlling one's behavior, while often a step in the right direction as it can reflect a desire to change one's mind, still does not change the thoughts of guilt, which merely become strengthened through their denial. Such a process can lead to "spiritual smugness," wherein one believes the problem of sin has been resolved. In reality, all that has occurred is repression, inevitably leading to thoughts of sin being projected elsewhere, either onto other aspects of one's life, or onto other people who stand condemned in our eyes for *our* sinful thoughts. The 19th century German poet Goethe understood this dynamic very well when he said that he was guilty of every sin and crime that had ever been committed. He himself had not committed that many, but he knew that at some point or another during his long life he had harbored all these "sinful" thoughts, and thus he was guilty of them. Guilt in our special relationships is always based on thoughts, never actions.

3. Form versus Content

The ego's emphasis on sex is clarified when we understand its confusion of form and content. The multitude of forms in this world conceals the simplicity of their content, which can be only two: God or the ego; truth or illusion. The ego attempts to convince us that our problems are on the level of form, either to be valued or avoided. In so doing, the ego's underlying goal of guilt and fear escapes notice and correction. Thus: "Only the form of error attracts the ego. Meaning it does not recognize, and does not see if it is there or not" (text, p. 442).

In its attraction to sex, the ego does not care if one values or avoids it. Encouraging sexual activity, the ego invites us to partake of various physical and psychological gratifications, all of which conceal the underlying pain brought on by reinforcing our belief in scarcity, using others as sexual objects, or being "forced" to maintain guilty secrets. These ego "gifts" can be observed in the following examples: the "Don Juan" whose goal is to seduce or make love to every woman in the world; women for whom sex is a symbol of being loved and desired; people tempted by promiscuity; and those lured into having secret alliances.

On the other side, the ego teaches that sex is a particularly unholy form of sin, and should be avoided. In many instances, such a position causes people to deny what is part of their lived experience, preventing their placing sexuality in its proper perspective as but a part of their ego-body identification, as are needs to eat, sleep, recreate, etc. To deny one's sexual feelings because they are deemed unholy or unspiritual would be to give them a power they do not have. As the Course says:

> *The body is merely part of your experience in the physical world. Its abilities can be and frequently are overevaluated. However, it is almost impossible to deny its existence in this world. Those who do so are engaging in a particularly unworthy form of denial. The term "unworthy" here implies only that it is not necessary to protect the mind by denying the unmindful (text, p. 20).*

When we fall into this ego trap of denial we are forgetting that one cannot leave this world of illusion without *first* correcting these illusions on the level where our belief is placed. The goal of *A Course in Miracles* is to transform the world not to transcend it, which is the step belonging to God when He lifts us back to Himself after all our misperceptions have been corrected by the Holy Spirit. While the Course places great emphasis on saving time, time is *not* saved through denial, but through undoing our guilt in our relationships where it is the most powerfully projected.

Moreover, to abstain from sexual activity out of fear, seeking to "protect the mind" against unholiness by struggling against sexual thoughts, impulses and actions, is to fall again into the ego's trap by confusing the levels of thought and behavior, cause and effect. Thus, the Course emphasizes: "It is extremely difficult to reach Atonement by fighting against sin" (text, p. 363). One need not be afraid of thoughts, therefore; one need only bring them to the light of the Holy Spirit that He might remove them from us. As the Course says, speaking of the original error of separation:

> *Call it not sin but madness, for such it was and so it still remains. Invest it not with guilt, for guilt implies it was accomplished in reality. And above all,* be not afraid of it. *When you see some twisted form of the original error rising to frighten you* [*as in sexual concerns*], *say only, "God is not fear but love," and it will disappear. The truth will save you . . . turn you to the stately calm within, where in holy stillness dwells the living God you never left, and Who never left you" (text, p. 348).*

In either form of the ego's plan, therefore, sex and the body have been made real, shifting the focus from the cause (mind) to the effect (body). To believe that sexuality is sinful because it is a body activity is the same error as believing it is holy because it has the power to join. Insisting that any form in this world is intrinsically good or evil is heads and tails of the same coin that makes illusions true. Indulgence or abstinence fulfills the same purpose if its value is based on form. Its true meaning can only come from its *content*, given it by the Holy Spirit. The early lessons in the workbook emphasize how we do not understand anything in our world because we do not understand its purpose. High on the list would be sex. Therefore, we should always guard against prejudging it (or any activity in this world) by what seems to be its meaning as taught by the varying standards of morality or criteria for mental health, as in, for example, believing that sexual expression is unholy or immoral, or that celibacy is unnatural or pathological. Judgment, as the Course repeatedly emphasizes, belongs to the Holy Spirit. He alone knows how the forms of sexuality fit into His plan for releasing us from our guilt.

In all our concerns over sexuality, then, the real problem of reinforcing guilt by making the separated body real is safely protected. Regardless of the path taken — pleasure-seeking or avoidance — the ego exalts in the denial of guilt.

No peace is possible until this guilt is released through learning the Holy Spirit's lesson of the inherent neutrality of the body, placing it solely under His guidance.

If it is an aspect of the Holy Spirit's curriculum for people to be celibate — for all or only part of their lives — and they remain faithful to their Teacher, sexual abstinence would be a joy and hardly a sacrifice. In fact, the sexual drive would actually decrease. If, however, the persons remain ambivalent about their vocation and secretly desire a sexual relationship, all the spiritual justifications in the world will not dissuade them that they are being cheated of something they really desire. Moreover, they will continually be plagued by sexual thoughts and feelings, conscious or unconscious. The joy that a celibate life can bring would quickly turn to bitterness, and beneath the bitterness would remain the guilt over one's continued failure before God.

On the other hand, if people live lives of sexual expression in the context of a relationship that God has joined, then their very sexuality can become, like all other forms of living, a means of achieving God's end. Their partners are not seen as sexual objects whose purpose is to fulfill certain special needs, but as persons through whom God will lead both closer to Himself. God remains the purpose, and so there will be no guilt for there has been no attack. God has not been displaced *by* a relationship, but sought *through* a relationship, the *form* whose special function it is to teach the *content* of forgiveness. In the end it will be His Presence that is loved, not a projection onto an idol. When sexuality is split off from the Holy Spirit's purpose of forgiveness, guilt must follow the use of another for one's personal gratification. It is not sex itself, nor any physical gratification that the Holy Spirit objects to, but the guilt that so often results from the pursuit of pleasure for its own sake.

Celibacy, then, finds its meaning only within a context of the change of mind the New Testament writers called metanoia: the act of conversion that places God at the center of all relationships and thoughts, making the guilt found in special relationships impossible. Without such a God-centering, one is left with a special relationship with celibacy, which is not celibacy at all. Seen within this perspective, then, a relationship between two people enjoying a full sexual life together can be as holy as the life of a consecrated celibate. A relationship that enables both people to find God through forgiveness remains faithful to the same goal of purity of heart sought in sexual celibacy.

The crucial issue, as always, is what the choice is *for*. If an action is a means of reinforcing guilt through substitution and attack, either in thought or deed, the choice will not be of God, and guilt and fear will be the result. However, if the purpose is to carry out the Will of God, then all of Heaven will bless the union which becomes an extension of God's love here on earth. We know which purpose we are serving by its fruits. If there is a consistent lack of peace in us, and those around us — fellow members in community or our families — experience unrest in our presence, then it is more than likely our principal attraction has been guilt and not love. However, if we are peaceful and this is shared by those with whom we live, we can be sure we have followed God's Will and have placed no other gods before Him. Guilt, then, has no place in a holy relationship where only love remains, and this love is shared by all we meet or even think about. Regardless of its form of expression, it will be God's love that is given and received as one, the lesson of forgiveness the Holy Spirit continually teaches us in our relationships.

Chapter 5

CONCLUSION: FAITH, PRAYER AND FORGIVENESS

The Holy Spirit's plan for our salvation asks two things of us: that we have faith in God, and practice His daily lessons of forgiveness. These concluding sections summarize these concepts.

The Need for Faith

We have already discussed faith in God as the foundation on which true forgiveness rests. Without experiencing Him as our center, we cannot know our invulnerability. Feeling vulnerable to the forces of the world, we would always experience threat and fear, and in fear's presence the love which forgiveness reflects could never be expressed. Moreover, by excluding God as the One to whom we turn in time of trouble, we are reinforcing the ego's belief that He is either non-existent or an enemy to be avoided. The original belief in separation from God is accorded reality, as is our guilt and sense of vulnerability. Thus is the ego's vicious circle maintained.

We can approach our need for faith from another perspective as well. The beginning stages of practicing forgiveness do not necessarily require any real faith in God. Regardless of one's religious beliefs, one can always learn to look differently at other people; to exchange a more charitable way of perceiving others' actions for one based on judgment and condemnation. However, as one approaches the deeper layers of the ego through the undoing of our projections, the harsh specter of guilt and fear suddenly arises before our eyes with a vengeance, as they are the obstacles to God.

To look at guilt and fear is frightening by definition, and also by experience. As we continue along the spiritual path, the pain of these experiences increases in intensity as do our feelings of hopelessness. We seem to be getting worse rather than better. In truth, however, we are merely drawing closer to the deeper, more repressed areas of guilt and fear, the very bedrock of the ego's system. In desperation the ego attempts to ward off this final step in its undoing and, in its "last ditch stand," seeks to attack us as it never has before.

Though its forms differ greatly among people, no one escapes this part of the path. For this reason, the Course refers frequently to the "periods of unsettling" and discomfort, not to mention terror, that are found along the way.[1] The Course describes the process:

> *The ego is . . . particularly likely to attack you when you react lovingly* [*i.e., respond to the Holy Spirit*], *because it has evaluated you as unloving and you are going against its judgment. The ego will attack your motives as soon as they become clearly out of accord with its perception of you. This is when it will shift . . . to viciousness when you decide not to tolerate self-abasement and seek relief. Then it offers you the illusion of attack as a "solution" (text, pp. 164, 166).*

The problem of our guilt must be recognized before it can be solved, and the ego always seeks to prevent us from this recognition. Now that the full terror of our guilt stands exposed, the ego becomes desperate, and this is where our temptation is the strongest to pull back and return to the ego's comfort. "Stop," it screams in our ear. "Go no further, for only oblivion and terror await you!" It literally tries to frighten us to death. "I told you so," it continues. "You never should have left me. Now look at the mess you are in, worse off than before. Return to me and I shall bring you peace, the security of the past." We are further told that our lives have been misguided, our spiritual strivings an illusion, and God nothing more than a myth or projection of some unresolved psychological disturbance or fantasy. Therefore, we are urged to return to "reality" and the inducements of the world. Tempted once again by the "gifts" of projection, we begin to attack, even including God and His helpers. People and devotions that had previously been sources of comfort and strength are seen as tools of the ego or the devil. All hope seems lost, replaced by increased terror.

[1]*See* Glossary-Index for "A Course in Miracles," *op. cit., p. 105.*

This stage is analogous to what Christian mysticism has called the "Dark Night of the Soul," the period of great aridity that ultimately precedes the final experience of union with God that traditionally has been the mystic's goal. Seen from another perspective, people have gone far enough along to recognize that "the world I see holds nothing that I want" (workbook, p. 227). The world's illusions can no longer serve as objects of our specialness to bring relief from guilt and anxiety. Possessions, fame, fortune, status, lovers or enemies, no longer are satisfying, for none of them lasts. These persons have advanced far enough to realize that all they desire is God, for only He is eternal. However, they have not quite reached the point where they can unequivocally make this commitment. Part of them still fears turning everything over to Him.

Caught in a "no man's land," they no longer desire the gifts of the ego, but cannot accept only the gifts of God. As the guilt and anxiety begin to mount, they have no place to turn for comfort. They have passed, as it were, the point of no return: they can neither return to the world, nor turn to God. The result is the bleak emptiness and sense of failure that is the sheer terror of life with an absent God: the dark night of the soul. One cannot transcend the ego without this experience. Moreover, it is not a stage that occurs once and once only. We experience its discomfort repeatedly as we continue along the path of forgiving our guilt.

The cult of self-worship or the mistaken belief that one is receiving special gifts or graces from God often find their roots in this stage. The fear of God has become so great that we are tempted to put our own self in His place, or at least to exalt it to equal status with our Creator. We may believe we are among God's chosen, given specific information, for example, about the end of the world, the Second Coming, or the cosmic plan to save humanity, and major if not primary roles in this plan. These mistakes, wherein the ego's voice sounds so similar to the Holy Spirit, are perhaps the most dangerous of all because of their subtlety and the strong investment placed in them, precluding any kind of persuasion to the contrary.

The fear and terror experienced here is almost beyond

belief, literally, for almost all belief was designed to keep us from this moment. Without knowing there is a Person within us who is not of us — a Person who can protect, comfort and lead us — it is highly unlikely this stage can be successfully worked through. We are thrown back on the utter desolation and hopelessness of the ego's life with which we have always identified. The self-hatred we sought to project onto others now confronts us head on, and suicide seems the most attractive solution of all. "There is an instant in which terror seems to grip your mind so wholly that escape appears quite hopeless. When you realize, once and for all, that it is you you fear, the mind perceives itself as split. . . . Now, for an instant, is a murderer perceived within you, eager for your death, intent on plotting punishment for you until the time when it can kill at last" (workbook, p. 365).

Often we need terrifying experiences to enable us to turn to the God we denied, that we may come to realize our utter dependence on Him: "This moment can be terrible, but it can also be the time of your release from abject slavery" (workbook, p. 319). This is not a stage which is approached too soon or in haste. If we were really on our own, in charge of the plan for our salvation, we would always be tempted to rush along too quickly. The ego would like nothing more than for us to steamroll ahead on the seeming path to God, only to become so frightened we turn away from Him to itself, convinced that we had done our part but God failed us once again. Guilt must be approached slowly so that we can gain the confidence and trust that we will not be torn asunder by its ravaging allies — fear and despair — bent on our destruction.

The Holy Spirit's curriculum is individually planned for us so we may approach this final step in the form most suitable for our learning. Step by step we are led through His lessons of forgiveness, "directed up the ladder separation led [us] down" (text, p. 553). Each one is basically the same, but we must learn the lesson in a myriad of forms until we reach the point where we understand its universal application. As the workbook says of its lessons: "Each contains the whole curriculum if understood, practiced, accepted, and applied to all the seeming happenings throughout the day. One is enough. But from that one, there must be no exceptions made. And so we need to use them all and let them blend as one, as each contributes to the whole we learn" (workbook, p. 376).

The Holy Spirit needs our patience and trust in not looking beyond the immediate lesson He has given. We are not aware of the deep extent of our fear, but our faith assures us we will never be presented with more than we can handle. When the going gets toughest we would learn that of ourselves we could not do it, but that of ourselves we do not have to. There is One beside us whose strength will become our own as we avail ourselves of it. He asks only that we accept the grace of His Presence that He can help us leave our nightmare world of fear, and walk into the light that fills the heart of each of us who knows that God is love.

Faith and Prayer: The Meaning of Abundance

Having faith in God is often understood to mean that God will provide all that is needed for our material and/or psychological well-being. The scriptural teachings on "Ask and it will be given you" — to be discussed in the second part of this book — are frequently cited in support of this belief. In New Age thinking, this principle is often labelled "Prosperity Consciousness"; namely, if we think prosperity, we will manifest it.

There is no question of the power that our minds possess, and indeed, when we consider that this *entire* phenomenal world is the product of our thought, we can begin to appreciate this power. As the Course says in terms of our learning ability:

> *No one who understands what you have learned, how carefully you learned it, and the pains to which you went to practice and repeat the lessons endlessly, in every form you could conceive of them, could ever doubt the power of your learning skill. There is no greater power in the world. The world was made by it, and even now depends on nothing else (text, p. 600).*

Since our minds made this world, they can also change

or modify it. Our minds can move mountains, literally as well as figuratively. If we practice enough self-discipline, as do, for example, many Indian yogis, we can perform unusual physical feats. And these need not exclude our manifesting external abundance, if this is what we wish to acquire. An objective observer cannot deny this power of mind, but it must be remembered that this is an ego mind. Our real Mind, which is of spirit and has never left is Source, does nothing: it merely is. In Chapter 3, we discussed the Course's distinction between magic and the miracle. It is the same distinction we can make between psychic ability and spirituality.

What renders a thought spiritual is its purpose. When the mind acts on its own, it is serving the ego's end, which is the belief that it *is* on its own, separated from God. But turned over to the Holy Spirit, abilities of the mind can be powerfully used on behalf of truth. This is especially so when these abilities can demonstrate to others and to oneself that the material universe is not what it seems. "Given to the Holy Spirit, and used under His direction, they are valuable teaching aids. . . . What is used for magic [the ego's purpose of making this world real] is useless to Him. But what He uses cannot be used for magic" (manual, p. 59).

There is a particular danger here, for one can gain worldly power through the training and exercise of the mind.

> *There is . . . a particular appeal in unusual abilities that can be curiously tempting. Here are strengths which the Holy Spirit wants and needs. Yet the ego sees in these same strengths an opportunity to glorify itself. Strengths turned to weakness are tragedy indeed. Yet what is not given to the Holy Spirit must be given to weakness, for what is withheld from love is given to fear, and will be fearful in consequence (manual, pp. 59f).*

Once this psychic ability or power is discovered by an individual and is identified with by that person, it is "no longer a genuine ability, and cannot be used dependably. It is almost inevitable that, unless the individual changes his mind about its purpose, he will bolster his 'power's' uncertainties with increasing deception" (manual, p. 60).

One can indeed receive what one chooses, if one puts one's mind to it. But there is a glaring fallacy that underlies this activity and reveals its basic purpose. To focus about a desired end, either through prayer, meditation or concentration, presumes to know what is best for us or others. In effect, we decide what we want — material benefits, "spiritual healing," or the like — and then pray that God grant our request; or else we leave God out of the picture entirely and ask ourselves for it. We have already discussed how impossible it is to know what is in our best interest, let alone anyone else's. However, there is One who does know and He is the One we should ask. Thus is our request changed from magic to the miracle. We are no longer praying for something that is external to us, but rather for the change in perception that alone can bring us peace.

We believe we ask for specific things, but these are merely forms that conceal the underlying content or experience: love or fear, forgiveness or guilt. These forms symbolize the experience we have asked for, and it is *this* we receive. We may or may not receive what we requested materially, but we *will* receive the guilt and fear that must accompany any thought or action that has excluded God. One recalls that Faust received what he requested, but at the price exacted by the devil. We too pay the price of our pact with the ego, as we have seen: if we believe the world can give us pleasure, it can also give us pain. As the Course explains:

> *The prayer for things of this world will bring experiences of this world. If the prayer of the heart asks for this, this will be given because this will be received. It is impossible that the prayer of the heart remain unanswered in the perception of the one who asks. If he asks for the impossible, if he wants what does not exist or seeks for illusions in his heart, all this becomes his own. The power of his decision offers it to him as he requests (manual, p. 51).*

It is a common misconception in spirituality that the

Holy Spirit answers our specific requests to change things in this world: from finding parking spaces and making us rich, to healing the sick and bringing world peace. This misconception stems from the same level of confusion that leads one to believe in magical remedies for sickness. When we pray to the Holy Spirit for changes in the world, we are assuming that He operates on the level of *effects*, solving our problems by overlooking the *cause* and remaining within the illusory problem world of the ego. If this were so, He would be following the same insane laws of the ego we do, abandoning the laws of truth. He would be paying attention to the effect and not the cause. The Holy Spirit cannot help us if He becomes part of the ego's world of illusions that we are trapped in.

We are asked to use this statement from the workbook whenever we are tempted by terror, apprehension or any form of suffering: "I will forgive, and this will disappear" (workbook, p. 359). What disappears is not the external form of the problem, for this is *not* the problem. What does disappear is our mistaken way of *looking* at the problem. As the Course says of itself: "This is a course in cause and not effect" (text, p. 432). It seeks to change the *cause* of our problems, which is our faulty way of thinking and perceiving, not the *effects* of these thoughts. Thus, if we are caught in a traffic jam and late for an appointment, we should not pray that the Holy Spirit disperse the cars so we will not be late, but rather we should pray that our mind be healed that feels anxious, worried or guilty. At that point, we can "place the future in the Hands of God" (workbook, p. 360), trusting that all will be well because He is in charge. How are we to know that it is in our best interest, not to mention others', to be on time? Perhaps there is unexpected benefit in coming to the appointment later? But there is One who does know. Turning to Him is our one responsibility and only concern.

The Course teaches that "the only meaningful prayer is for forgiveness, because those who have been forgiven have everything" (text, p. 40). It is a prayer that "is nothing more than a request that you may be able to recognize what you already have" (text, p. 40). What we "already have" reflects the principle of abundance: God has given us everything in our creation. This abundance has no referent to anything in the material world. Abundance is only of God, and cannot be expressed in what is not of Him. Thus, there can be no connection between the worlds of spirit and materiality, as they reflect mutually exclusive levels: one real, the other illusory. What does unite them, however, is the purpose of the Holy Spirit, who comes to this world of illusion and helps us change our minds about what reality is. Since we are the ones who thought up this insane world, we can only become free by changing our thoughts. They cannot be changed for us. Without this purpose the world is meaningless, along with its values and pursuits.

Thus, it is a distortion of the principle of abundance to believe that by becoming more "spiritual," as it were, we will receive the material abundance we desire. To pray for money or any expression of this world's "gifts" is the same mistake as praying for a physical healing. What we receive when we do become more "spiritual," or right-minded, are God's gifts of the spirit, encompassing His love, peace, joy and eternal life. There *are* no other gifts. The miracle corrects this distortion; magic increases it. Forgiveness expresses the miracle, and is our one function while we are here, for it is our one need. Undoing our guilt, forgiveness restores to our awareness the memory of God's love and His abundance.

In the Course, Jesus writes of the "limitation" of his power:

> *You may still complain about fear, but you nevertheless persist in making yourself fearful. . . . you cannot ask me to release you from fear. I know it does not exist, but you do not. If I intervened between your thoughts and their results, I would be tampering with a basic law of cause and effect; the most fundamental law there is. I would hardly help you if I depreciated the power of your own thinking. This would be in direct opposition to the purpose of this course (text, p. 27).*

What Jesus and the Holy Spirit *do* do, however, is teach us that we have made a mistake in our thinking, which has resulted in the problem of fear that we have now externalized.

They have come to us to represent another way of thinking, that we may choose again. The Course speaks of the role of each of us as teachers to the other in the role of healer. To all who have become immersed in the ego's quicksand, these teachers

> *come, to represent another choice which they had forgotten. . . . [The healer's] thoughts ask for the right to question what the patient has accepted as true. As God's messengers, His teachers are the symbols of salvation. . . . They stand for the Alternative. . . . They seek for God's Voice in his brother who would so deceive himself as to believe God's Son can suffer. And they remind him that he did not make himself, and must remain as God created him. . . . The truth in their minds reaches out to the truth in the minds of their brothers, so that illusions are not reinforced (manual, p. 18).*

Each of us, then, becomes the instrument of the Holy Spirit, the Voice that speaks for Christ, our real Self. He does not change the external world, but seeks instead to change our internal world — our thoughts — by appealing to the power of our decision.

> *In every difficulty, all distress, and each perplexity Christ calls to you and gently says, "My brother, choose again." He would not leave one source of pain unhealed, nor any image left to veil the truth. He would not leave you comfortless, alone in dreams of hell, but would release your mind from everything that hides His face from you (text, p. 620).*

Thus, when external difficulties seem to lift, all that has happened is that we have changed our mind about them. Where we saw the world as serving to punish us for our sins, now we see it with the Holy Spirit's benediction upon it, that it can serve to teach us that we have not sinned. The seeming change in the world has only reflected the change in our thoughts — the miracle that shifted our allegiance from the ego to the Holy Spirit.

In summary, then, when we pray we ask merely for the Holy Spirit's help that we look at the situation as He does. To ask that He intervene to change something in the world will conceal the true cause of the problem, and this will prevent healing. This is the real meaning of prayer, and on this level He answers all prayers. If we pray for help in *this* world, we are praying to the ego, subscribing to its smokescreen of reversal of cause and effect. On this level, too, our prayers will be answered, but by the ego, since it is the ego we called upon. Its answer may be welcomed and seem to bring us what we want, but its "gift" is fear, camouflaged as love. True peace will never result from this. The Course states: "If you would know your prayers are answered, never doubt a Son of God" (text, p. 153). We translate this in our daily life by hearing only the Voice for God in him, reinforcing the Holy Spirit in ourselves. Only on the level of mind is this possible.

Our Function of Forgiveness

Our sole function on earth is forgiveness, for through it we are led out of hell and learn the specific function God has given us, realizing we have everything we need to fulfill it. Thus are we freed of our guilt and fear to do specific work on behalf of God's kingdom and receive its gift of peace.

Forgiveness requires a shift in perspective of how we view the world of illusion. While we see it as a place wherein we find pleasure and seek to avoid pain, we will become dependent on what is outside: loving what can satisfy us, hating what we believe can hurt us. In such a perception peace is impossible, for worldly pleasure or pain can bring only conflict: If we believe something can give us pleasure we must also believe it can give us pain. Thus, an inherent ambivalence is built into all things of the world, and unconditional and permanent love becomes impossible. The world becomes separated into two camps, and God's single creation of love denied.

Pleasure and pain, therefore, do not represent a real choice since they represent a choice between illusions, giving the world a meaning it does not have. Going home to God is its only meaning. He is unchanging, but our perceptions and needs are always changing. One day we are attracted to this person, object or devotion, and the next our preferences shift to something else. All these are nothing but "little, senseless substitutions [for truth], touched with insanity and swirling lightly off on a mad course like feathers dancing insanely in the wind. . . . They fuse and merge and separate in shifting and totally meaningless patterns . . . " (text, p. 348).

This hardly means that one should live without needs and preferences. We would not be living here in the body if this were so. However, when we place our lives under the Holy Spirit's guidance He helps us recognize where our true needs are. He uses everything that is unique to us — our virtues as well as faults — to teach us His lessons. His lesson plan is gradual and gentle, and we are never asked to give up anything at all. The Course says of itself: "[It] requires almost nothing of you. It is impossible to imagine one that asks so little, or could offer more" (text, pp. 409f). The Holy Spirit asks merely that we look at our preferences that He may teach us the difference between what makes us truly happy and unhappy, and choose again which we really prefer. The Course says to us: "You no more recognize what is painful than you know what is joyful, and are, in fact, very apt to confuse the two. The Holy Spirit's main function is to teach you to tell them apart" (text, p. 124).

Once we experience that it is *our* choice to let go of our investment in worldly things, hoping that they will bring salvation or happiness, resentment and a sense of loss or sacrifice become impossible. When we finally realize all that God has given us, we "will think, in glad astonishment, that for all this [we] gave up *nothing*" (text, p. 323)! The path to God is meant to be a joyful one because of the One to whom it leads, for when our desire is brought into accord with the Holy Spirit, only joy and peace can result. In that union of wills, the ego is undone and its seeming gifts disappear, eclipsed by the one gift of God.

The purpose of forgiveness is to help us achieve the unified perception that this world has nothing to offer because nothing here is lasting and "we can't take it with us." Only God endures, and so the real value of worldly things lies in their helping us learn this lesson the Course would teach: the purpose of the world is to teach us that there is no world. In and of themselves, the things of the world are neither good nor evil. It is the purpose we give them that determines their worth. Real pleasure comes from fulfillment of function, doing the Will of God in the context of our everyday lives. Pain results from function unfulfilled, the denial of the Holy Spirit's lessons of forgiveness. Without keeping this larger perspective in mind, we find ourselves thrown back on experiencing the needs that have not been met in the past or present.

We learn the Holy Spirit's lesson of forgiveness through our relationships and life situations. The difficult people we meet, trials we undergo, sufferings we experience — all have the same basic purpose of giving us the chance to look through the forgiving vision of the Holy Spirit rather than the guilt-reinforcing eyes of the ego, to forgive others and ourselves. This is not to deny that things occur in the world that should not, but simply that there is another way of looking at them that provides the ultimate release from all suffering: the deep faith in God's abiding Presence in our hearts which can transform pain to joy. As stated in the Course: "No form . . . of suffering can long endure before the face of one who has forgiven and has blessed himself" (workbook, p. 346).

Since there is one problem there is only one solution. Forgiveness corrects guilt, and to do it truly is to do it forever. Failing to forgive we are condemned to a seemingly endless cycle in which the past repeatedly recurs in the present, what Freud termed the repetition compulsion. The lessons we failed to learn at an earlier period in our life are presented again, offering us repeated opportunities until the lesson is learned. This is not the Holy Spirit's cruel idea of a joke, but His loving way of helping us work through a problem of guilt we otherwise could not have done. If we choose to see the lesson as an added burden and curse, we will remain condemned by the guilt that is reinforced through projecting blame onto others. When we decide to learn the lessons and choose to forgive, we correspondingly forgive all those unforgiven in the past.

To summarize, working out a problem through forgiveness is a process of first recognizing that others are not responsible for our unhappiness, and secondly that all our needs and lacks have been met and but wait for our acceptance. "Let me recognize my problems have been solved" (workbook, p. 141). Beyond our guilt is the abundance and fullness of God. Our decision to want only that abundance for ourselves and for all others is the decision to forgive. It is a decision that allows the Holy Spirit to help us fulfill the only function we truly have, for it is the one given by God that makes all the others possible. Only here is real pleasure found; for only in the peace of God do we find rest unto our souls.

The decision to have the Holy Spirit make our decisions for us is insulting only to the ego, and it would accuse us of quietism or neurotic passivity. However, our passivity lies merely in leaving our ego behind so that the impetus for our life comes from God. Energized by His power, we step out into the world to do the Holy Spirit's work, having Him be our guide instead of the ego. We become passive to the whims of the ego but active to the Will of God. This ensures that His Will is done in our hearts and throughout the world, that all may find peace in the midst of war, unity in divisiveness, and love in the face of hate.

The Holy Spirit asks us to see all things as lessons in forgiveness that God would have us learn. Thus we walk the world in a spirit of gratitude for the opportunities for release from guilt that are offered us. Every situation can teach this as long as we are open to accept its gift. What we ask for *is* given us. If we look out on a world of fear, seeing there the fear that really lurks in our hearts, it is this fear we shall receive. If instead we offer forgiveness to the world, seeing in all attack a desperate cry for help, it will be our own forgiveness we shall find.

The prisons of guilt and fear we establish for ourselves and others, when given over to the Holy Spirit, become transformed into shrines of forgiveness. There are our "secret sins and hidden hates" undone as they are seen in another and then let go, bringing peace at last to all those who wander "in the world, uncertain, lonely, and in constant fear" (text, p. 621). We wander among them, and so we are brought time and time again to this holy place by the Holy One Himself, that we may choose to recognize in each other the holiness we have forgotten, and which our forgiveness now recalls to us.

Would we not feel grateful, then, for what had once seemed like misfortune's curse? Would we not let the song of gratitude fill our heart that Heaven had not left us alone in our prison house of fear, but had instead joined with us there that all God's children be free? And would we not awaken each morning with this prayer of thanksgiving on our lips, thanking God for the opportunities the day will bring?

> *Father, help me see only Your Will this day in every one I meet; that I may teach the single lesson you would have me learn: that all my sins have been forgiven me because I have forgiven them in all my brothers and my sisters You have sent. Help me not to be tempted by my fear to hate or to condemn; but only let forgiveness rest upon my eyes that I may see Your love in all I meet today, and know that it is in myself as well.*

PART II:
NEW TESTAMENT TEACHINGS

INTRODUCTION

When asked which was the greatest commandment, Jesus answered, from the Old Testament: "You must love the Lord your God with all your heart, with all your soul, and with all your mind," adding that the second greatest commandment was like the first: "You must love your neighbor as yourself" (Mt 22:37-40). Throughout the gospels we find Jesus speaking of his Father's love and trusting in His providence, as well as forgiving and not judging others, culminating in the "new commandment" he left his disciples: "Love one another" (Jn 13:34). These two commandments can be translated into faith and forgiveness, the key principles of *A Course in Miracles*, and what we referred to as the Holy Spirit's plan of salvation.

It is with great humility that a psychologist (not to mention a student of *A Course in Miracles*) opens up the pages of the New Testament to find statements with such great psychological implications — 1900 years before Freud! Jesus was a brilliant psychologist, as was the apostle Paul, and many basic insights of twentieth century psychology which form the cornerstone of the Course's teachings are clearly foreshadowed in the New Testament writings. In this second part we shall explore these writings in depth, integrating both the teachings of Jesus as well as the Epistles with examples from Jesus' own life.

It is important to note that the writers of the New Testament were attempting to understand the sudden bolt of lightning that Jesus radiated into the heart of the ego's darkness within the limitations imposed on them by their cultural and religious backgrounds, not to mention their own ego needs and projections onto the ego needs of others. The four gospels as we have them today are the end product of a long oral and written tradition of continued tellings, retellings and editing of the life of Jesus. The earliest gospel, Mark, was not written down until at least thirty years after Jesus' death, while John's gospel, the least historical and most theological of the four, was not composed until well into the final decade of the first century, over sixty years from the crucifixion. Each of the four reflects the specific needs faced by the early Church, and its narration and interpretation were very much colored by these needs. The evangelists often placed — consciously and unconsciously — words in Jesus' mouth that would be the most helpful to a politically and religiously persecuted group struggling for its existence, rather than faithfully adhering to what he actually said and did.

The unique psychological insights of *A Course in Miracles* help us to understand how these ego factors influenced and distorted the comprehension of the people who knew and experienced Jesus, both in his earthly life as well as after his resurrection. In Chapter 9 we shall consider some of these distortions as they relate to the scriptural and traditional understanding of the crucifixion. Our discussion of the New Testament teachings is not primarily historical or theological, although the influence of scripture scholarship and theology is apparent in many places. Rather, these chapters reflect a psychologist writing from the perspective of the Course, whose emphasis is on experience, not theology. As it states: "A universal theology is impossible, but a universal experience is not only possible but necessary" (manual, p. 73). Therefore, the Biblical teachings — both Old and New Testaments — should be interpreted in light of the insights, language, and needs of their respective ages, not to mention our own. We in the 20th century are subject to the same limitations, and no doubt our mistakes will require correction in the centuries that follow.

One potential difficulty in interpreting the Bible is the confusion between form and content we have already noted in Part I. This confusion is a major source of misunderstanding regarding spiritual practices based upon scriptural texts. Aside from the difficulty of knowing exactly what Jesus or the New Testament writers meant, let alone what they said, there is the added problem of knowing when a teaching may originally have been aimed at answering a specific question or need, but now would have a more generalized meaning, answering a different kind of question. For example, some scholars believe that Jesus' strictures against divorce (Mt 5:31f, 19:3-9) were meant to protect women since, under Jewish law, it was virtually impossible for them to divorce their husbands, but relatively easy for husbands to divorce them. The meaning of this teaching for us today would be quite different, as we shall discuss in Chapter 7. The confusion between form and content in Jesus' exhortations to "take up one's cross" (Lk 9:23) has led to a glorification of suffering and sacrifice, masking its call to release our special relationships, which we explore in the opening section of the following chapter. Our treatment of these and other texts is based on the principles of *A Course in Miracles* presented in Part I.

Part II is divided into six chapters. The first, Chapter 6, treats the world of the ego from which Jesus came to save us. This is the separated world of the special relationship, for which forgiveness — the theme of Chapters 7 and 8 — is the solution. Jesus' teachings on forgiveness are discussed first, followed by his personal example of these teachings, which culminate in the crucifixion. Chapter 9 treats the misunderstandings of the crucifixion, showing how people unknowingly embraced the ego's path of suffering and sacrifice, reinforcing the very guilt and separation the cross was meant to undo. In Chapter 10 we present Jesus' teachings on God's love, the correction for the belief, prevalent in his time as well as our own, that God will punish us (or others) for our sins. The final chapter summarizes the important gospel teachings on decision, appealing to the power of our mind to follow God's Voice of forgiveness, once we have chosen to follow the ego's voice of guilt.

Chapter 6

THE WORLD OF THE EGO: THE SPECIAL RELATIONSHIP

We have seen how the ego's world of separation is most heavily secured by the special relationship, which can properly be called *the* problem of the world. It is the most seductive of the ego attempts to keep us in darkness, and there is no more serious obstacle to finding the peace of God than this subtle shift in allegiance from God to the ego. In our world of guilt and fear, moreover, it is impossible not to be involved with others in special relationships, and thus use them as defenses against our relationship with God.

In Chapter 1, we noted that special relationships involve not only people but can include objects, situations, addictions, etc. Thus, for example, people who cannot tolerate their anxiety may form a special relationship with alcohol, drugs, sexuality, food, work, etc., using any of these as a means of avoiding what is painful. Pursuing worldly pleasures, security, fame and power are other means whereby the ego would strive to anchor us in the world of illusion. In all of these, regardless of their form, we recognize the same ego dynamic of substituting for God, for it is He alone who can bring us pleasure and protect us from our pain.

The ego denies God by elevating guilt on His throne, and then convinces us to seek outside ourselves for salvation from this guilt in the form of idols to be worshipped or avoided. As the Course teaches, however: "An idol cannot take the place of God . . . Seek not outside your Father for your hope" (text, p. 575). The gospels provide us with numerous teachings and examples of this problem, and it is these we shall explore in this chapter.

Taking Up One's Cross

We begin with the teaching of Jesus that has probably justified more ego interpretations — albeit unconsciously motivated — than any other. In Luke's gospel, Jesus tells his disciples: "If anyone wants to be a follower of mine, let him renounce himself and take up his cross every day and follow me" (Lk 9:23). This statement has often been interpreted as a call to emulate Jesus' apparent suffering, thereby justifying a life of sacrifice and pain, the ego's perennial goal. Underlying this idea of a sacrificial life was the belief that because Jesus sacrificed his life for us, suffering for the atonement of our sins, we must do the same. Many sincere Christians would suffer misfortune gladly, "offering it up" to their Lord, believing that the more they sacrificed the closer salvation would come to themselves and others.

We have already seen how a life of suffering stems from an interpretation of oneself as a victim, and can never be God's Will for us. Sacrificing something has the same psychological effect as embracing it, for it establishes a value nothing here can have. One does not fight against something unless one believes it is real and that there is a value in opposing it. Jesus' teachings on "renunciation" express a change of *attitude* — from the ego to God — not a course of action. We give up our investment in the things of the world, which is always an investment of guilt, not the things themselves. However, we can view this scriptural exhortation to "take up one's cross" in another light which does make good sense.

The twin parables of "The Treasure" and "The Pearl" (Mt 13:44-46) provide a perspective in which we can better understand Jesus' teaching. When we have at last found the treasure hidden in the field, or the pearl of great price, we become joyful ("go off happy") and sell everything else that we may have it. When the things of the world are measured against the treasures of the kingdom, who in his right mind would not choose that treasure and lay aside what is valueless? As the workbook lesson states: "The world I see holds nothing that I want . . . [for] nothing is here to cherish. Nothing here is worth one instant of delay and pain; one moment of uncertainty and doubt" (workbook, p. 227.)

The emphasis here is not on giving things away, but rather on the great joy that is experienced so that all things, once seen as valuable, can now be looked at differently. Sacrifice, then, plays no part, for one has in fact "given up" what means nothing. "It takes great learning both to realize and to accept the fact that the world has nothing to give. What can the sacrifice of nothing mean?' (manual, p. 32) Thus, it is not important *what* is given up, but *why*, recognizing what alone is true. Great joy inevitably results, for seeing the Holy Spirit's meaning in all things is the joy of knowing God's love for us. When we have found Jesus, the messenger of the kingdom, we are impelled by our newly awakened love for him to leave "our nets behind," like the fishermen when they were called, and follow him. But what is it that we leave behind, and what is the path we will follow?

Jesus was the most complete expression of a life that has totally transcended the ego. If the cross, or crucifixion, is the symbol of the ego, then taking up one's cross means to follow the path of ego-transcendence that Jesus did. We can identify with undoing our ego's guilt, rather than with the trials and pains of giving up this guilt. As the Course states: "Crucifixion is always the ego's aim. It sees everyone as guilty, and by its condemnation it would kill" (text p. 264). As the special relationship is the home of guilt, the path of the cross consists of undoing these destructive relationships.

This path, which is the process of accepting the Atonement for ourselves, is certainly not without its difficulties. However, these difficulties are not to be glorified or spiritualized, but rather understood within the context of the ego's need to "strike back." Divesting oneself of investment in special relationships is bound to induce feelings of pain. It is impossible to change these relationships that represented our security and protection from guilt without experiencing guilt. Since it has been our fear of this guilt that has caused us to listen to the ego's voice for specialness, it is the same fear that will be aroused once the investment in special relationships begins to shift and the guilt allowed to surface in our conscious experience. In discussing the shift from a special to a holy relationship, the Course says that the relationship may "seem disturbed, disjunctive and even quite distressing" (text, p. 337). Looking at guilt and fear is fearful, as we have seen, and where there is fear, pain and suffering cannot be avoided.

The Course repeatedly emphasizes the process of bringing the darkness to the light, our illusions to the truth of the Holy Spirit, and at one point terms part of this process a "period of unsettling" (manual, p. 10). In the gospel, Jesus cautions us to expect this, even while he encourages us to follow him. The pain of *not* following him, holding the ego's hand instead, far eclipses the anxiety of learning to trust only him. Placing our trust in the ego's nothingness must lead to increased despair. Even more to the point is the conflict of continually going against what we truly want, the conflict between ourself and our Self. Friction and tension are inevitable, and joy impossible. Our idols of fear, masquerading as defenses, must be abandoned if we are to find God's true representative, not an illusory substitute. The pain of the cross is experiencing our fear and guilt so that we now may make another choice — forgiveness instead of specialness — and come at last to find the joy of Heaven.

We come to this joy by the straight and narrow path, leaving our illusion of false gods on either side: "Between these paths [renouncing or choosing the world] there is another road that leads away from loss of every kind, for sacrifice and deprivation both are quickly left behind. This is the way appointed for you now" (workbook, p. 284). The gospels are quite explicit about the difficulties of this path, and Jesus makes it clear to his disciples what it means to be called out by him and sent into the world: "Provide yourselves with no gold or silver, not even with a few coppers for your purses, with no haversack for the journey or spare tunic or footwear or a staff" (Mt. 10:9f). We are to be like the "lilies of the field," relying on the providence of God for all that we need. We are sent as lambs among wolves, with nothing to protect ourselves but the innocence and invulnerability that does not come from ourselves or the world, but from our Heavenly Father.

These instructions have usually been taken to mean complete poverty, and they would certainly appear to be highly impractical, for all apostles (teachers of God) have earthly needs. We have already seen that to apply this teaching to actual material things distorts their true meaning, which refers to the poverty of spirit reflected in the Matthean beatitudes. In reality, of course, spirit is not poor, and poverty here refers to the part of the spiritual path where we relinquish our attachments to the things of this world and abandon ourselves to the Will of God. As St. Paul writes: "What we have to do is to give up everything that does not lead to God, and all our worldly ambitions; we must be self-restrained and live good and religious lives here in this present world" (Tt 2:12). St. Benedict, the father of Western monasticism, instructed his monasteries to have these words printed in full view within the community room: "Let them [the monks] prefer nothing to Christ."

Thus, Jesus is instructing us to change our mind from the ego's way of looking at the world to the Holy Spirit's. It is the ego's distortion of this central teaching that fastens it to specific things, rather than to the underlying principle. The problem is not the body, but how we *think* about the body. What we "sacrifice" is our *thoughts* about materiality, not materiality itself. Otherwise, we merely practice the false asceticism of giving up what is never real, thereby keeping the thought real in our minds. The Course comments on this mistake, referring to Freud's four motivations:

> *There is no sacrifice in the world's terms that does not involve the body. Think a while about what the world calls sacrifice. Power, fame, money, physical pleasure; who is the "hero" to whom all these things belong? Could they mean anything except to a body? Yet a body cannot evaluate. By seeking after such things the mind associates itself with the body, obscuring its identity and losing sight of what it really is (manual, p. 32).*

When our minds are centered on our true identity, which Jesus manifests to us, there can be no interference with the free flow of Heaven's plan, and all our needs for the journey will be met. As we have seen, it is not God who meets these worldly needs but ourselves. Once our minds are properly focused and healed of the guilt that manifests itself in punishment, all hardship disappears and we receive the love that we know we are, in the form we need and can accept.

We can see the same principle expressed in this series of gospel teachings on concerns over the future or need to retain the past. We are to leave the past behind, Jesus is telling us, as well as all worries about what will be, echoing the workbook lesson: "I place the future in the Hands of God" (workbook, p. 360). Three men come to Jesus as he and the disciples are traveling, expressing an interest to join them (Lk 9:57-62). To one of them Jesus says: "Foxes have holes and the birds of the air have nests, but the Son of Man has nowhere to lay his head": following Jesus means giving up security in worldly or ego things. The second man, who first wishes to bury his father before coming with Jesus, is told: "Leave the dead to bury their dead; your duty is to go and spread the news of the Kingdom of God": what is done is done, Jesus is saying, for to follow me is to leave the dead of the past, setting out on the road to life in the present, the window to eternity. This principle is reiterated in Jesus' response to the third man who asks first to say good-bye to his family: "Once the hand is laid on the plow, no one who looks back is fit for the kingdom of God": the investment in holding on to the past precludes accepting the gifts of the kingdom.

On first reading, these teachings sound harsh, cruel and demanding. However, when seen in another light —beyond the form to the content — their message is understood as gentle and loving: because God is our need, to follow Jesus is our only joy. If we were not afraid of letting go of our previous "joys" — the real source of our pain — this path would involve no suffering or fear of any kind.

Our most secret investments in the securities of the world must be released from our unconscious mind where they can never be corrected. As Jesus taught: "There is nothing hidden but it must be disclosed, nothing kept secret except to be brought to light" (Mk 4:22). It is the very process of bringing the darkness of our guilt and fear into the light that is fearful, not the supposed object of our fear. Our trust in Jesus allows us to move beyond this fear, for he continually reminds us: "Be not afraid." As long as we take his hand, as he urged Peter on the water, we will never sink into the ego's waters of fear, anxiety and guilt.

It is crucial, then, not only to take up one's cross of moving beyond the ego, but to take Jesus' hand and follow him. Without his guidance we can never go through the fear and pain that the cross can represent. Instead, we inevitably will identify with the fear, making it our only reality. Another story whose title and author I cannot recall well illustrates the tragic consequences of making fear real without trusting in the God who always protects us by His love.

A man wagered his friends he could stay overnight in a house that was reportedly haunted. Though secretly afraid, he suppressed his anxiety and proceeded to spend the night. Later in the evening he heard sounds and, becoming frightened, moved away from them. As he quickened his steps, he suddenly felt a tight grip around his neck. He struggled hard to free himself, lunging forward, but the more forceful he became the tighter the grasp around his neck. He struggled desperately to breathe, but it was a losing battle. The grip was relentless, and the man finally collapsed, lifeless, on the floor. The next morning his friends found him, choked to death by his scarf which had caught on a nail: the more he had struggled against the scarf the tighter it had become. The man's fear of his unreal attacker became his murderer.

In summary, then, it is unavoidable that we pass through the temporary anxiety and suffering of ego transcendence if we are to reach the peace and joy that is the true inheritance of our Father, whose "Will for me is perfect happiness" (workbook, p. 179). To be willing to take this path is to desire this peace, and a goal cannot be attained without its means. Our goal is the eternal life Jesus holds out to us, and it is this goal of freedom that should be our focus, not the pain of leaving behind our special relationships. We should be of good cheer because what died on the cross was fear, and Jesus teaches us now to overcome our fear by "taking up his cross" of forgiveness.

Jesus' Teachings on Special Relationships

There are few places in the gospels where Jesus is more emphatic or seemingly harsh than in his statements that the disciples avoid becoming falsely involved with others. This central teaching occurs five times in the synoptic gospels, and its strongest statement comes in Luke: "If any man comes to me without hating his father, mother, wife, children, brothers, sisters, yes and his own life too, he cannot be my disciple" (Lk 14:26). Matthew's version softens the instruction, as well as clarifying what is meant: "Anyone who prefers father or mother . . . son or daughter to me is not worthy of me" (Mt 10:37).

This statement has been taken, in its most extreme form, to mean that one traveling the spiritual path must physically leave one's home, sever relationships with one's parents and, in effect, live as if they no longer existed. This sacrifice was seen as the "price" Jesus exacted from us in order to follow him, and the "price" paid by the parents for having such a child, whether *they* believed in this principle or not. No one who followed this line of interpretation could escape the conclusion, even if buried under a cloud of denial, that God is cruel to demand such a sacrifice. We have already seen how a loving Father never demands sacrifice of His children. We have also seen how prone we become to falling into the ego's trap of mistaking form for content, as well as rationalizing our ego need for sacrifice by invoking spiritual motivations. Here, as elsewhere, Jesus is speaking of the *meaning* of the principle, not its literal or specific expression.

Jesus certainly is not advocating violating the fifth commandment to honor our father and mother. In fact, Jesus elsewhere upholds this very commandment against the practices of the scribes and Pharisees (Mt 15:1-9), whom he criticizes for hypocritically preferring *their* tradition of dedicating their material goods to the Temple as opposed to supporting one's aged parents. Jesus says: "And why do you . . . break away from the (fourth) commandment of God for the sake of your tradition?" (v.3) Rather, Jesus is teaching that we must always put him first in our hearts and minds, otherwise the love and attention we give to others will be tainted by the ego. The true follower of Jesus "must" love him as he loves his God —with all his heart, soul and mind — because this is the only love there is. As the Course says: "For God created the only relationship that has meaning, and that is His relationship with you" (text, p. 299).

For us Jesus *is* the love of God. The Course states: "[his name] stands for love that is not of this world . . . .It becomes the shining symbol for the Word of God, so close to what it stands for that the little space between the two is lost" (manual, p. 55). Moreover, "in remembering Jesus you are remembering God. The whole relationship of the Son to the Father lies in him" (manual, p. 55). Thus, to "prefer" others to Jesus is to replicate the same "sin" of substitution that was our choice in the separation, choosing our ego self to take the place of our true Self. We have seen how this original substitution becomes chosen over and over in our special relationships.

In one sense, it may be said that we are asked to form a "special relationship" with Jesus. Unlike all other relationships, however, this one would not be based upon guilt or substitution, but upon love, the means of leading us beyond all special relationships. Loving Jesus, then, would be a love that would include all people, denying specialness' demand for exclusivity. Since choosing to follow Jesus in our daily lives represents a decision to give up the ego, it could only be his voice that would guide us. As Jesus says in the Course: "When you unite with me you are uniting without the ego, because I have renounced the ego in myself and therefore cannot unite with yours. Our union is therefore the way to renounce the ego in you" (text, pp. 136f). Excluding him from this place in our hearts we must fill the void, and in that need is born all our special relationships.

The ego warns that to let go of our special relationships is to give up something valuable, without which we would be miserable and lonely. It cautions against such great sacrifice. This warning underlies Peter's question to Jesus about giving up all worldly possessions: "What about us?' he asks Jesus, "We have left everything and followed you. What are we to have, then?" (Mt 19:27). Though put in question form, Peter's words are really a statement: if we let go of what has meaning for us in the world, there will be nothing left. But Jesus answers him: "Everyone who has left houses, brothers, sisters, father, mother, children or land for the sake of my name will be repaid a hundred times over, and also inherit eternal life" (Mt 19:29).

Again, we can understand that Jesus is not urging his followers to sacrifice or give up anything, but rather to see their earthly lives in their proper perspective. When asked to intercede on behalf of a man's inheritance, Jesus replies: "Watch, and be on your guard against avarice of any kind, for a man's life is not made secure by what he owns, even when he has more than he needs" (Lk 12:15). This is followed by the parable of "The Rich Fool" (Lk 12:16-21). A rich man seeks to build bigger barns to house his goods, to prepare for the years ahead. But God says to him: "Fool! This very night the demand will be made for your soul; and this hoard of yours, whose will it be then?' (v.20) The word "fool" is used in the God-denying sense of the psalms: "The fool says in his heart, 'There is no God!'. . . . [He] will be struck with fear, fear without reason" (Ps 14:1,5). Those are the "fools" who deny God, who seek to place their security within the ego's world. Only investing in God brings true reward, for only God is our security. Thus, Jesus ends the parable, saying: "So it is when a man stores up treasure for himself in place of making himself rich in the sight of God" (v. 21). Things of this world pass, but the kingdom is for all time. We must choose which is to be our treasure.

In the parables of "The Tower Builder" and "The King Contemplating a Campaign," (Lk 14:28-33) Jesus teaches that one should never begin a construction job without first weighing the costs to complete it, or to plan a military campaign without knowing if one's army is sufficient to defeat the enemy. To do so risks the taunts of onlookers: "Here is a man who started to build and was unable to finish" (v.30). Jesus is cautioning his followers as to the nature of his path. To retain even a small part of our ego attachments is enough to prevent us from accepting the love of God. To uphold any aspect of the ego's system is to uphold it all, including the guilt that denies God's love and "forbids" us from experiencing it. Such a compromise makes us look foolish, for then one has neither: not completing the process of forgiveness reinforces guilt, while holding on to the ego and denying God strengthens our fear of Him. We are, in effect, left nowhere. This is the great difficulty of following Jesus' path: the lack of compromise that ultimately is asked of us. As the Course states: "There is no compromise that you can make with guilt, and escape the pain that only guiltlessness allays" (text, p. 255). In the end, all ego defenses must be abandoned; only then can we truly find peace.

These two parables, then, are not so much of self-renunciation or denial as ones of self-examination. Jesus is asking us to look within for any spots of ego darkness that would obstruct Heaven's light from shining. His message to us is: "None of you can be my disciple unless he gives up all his possessions" (v.33). Here again we see that Jesus is not asking us to "give up" material possessions in a spirit of sacrifice, but rather to give up our investments in them, for they no longer mean what they did. Jesus asks us to live our lives to the full by completing the process of forgiveness so that our joy may be equally as full. As long as one "spot of darkness" remains within us, the light of Christ is obscured, and Jesus would have us be the pure channel of light that he is. He tells the disciples: "See to it then that the light inside you is not darkness. If, therefore, your whole body is filled with light, and no trace of darkness, it will be light entirely, as when the lamp shines on you with its rays" (Lk 11:35f).

Therefore, Jesus instructed the disciples: "Anyone who wants to save his life will lose it; but anyone who loses his life for my sake will find it" (Mt 16:25). By seeking to secure our ego lives by holding on to our special relationships we are really losing our life, for we have placed our faith in nothing. In letting these attachments go – choosing a holy relationship instead of specialness – we make the one decision that restores our true life in God to our awareness. Thus we find life's real meaning and realize, "in glad astonishment, that for all this [we] gave up *nothing!*" (text, p. 323).This is the pearl of great price, represented for us by Jesus, when we place him first in our hearts and minds.

This same teaching is found in Jesus' statement about making ourselves eunuchs for the sake of the kingdom (Mt 19:12). As we have seen in Chapter 4, Jesus could not be advocating the *form* of celibacy, withdrawing from sexual relationships that we remain "pure" for him alone. Rather, he is urging us to make the interior act of choosing him first. Thus, all our relationships, regardless of their form, can flow from his love. Once he is at the center of our relationships we can experience the truth of his words: "Anyone who does the will of my Father in heaven, he is my brother and sister and mother" (Mt 12:50). Only by resting secure in God can we recognize our relationships as being learning opportunities that enable us to extend Jesus' love to all people.

Thus, it is not enough to withdraw our investment in the world, the meaning of "go and sell everything you own." We must also "give the money to the poor" (Mk 10:21), which is to share the fruits of our "ego-emptying" with others. These are the "poor" whom Jesus sends to us — all those who hunger for the love of God, believing they are separated from it. In our sharing this love with them we all come together in His Presence. It is the natural condition of love, unlike special love, to embrace all people as our Father embraces us.

This does not mean that we love all people in the same way. Rather, it is the *content* of our love that is important, not the form in which it is expressed. In this world of separation, it is not possible to have God's universal love manifest in the same manner to all. For example, we observe holidays with our own families, or have certain friends for dinner but do not include others. This "selectivity" does not mean that our family members or closest friends are "better" than the rest of the world's population, but simply that these relationships are part of the Holy Spirit's plan to help us learn and teach His lessons of forgiveness. What is essential is that our egos do not exclude others from our circle, but that we let the Holy Spirit make these decisions for us. In this way all our relationships, regardless of their level of intensity or intimacy, will become holy. The Course calls these holy relationships "heralds of eternity," wherein "two voices raised together call to the hearts of everyone, to let them beat as one. And in that single heartbeat is the unity of love proclaimed and given welcome" (text, p. 405).

Jesus told us he came to bring peace (Jn 14:27), but the false and fleeting sense of safety that results from relationships built on special love dependency is not the peace that Jesus offers us. Rather, we must learn to relinquish the false self that would have us seek out such relationships, choosing instead the one relationship with him that unites all the others in itself. We must disengage ourselves from attachments to everything that is not of God so that we may finally be united with our true reality. To help lead us from the hell of our ego lives to the Heaven of the life in God, Jesus sends us each other, his messengers, bringing us tidings of great joy. But unless he himself remains at the center of our relationships, their message of forgiveness, joy and happiness will be lost in guilt, pain and misery. In each relationship, therefore, Jesus calls out to us: "Come to me, all you who labor and are overburdened, and I will give you rest" (Mt 11:28). Thus is the guilt and fear of our special relationships transformed, through forgiveness, into the reflection of the love of God.

Special Love for Jesus

This shift from guilt to love, through forgiveness, is clearly demonstrated in the disciples' own relationship with Jesus, with whom they had formed a special relationship. Recalling the ego's dynamics of guilt, we can understand the disciples' proneness to specialness. The universal belief that we are separate from God leads to feelings of unworthiness, emptiness and lack, and thus a need to be special, different and better than others. Sharing this belief and thus desiring this special recognition, the disciples demanded concrete demonstration of this special love from Jesus, fulfilling the ego's purpose of concealing their underlying feelings of unworthiness. The gospels provide several examples of this need and demand.

In Mark 9:38 we see John complaining to Jesus that another who is "not one of us" was casting out devils in Jesus' name, and that the disciples had tried to stop him. John, speaking for the others, was expressing the belief that *only* they were able to perform this healing, for *only* they were the true followers of Jesus. If their Master could have angrily struck this outsider dead with a thunderbolt, they would undoubtedly have been satisfied. Jesus' response, however, was not what they expected: "You must not stop him: no one who works a miracle in my name is likely to speak evil of me. Anyone who is not against us is for us" (Mk 9:39f).

Luke's account of the same interchange is followed by the incident of the Samaritans' inhospitality towards the messengers Jesus had sent ahead as he made his way from Galilee to Jerusalem. James and John, elsewhere referred to as the "sons of thunder," came to Jesus, upset over the Samaritans' seeming rejection of them. They asked: "Lord, do you want us to call down fire from heaven to burn them up?"(Lk 9:54).The evangelist describes Jesus' response: "He turned and rebuked them, and they went off to another village" (Lk 9:55f).

Jesus' two responses echo his words in the Sermon on the Mount: "It is not those who say to me, 'Lord, Lord,' who will enter the kingdom of heaven, but the person who does the will of my Father in heaven" (Mt 7:21). We are all special in the eyes of the Father, who loves us as one. By doing his Will, we affirm His Fatherhood. By denying His Will, as did Adam and Eve, we unconsciously seek to destroy this Fatherhood and sever our relationship with Him. Being a literal follower of Jesus is not essential. We express our discipleship by our love for one another; in thought and actions, not words. God asks only this of us, Micah said: "to act justly, to love tenderly and to walk humbly with your God" (Mi 6:8). Thus, Jesus accepts his unity with those who are not his followers, and even those who reject him. His love and respect for all people is his lesson to the disciples, that they may learn to love as he loves.

Jesus here is reflecting the traditional Jewish theological belief in the Noatic Code, based upon God's covenant with Noah. After the Flood, God promised never to destroy the earth, binding *all* people to keep their part of the covenant not to shed the blood of anyone: "He who sheds man's blood, shall have his blood shed by man, for in the image of God man was made" (Gn 9:6). As long as people obey this basic law, which we may extend to seeking never to harm another, they have kept to their agreement. Since all the nations of the world stem from Noah's three sons (see the genealogy in Gn 10), this covenant embraces all people, not just the children of Israel. Thus, Jesus is teaching his disciples that all people are his brothers and sisters, regardless of their religious path or spiritual teacher.

Scripture scholars suggest, after Luke's statement in 11:1, that Jesus gave the Lord's Prayer in response to the disciples' desire to have something that would distinguish them from all other groups, notably the followers of John the Baptist. They wished to be special and have a prayer no one else had. If this hypothesis is correct, it provides an instructive example of how Jesus can turn a request of the ego into a means to lead us beyond the ego.

Not only did the disciples wish to be different from other groups, but they fought among each other to be first in Jesus' affections. We see the sons of Zebedee, James and John, asking Jesus to sit at his right and left hands when he is in his glory (Mk 10:35-37). In Matthew's version it is their mother who makes the request (Mt 20:20-23). Elsewhere, the disciples argue among themselves who is the greatest (Mk 9:33f; Lk 9:46; 22:24), or pose the question to Jesus himself (Mt 18:1).

That Jesus recognized the problem of specialness is evident in his response to the disciples' plea for unique roles in his ministry and special places in his heart. His characteristic answer was a call for humility: "If anyone wants to be first, he must make himself last of all and servant of all" (Mk 9: 35); and even more pointedly:

> *Among pagans it is the kings who lord it over them, and those who have authority over them are given the title Benefactor. This must not happen with you. No; the greatest among you must behave as if he were the youngest, the leader as if he were the one who serves. For who is the greater: the one at table or the one who serves? The one at table, surely? Yet here am I among you as one who serves! (Lk 22:25-27).*

Jesus himself provided an example of this humility in washing the feet of his disciples at the Last Supper. Peter strongly objects, but Jesus' reply epitomizes the principle of love's equality: "If I do not wash you, you can have nothing in common with me" (Jn 13:8). In effect, Jesus is saying: "If you insist on separating me from yourself by making me special, you will not be able to share in our Father's kingdom, where all His children are equal." In the gospel, Jesus says: "I tell you most solemnly, no servant is greater than his master, no messenger is greater than the man who sent him" (Jn 13:16). Similar sentiments are found in Jesus' response to the rich, young man who addresses him as "Good master": "Why do you call me good? No one is good but God alone" (Mk 10:18); and to the disciples:

> *You . . . must not allow yourselves to be called Rabbi, since you have only one Master, and you are all brothers. You must call no one on earth your father, since you have only one Father, and he is in heaven. Nor must you allow yourselves to be called teachers, for you have only one Teacher, the Christ. The greatest among you must be your servant. Anyone who exalts himself will be humbled, and anyone who humbles himself will be exalted (Mt 23:8-12).*

By this last statement, we can see that Jesus was not diminishing his own authority. This is also clear in the verse following his washing of the disciples' feet: "You call me Master and Lord, and rightly; so I am" (Jn 13:13). Rather, Jesus is urging his followers not to put themselves down any more than they should puff themselves up. He is emphasizing equality and the absence of specialness: "If I, then, the Lord and Master, have washed your feet, you should wash each other's feet. I have given you an example so that you may copy what I have done to you" (Jn 13:14f). We shall return to this issue of Jesus and "spiritual specialness" in Part IV.

One of the most important examples of Jesus' treatment of the problem of specialness is also from John's account of the Last Supper. The disciples believed that their power to heal and forgive came from Jesus. However, they understandably mistook the base of this power to be rooted in the physical person of Jesus who lived and walked with them. If this were so, their ministry would have been restricted to the time of Jesus' earthly life. The final lesson Jesus was to leave the disciples was that his power and authority was *inside* them. Because this power was of the Holy Spirit, it could not be limited by time or place. One person having this power did not exclude its presence in another. This idea, of course, flies in the face of specialness, which by definition limits love's manifestation to certain special people within a specific temporal and spatial framework. Specialness is exclusive and limited; true love, inclusive and limitless, embraces all people without exception.

This, then is a question of faith, faith in a different order of reality that cannot be known through the five senses. It was an essential part of Jesus' mission to direct our attention, mind and heart to this other order of reality. After his resurrection, he appeared to the disciples who had lived with him during his earthly ministry; to the doubting Thomas he said the words which held such great meaning to the followers who did not know him during his lifetime: "You believe because you can see me. Happy are those who have not seen and yet believe"(Jn 20:29).Thus, Jesus prepared his disciples at the Last Supper: "In a short time you will no longer see me, and then a short time later you will see me again" (Jn 16:16). It was not with their body's eyes that they would see Jesus, but through the vision born of faith in the reality of spirit, through which is experienced the living Presence of God who is beyond time, space and the material world. It was to transcend the limitations of this world of separated forms that Jesus taught his lessons of forgiveness, and exemplified them with such perfect purity. With his life, he set into motion the lesson of the prophets who preached the opening of the eyes and ears of the people: that glorious time when "the eyes of those who see will no longer be closed, the ears of those who hear will be alert, the heart of the hasty will learn to judge, the tongue of the stammerer will speak clearly" (Is 32:3-5).

Because one of Jesus' major purposes was to help those who were to do his work on earth learn to hear the Voice from Heaven, it was essential they be taught that the kingdom of God is within, not outside them. However, as long as Jesus remained physically present to the disciples and an object of their dependence, they could never have learned this lesson. The need for their Lord was too great. Thus, Jesus speaks these consoling words of his imminent death: "Still I must tell you the truth: it is for your own good that I am going because unless I go, the Advocate [the Holy Spirit] will not come to you; but if I do go, I will send him to you . . ." (Jn 16:7). "Unless I leave," Jesus is explaining to them, "you will never understand that I live within you. After my departure, you will recognize that the Holy Spirit carries me with you no matter where you are, I can speak within you all at the same time."

Therefore, if Jesus were to have remained with his disciples, their special love relationship with his physical and psychological self would have prevented their ever recognizing the living Presence of the Spirit within them. They would have been reinforcing the very lesson of specialness they were supposed to unlearn. Jesus did not want them or anyone to become dependent on his actual physical presence, or to have our awareness of him limited to it. It would hardly serve the lesson of the limitlessness of God if Jesus himself were limited by the very ego laws he was teaching us to transcend. This, then, remains the crucial point in faith: that we withdraw our faith in what we see, hear and understand, recognizing, with Hamlet, that there are more things in Heaven and earth than are dreamt of in our philosophy. Through his living example, Jesus showed us what these "more things" truly are. His continued presence in our lives reveals this truth: God is limitless, and this freedom of spirit we share with Him.

It is this ongoing contact with God's Voice, of which Jesus is the manifestation, that frees us to be anywhere and with anyone, to do anything in this world with the perfect awareness that we are not alone. Our Teacher is always with us, even to the end of time. Since this Voice is not bound by time and space, neither are we. We are free to walk the world in perfect freedom, in perfect confidence and trust that our Teacher, Comforter and Advocate goes with us. As Jesus states in the Course: "You do not walk alone. God's angels hover near and all about. His Love surrounds you, and of this be sure; that I will never leave you comfortless" (workbook, p. 478).

When we are free from dependence on external forms, we are ensured of the direct communication between us and the Holy Spirit. Communication through Him, unlike communication in the physical world, knows no boundaries. Because of this, Jesus can be with us always and equally, and the problem of specialness is undone. As the Course states: "Communication is not limited to the small range of channels the world recognizes. If it were, there would be little point in trying to teach salvation. It would be impossible to do so. The limits the world places on communication are the chief barriers to direct experience of the Holy Spirit, Whose Presence is always there and Whose Voice is available but for the hearing" (manual, p. 59). Thus we are able to recognize that this Voice speaks for us, for our true Self that we have forgotten and denied. By this link, the fundamental unity of God and ourselves is reinforced, even as we continue living within an ego framework. God uses our belief in the reality of separate voices to teach us ultimately that there is only One.

Jesus' words and his message at the Last Supper must have fallen on deaf ears, certainly on non-comprehending ones. The disciples could hear their Lord only through the veil of their own specialness, the fear and guilt of their ego selves. It would not have been until after they experienced his resurrection that the disciples could begin to know the tremendous gift of love Jesus had given them. But first they would have to go through the most difficult lesson of all: the crucifixion.

The Web of Specialness: Special Hate for Jesus

It would be most difficult to place ourselves in the disciples' shoes during that period beginning with Jesus' arrest in the Garden of Gethsemane until he appeared to them Sunday evening in the upper room. The gospel narratives, moreover, offer precious little beyond some tantalizing clues. The rest is left to our imagination, guided by the psychological insights we have discussed in Part I. We can safely say, however, that this group of loyal followers would have been psychologically shattered by the startling reversal of the events of these days.

For many months, they had built up their faith and trust in Jesus which climaxed in his triumphant entry into Jerusalem on Palm Sunday. They saw in him the realization of their hopes for the coming of the Messiah who would reign on David's throne, establishing God's kingdom of peace and justice on earth, the incarnation of the one spoken of in the psalms: "Yahweh's oracle to you, my Lord, 'Sit at my right hand and I will make your enemies a footstool for you'" (Ps 110:1). The many "signs and wonders" they witnessed throughout Jesus' ministry would have reinforced this belief, not to mention their personal experience of their Lord's love for them.

However, the gospels repeatedly portray the disciples misunderstanding the true nature of the kingdom that Jesus preached, and of the meaning of his life and coming death. Peter, for example, remonstrates with Jesus after being told of his future death: "Heaven preserve you, Lord . . . this must not happen to you" (Mt 16:22). When Jesus repeats it, the disciples respond with "great sadness" (Mt 17:23). In his account, Mark comments: "They did not understand what he said and were afraid to ask him" (Mk 9:32), while Luke observes: "They could make nothing of this; what he said was quite obscure to them, they had no idea what it meant" (Lk 18:34). Finally, John's version of the Last Supper has several of the disciples asking Jesus to clarify what they are unable to understand. To Philip, Jesus replies: "Have I been with you all this time . . . and you still do not know me?" (Jn 14:9).

Given their own as yet limited comprehension, they could not have done otherwise. The metanoia or change of mind that Jesus taught was translated by the disciples into something external. Not until the resurrection could the disciples' understanding begin to shift, when they would recognize that the temple that was to be destroyed and rebuilt in three days referred to Jesus himself, not an external structure (Jn 2:19-22). The "failure" of Jesus' mission to establish an earthly kingdom would inevitably have devastated them. Viewed in retrospect, the few short days separating Good Friday from Palm Sunday must have seemed infinite. All hope had gone, and nothing remained except desolation and the bitter memories of broken dreams.

This background underscores the problematic nature of the disciples' special relationship with Jesus. Seeing in

Jesus the promised Messiah of scripture, they transferred onto him their psychological need for a savior, believing that their own self-worth lay in him and in the success of his mission. Not feeling worthy in themselves, they needed to feel special through their relationship to him.

In Chapter 1, we saw how quickly love turns to hate when the object of this love fails to meet the demands and obligations placed on it. We may infer a similar process now building to its climax, beginning with Jesus' arrest and culminating in the post-crucifixion scene of the disciples huddled together in the upper room.

Having projected onto Jesus their special need for an ideal savior who would meet all their needs, what now remained with Jesus gone, particularly his having died under such demeaning circumstances? The dynamics of the ego first demand the reinforcement of their own guilt: what happened to Jesus was their fault; Jesus died because of their sins against him. These "sins" would have included: not fully believing in him or his message; murmuring among themselves behind his back; doubting his promises and assurances; falling asleep at Gethsemane; denying him three times after his arrest; hiding in fear for their lives during his trial and crucifixion — in general, abandoning him at *his* hour of seeming need, after all he had done for them in *their* need.

In all, it would have been almost impossible for the disciples not to have felt, consciously or unconsciously, that their own betrayal, abandonment, and lack of faith were responsible for the actual betrayal and murder of their Master. Even if they did not yet recognize the full extent of Judas' actions, they would have themselves felt guilty of the same action. Freud has helped us understand this dynamic by describing the child's "omnipotence of wishes": If a parent should die, the child's unconscious angry thoughts against that parent would make him or her feel responsible for the death. Jesus taught the same principle by emphasizing the importance of our thoughts, which we shall discuss in the following chapter. Having attack thoughts is sufficient to make us guilty, even if the anger is unexpressed or out of awareness. Thus, the disciples' feeling responsible for Jesus' death would have reinforced the guilt already present in their special relationship with him.

Now arises the most painful of all the ego's weapons: fear. If indeed the disciples believed that they had committed such terrible sins against Jesus, as their guilt affirmed, how terrible then would be the punishment they would inevitably and justifiably receive. John writes: "In the evening of that same day, the first day of the week, the doors were closed in the room where the disciples were, for fear of the Jews" (Jn 20:19). On the one hand, we can appreciate the disciples' apprehensions that the people or the Sanhedrin would not be satisfied with the death of Jesus. Wishing to stamp out what they believed was a threat to their authority, the leaders would seek to kill off the rest of Jesus' "conspirators." However, we have already seen that the ultimate source of fear is not external situations, but rather the expectation of punishment demanded by our guilt. As it was impossible for the disciples not to have felt guilty over their believed sinfulness, specifically as it related to *their* behavior and thoughts regarding Jesus, it would have been equally impossible for them not to fear reprisal. If the people crucified Jesus who was totally innocent, their unconscious would reason, what would they do to us who are so sinful?

At its root, fear comes from only one source: when we believe we separated from God, our guilt over this believed sin of having attacked our Creator demands that He will retaliate in kind. When understood in this context, the disciples huddled in fear behind closed doors recalls Adam and Eve's attempt to hide in the garden. They feared the God who would punish them for their sin against Him, a fear their own guilt set into motion and reinforced. Thus, their fear of capture by the Jews was really an expression of the unconscious fear of God. They sought to hide from Him, magically hoping to conceal themselves behind the locked doors.

Once God is established as our enemy instead of Friend, another source of fear enters. Without the God who alone is our shield and protector, who is there to protect us from the harsh cruelties of the separated world in which we now feel so vulnerable, alienated and alone? Our guilt has cut us off from the only One who can help, at the same time that One becomes the object of our greatest fear. Thus, every individual expression of sin or separation, such as anger or fear, will unconsciously remind us of our separation from God. How much more of a reminder would this be when the occasion of "sin" involves the messenger of God Himself? Suddenly faced with their external protector taken from them, and not seeing him act as the messianic king their expectations dictated, they had no choice but to fall back on their ego. Forgetting that their safety lay in the God of Israel who was their true rock and salvation, they fled to the ego for security and thus right into the waiting arms of projection.

At the same time this guilt was being reinforced, the fear of confronting it would lead the disciples to project the guilt onto someone else, attempting to affix to that person the guilt they really believed was their own. It would not have been difficult at that moment for the disciples to find suitable objects on whom to project. There would be Judas, Peter, or any of the other disciples; the leaders of the Sanhedrin who had clamored for Jesus' death; the Romans who carried out the crucifixion; or even God, who permitted this horrible tragedy to occur. Perhaps the most devastating to them of all the scapegoats, however, would have been Jesus himself: Jesus, the all-knowing savior who walked open-eyed into the trap; Jesus, the miracle worker who never stopped the inevitable from happening, even though he surely could have saved himself; Jesus, the messianic king now turned weak and disgraced. Above all others, then, it would have been Jesus who was most responsible for the misery the disciples felt. Their special love's defensive cover had suddenly been seized from them, and their tremendous loss could only be due to *his* failure. In their guilt-ridden minds, protected by projection, it was not they who had abandoned Jesus and betrayed his trust, but Jesus who abandoned and betrayed them. All doubts they once entertained about the strategy of his messianic mission now seemed totally justified.

At this point,the insidious guilt-attack cycle, the bulwark of the ego's system, is set into motion. The guiltier the disciples felt about their unconscious involvement in Jesus' death, the greater their need to project responsibility onto others. This merely increased their guilt, especially when the one on whom they projected the most (because their guilt towards him was the greatest) was Jesus himself. Their loss was unfathomable; their guilt, overwhelming; their hatred, terrifying — their world had suddenly come to an end, inexplicably shattered by events that seemed beyond their control.

The combination of sin, guilt and fear the disciples experienced after the crucifixion would seem beyond our comprehension, too terrifying to contemplate. Yet, as we have seen in Chapter 1, each of us carries these feelings within us for we share the same collective ego, similar in one sense to Jung's concept of the "collective unconscious." It shatters our minds even to think of it. Without the mechanisms of denial and projection, it would be impossible for us to survive. These same defense mechanisms, however, ensure that this survival will be one of pain, suffering, terror and death. The disciples huddling together in the upper room are symbolic of everyone. Those terrifying hours that occurred once in history recur daily, albeit in different forms, in our lives. "Each day, and every minute in each day, and every instant that each minute holds, you but relive the single instant when the time of terror took the place of love" (text, p. 513). Then, suddenly, in the midst of the terror of our ego's darkness, Jesus appears with his salvific message of forgiveness. The next two chapters will discuss this message of forgiveness, culminating in Jesus' forgiveness of his disciples and of us all.

Chapter 7

FORGIVENESS: THE TEACHINGS

Before we discuss Jesus' message of forgiveness to his disciples in the upper room, we shall consider the principles of forgiveness as they are given in the New Testament. In the previous chapter, we spoke of the process of detachment, or changing our mind about the things of the world. In his practice of spiritual direction, the 16th century Spanish mystic, St. John of the Cross, emphasized that this issue never rested in the worldly things themselves, but rather in our attachments to them. This important caution helps us shift the focus from externals to our interior disposition, the same shift we noted in our discussion of Table 2 in Chapter 3. This shift is the basis for forgiveness, for it brings the problem of our guilt back inside our minds where it can be removed for us by the Holy Spirit. As the Course describes the process: " . . . seen within your mind, guilt and forgiveness for an instant lie together, side by side, upon one altar. There at last are sickness and its single remedy joined in one healing brightness. God has come to claim His Own. Forgiveness is complete" (manual, p. 82).

Reviewing the principles discussed in Chapters 1 and 2, the core of our ego or separated self is our guilt, which the ego has convinced us is our true self. Teaching us guilt is fearful, the ego next proceeds to convince us that we can never approach it directly. Thus, guilt lies buried in our unconscious mind, "protected" from correction. However, we *are* able to deal with it after we have projected it onto others. By looking beyond the ego darkness we have projected to the light of Christ that still shines, we are able to recognize the same light shining in ourselves. This recognition, or shift in perception, is the essence of forgiveness: forgiving others that we may forgive ourselves.

The most concentrated presentation of this theme occurs in the Sermon on the Mount, found in Chapters 5-7 in Matthew. In Chapter 5, Jesus chooses six Old Testament standards of behavior and extends them. As he said as preface to this: "Do not imagine that I have come to abolish the Law or the Prophets. I have come not to abolish but to complete them" (Mt 5:17). Thus, each one comes in the general form: "You have learned how it was said. . . . But I say this to you": Four of the six specifically reflect the gospel message of forgiveness and will be taken up in the first three sections of this chapter. The first section considers forgiving those we have attacked, reversing our projection. This is based upon the first of these Old Testament texts, dealing with anger. The next section extends this idea by presenting Jesus' two teachings on forgiving our enemies,which his own life so powerfully exemplified. The third section treats the question of divorce, based upon the fourth of the Old Testament texts. We shall consider this from the perspective of healing our special relationships. The final two sections in this chapter treat the relationship between forgiveness and God's love, and Jesus' frequently misunderstood love for the sinful and poor.

Anger

> *You have learned how it was said to our ancestors: You must not kill; and if anyone does kill he must answer for it before the court. But I say this to you: anyone who is angry with his brother will answer for it before the court. . . . So then, if you are bringing your offering to the altar and there remember that your brother has something against you, leave your offering there before the altar, go and be reconciled with your brother first, and then come back and present your offering (Mt 5:21-24).*

Jesus is teaching that it is not enough to refrain from killing; we should not even become angry. As in the rest of the Sermon, we are presented with an ideal for behavior. Only a saint of saints, an advanced teacher of God, would be totally beyond anger, being totally beyond guilt. Nonetheless, this is an ideal we should strive to attain. Jesus explains this in the passage about bringing our offering to the altar, which summarizes the importance of forgiveness. If people hold grievances against us which we find upsetting, or we against them, true peace of mind is impossible and we cannot approach God's altar. The lack of forgiveness between us protects the underlying guilt and is sufficient to maintain our belief in separation from God. Guilt, by demanding our punishment, convinced us that God could not possibly love us.

Thus, it is not that God will not accept our gift, but that our fear would not allow us to accept His. Through reconciling ourselves with one another, the guilt is undone and we are free to come before our Father, ready to receive His gift of love. Our offering to Him is our willingness to let go of our guilt (steps 1 and 2), and in return we receive His merciful love, Heaven's equivalent of our forgiveness (step 3). Jesus continued this teaching later in the Sermon when he taught: "If you forgive others their failings, your heavenly Father will forgive you yours; but if you do not forgive others, your Father will not forgive your failings either" (Mt 6:14f).

Our willingness to turn our guilt over to the Holy Spirit is an example of what we referred to in Chapter 3 as "healthy guilt." This expresses our desire to release this obstruction to our relationship to God, and thus return to Him through our forgiveness. Psalm 32 offers a clear portrait of the effects of both ways of handling our guilt:

1) retaining it inside ourselves:

All the time I kept silent, my bones were
wasting away with groans, day in, day out;
day and night your hand lay heavy on me;
my heart grew parched as stubble in summer
drought.

2) releasing it by defenselessly giving it to God:

At last I admitted to you I had sinned;
no longer concealing my guilt,
I said, "I will go to Yahweh and confess my
fault."
And you, you have forgiven the wrong I did,
have pardoned my sin.
That is why each of your servants prays to
you in time of trouble;
even if floods come rushing down,
they will never reach him.

You are a hiding place for me,
you guard me when in trouble,
you surround me with songs of deliverance.
(Ps 32:3-7)

This principle underscores the law from the book of Numbers: "If a man or woman commits any of the sins by which men break faith with Yahweh, that person incurs guilt. He must confess the sin he has committed . . . " (Nb 5:6f). In John's first letter we read: "If we say we have no sin in us, we are deceiving ourselves and refusing to admit the truth; but if we acknowledge our sins, then God who is faithful and just will forgive our sins and purify us from everything that is wrong" (1 Jn 1:8f).

Therefore, a decision to hold on to our anger, justifying the grievances held against another, is in reality a decision to hold on to our guilt. This form of defensiveness is sufficient to keep us in a "state of sin" — separate from God — for this is what guilt upholds. As James taught in his letter: "God's righteousness is never served by man's anger" (Jm 1:20); and Paul: "Never let the sun set on your anger" (Ep 4:26). Once we are angry, all the love of Heaven will not break through this prisonhouse of the ego. We shall stand alone in our deluded minds, estranged from the world and from God, never recognizing the true cause of this experience of isolation: our decision to remain unforgiving, and therefore in a state of sin and guilt.

Jesus' teaching on anger seems to conflict with his own behavior late in his ministry when he expelled the money-changers from the Temple, shortly after his final entry to Jerusalem. The incident is described in this way by Mark:

So they reached Jerusalem and he went into the Temple and began driving out those who were selling and buying there; he upset the tables of the money changers and the chairs of those who were selling pigeons. Nor would he allow anyone to carry anything through the Temple. And he taught them and said, "Does not scripture say: 'My house will be called a house of prayer for all the peoples?' But you have turned it into a robbers' den" (Mk 11:15-17).

Jesus' actions here seem to reflect those of an angry man. But do they? It should first be noted that nowhere in any of the four gospel accounts of this scene does it say Jesus was angry. The accounts merely describe his behavior or actions. Notwithstanding this, there are at least three ways of understanding this episode.

1) *The scene described in the gospels did not really occur in that manner.* Scripture scholarship has taught us how much of the gospel material has been filtered through the perception of the early Church, which read back into Jesus' words and actions what they needed to hear for themselves as a persecuted and persecuting group. The searing indictment of the scribes and Pharisees found in the twenty-third chapter of Matthew would be a case in point. It would be very difficult to conceive of the Prince of Peace and messenger of God's mercy and love ever speaking this way. In the case of the temple scene, it is possible that the early Church elaborated on such an event, having Jesus verbalize the accusation against the Jews that they really wished him to say, justifying their own need to perceive in others a lack of understanding God's plan.

2) *The event occurred as it was reported in the gospels, but has a different interpretation; namely, Jesus was not personally angry.* There are at least three specific characteristics we can note in a personal response of anger: first, at the moment we are angry there is an absence of peace: anger and peace are mutually exclusive states; secondly, when we are angry, God is the farthest thing from our minds: all our attention is focused on the object of our wrath; and thirdly, the objects of our wrath are perceived as enemies, separated from us by our anger: thus, we lose sight of them as our brothers and sisters, united as one family in God's love.

It seems inconceivable that these three characteristics would apply to Jesus, especially this late in his life (only John places the episode at the beginning of Jesus' public ministry). Would Jesus be unpeaceful, not fully conscious of his Father or his Father's business, and see himself separated from the very people he loved and came to help?

However, if Jesus were not angry, what *did* happen in the Temple? Conceivably, Jesus was teaching the people a lesson in the form that was best suited to the circumstances and which would have the greatest impact. Like all good teachers, Jesus presented his lessons so that his pupils would learn best. He tailored these lessons to the form most suitable to his audience. The gospels offer many examples of Jesus speaking one way to the multitudes, and quite another to an individual person. To the former he could sound harsh, while to the latter he was compassionate and forgiving. A classroom teacher presents a lesson one way to a class of forty, and quite another way to a group of two or three. In the expulsion of the dealers from the Temple, we see Jesus making a dramatic point in a dramatic situation. This was just before the Passover, when Jewish Law demanded that all Jews in the country go up to the Temple to worship. Because thousands were congregating in the Temple at this time, Jesus had to speak and act in bold, dramatic strokes to capture the people's attention and convey the message that they had misunderstood the meaning of worship. His actions were motivated by love, designed to reach his erring brothers and sisters in the most effective way possible, recalling to them the true meaning of the Temple as a house of prayer.

3) *Jesus did, in fact, become personally angry.* However, even if one accepted this third alternative, seeing Jesus' anger as proof of his "humanness," of having an ego, the question would still remain: why would we wish to identify with his ego, citing this incident in the Temple as a justification for our anger, forgetting all that Jesus taught us — especially in the Sermon on the Mount — about *not* getting angry, not to mention his personal example at the very end of his life when no man would have been more justified in becoming angry, yet he did not?

One of the most basic lessons Jesus' life witnessed to was that anger is never justified, for only a response of forgiveness and love can be God's Will. Nothing can ever justify separating us from each other, or from the One who created us as one family. As the prophet Malachi wrote, four to five centuries before Jesus: "Have we not all one Father? Did not one God create us?" (Ml 2:10). Anger and attack deny this statement; forgiveness affirms it.

Forgiveness of Enemies

You have learned how it was said: Eye for eye and tooth for tooth. But I say this to you: offer the wicked man no resistance. On the contrary, if anyone hits you on the right cheek, offer him the other as well; if a man takes you to law and would have your tunic, let him have your cloak as well. And if anyone orders you to go one mile, go two miles with him. Give to anyone who asks, and if anyone wants to borrow, do not turn away (Mt 5:38-42).

You have learned how it was said: You must love your neighbor and hate your enemy. But I say this to you: love your enemies and pray for those who persecute you; in this way you will be sons of your Father in heaven, for he causes his sun to rise on bad men as well as good, and his rain to fall on honest and dishonest men alike. For if you love those who love you, what right have you to claim any credit? Even the tax collectors do as much, do they not? And if you save your greetings for your brothers, are you doing anything exceptional? Even the pagans do as much, do they not? You must therefore be perfect just as your heavenly Father is perfect (Mt 5:43-48).

These two Old Testament texts extended by Jesus are perhaps his most famous teachings of the principles of forgiveness: turn the other cheek and love your enemies. In the first, Jesus teaches that we should offer our enemy no resistance. Rather than the old standard of an eye for an eye, repaying another for what has been done to us, we are told to turn the other cheek. If an unreasonable demand is made upon us, we should respond to the extent of giving twice what was asked of us: our cloak as well as our tunic, walking two miles instead of one.

By the standards of the world this thinking makes no sense. To behave in such a fashion seems merely to invite people to walk all over us, letting them get away with various forms of injustices. But what if these standards are incorrect? We have seen that a thought system may be logical with its conclusions following from its premises, but its rigor in logic does not make the system true. Only valid premises can do that. Jesus came to show us that the premises on which this world rests are faulty, for they reflect a world in which God is absent.

The premises of our ego's world rest on vulnerability, fear and defensiveness. These are most clearly reflected in our interpersonal behavior, especially our responses to the attacks or criticisms of others. Here, at the end of the fifth chapter of Matthew, Jesus gives us explicit guidelines for our behavior; principles that result from a totally different set of premises: our invulnerability as children of God and the absence of fear, which allows us to be defenseless in the face of seeming attack. Peter echoes these principles in his first letter: "No one can hurt you if you are determined to do only what is right; if you do have to suffer for being good, you will count it a blessing. There is no need to be afraid or to worry about them. Simply reverence the Lord Christ in your hearts. . . . " (1 P 3:13-15). And if another seeks to hurt us, "Never pay back one wrong with another, or an angry word with another; instead pay back with a blessing. That is what you are called to do, so that you inherit a blessing yourself" (1 P 3:9).

This attitude leads to a perception of all people as our brothers and sisters, transcending the dichotomy between good and bad, friend and enemy. Such distinctions are unknown in Heaven, where our Father causes his sun and rain to fall on *all* people as one. God, we read in Deuteronomy, is "never partial" (Dt 10:17). Without the defensiveness born of guilt and fear, what remains is the awareness of the unity of all people in God, children of the one Father. As St. Peter addressed the crowd in Cornelius' house: "The truth I have now come to realize . . . is that God does not have favorites. . . . Jesus Christ is the Lord of all men" (Ac 10:34,36). James urges us not to make "distinctions between classes of people" (Jm 2:1), for once we do we "are committing sin, and under condemnation for breaking the Law" (Jm 2:9). When we define sin as being a lack of love, or "missing the mark" in one of its original Hebrew meanings, this teaching becomes even more relevant, as love does not separate. To the Ephesian slave owners, St. Paul taught that slave and free deserve respect, for both "will be properly rewarded by the Lord. . . . They and you have the same

Master in heaven and he is not impressed by one person more than by another" (Ep 6:8f).

The implications of this principle are that we are to love all people, regardless of their position, station in life, or their behavior. A subtle way in which the ego has maintained its need to project guilt and separation has been to segregate out groups of people whose beliefs and behaviors differ from our own. In the name of righteousness and truth, we unconsciously condemn in others the guilt we wish to deny in ourselves. This is the mistake of confusing form and content. Focusing on form will always separate, as forms *are* separate by definition, while God's content of love must always unite. Thus the Course states: "The ego analyzes; the Holy Spirit accepts" (text, p. 190).

St. Paul was well aware of this error, though perhaps he did not recognize its full generalizability. In this long exhortation to the Romans, he warns against judging others, specifically regarding problems which had arisen within the Roman community around the question of clean and unclean foods, and the keeping of holy days:

> *If a person's faith is not strong enough, welcome him all the same without starting an argument. People range from those who believe they may eat any sort of meat to those whose faith is so weak they dare not eat anything except vegetables. Meat eaters must not despise the scrupulous. On the other hand, the scrupulous must not condemn those who feel free to eat anything they choose, since God has welcomed them. It is not for you to condemn someone else's servant; whether he stands or falls it is his own master's business. . . . If one man keeps certain days as holier than others, and another considers all days to be equally holy, each must be left free to hold his own opinion. . . . You should never pass judgment on a brother or treat him with contempt. . . . Far from passing judgment on each other, therefore, you should make up your mind never to be the cause of your brother tripping or falling. Now I am perfectly*

well aware, of course, and I speak for the Lord Jesus, that no food in unclean in itself; however, if someone thinks that a particular food is unclean, then it is unclean for him. And indeed if your attitude to food is upsetting your brother, then you are hardly being guided by charity. . . . The kingdom of God does not mean eating or drinking this or that, it means righteousness and peace and joy brought by the Holy Spirit. If you serve Christ in this way you will please God and be respected by men. So let us adopt any custom that leads to peace and our mutual improvement; do not wreck God's work over a question of food (Rm 14:1-20).

We are all part of the one body of Christ, and judgment based on separation belies this inherent unity. Thus, Paul urges: "Bear with one another charitably, in complete selflessness, gentleness and patience. Do all you can to preserve the unity of Spirit by the peace that binds you together. There is one Body, one Spirit, just as you were all called into one and the same hope when you were called" (Ep 4:2-4).

Jesus, therefore, teaches that it is not enough to love our neighbors, we must love our enemies as well. We must love our enemies because they are *not* our enemies: "We are all parts of one another" (Ep 4:25). Perceiving others as separate from us reflects our need to protect what we are most afraid of in ourselves. Thus, perceived enemies are really our saviors, for in them we see the projected image of the enemy within. Unable to deal with our repressed guilt by ourselves, we can now forgive it when seen in another.

We have already discussed how it is psychologically impossible to love someone once he or she has been judged to be an "other" or an "enemy." True forgiveness can never occur once another has been perceived as a threat or having inflicted harm. Only when the perceived (seeming) attack has been understood as a call for help can the "enemy" be forgiven and seen as a friend. As St. Paul said: " . . . you are not to regard him as an enemy but as a brother in need of correction" (2 Th 3:15).

Jesus' words that we should pray for those who persecute us can be understood as a call to see them as he does, what the Course refers to as the "vision of Christ." In so doing we have changed our perception from enemy to friend, looking beyond the other's ego to the Christ, seeing the same Christ in ourselves: the one Self we all share. The guilt inside that we had projected onto this "enemy" is forgiven, and the love that is our true identity in God is restored to our awareness, as we also see that love in another. In this way we become "perfect just as [our] heavenly Father is perfect." To be perfect is to be without sin and guilt; to be, as Paul writes: "Holy and spotless, and to live through love in [God's] presence" (Ep 1:4). God's perfection is in each of us, both "good" and "bad" alike. To help us realize this, the Holy Spirit reinterprets those on whom we would be most tempted to project "good" and "bad," based on our own ego needs. He asks us to see only Christ in these people, that we may come to remember His love, seeing only Him in ourselves. Thus we are to "continue to love each other like brothers, and remember always to welcome strangers, for by doing this, some people have entertained angels without knowing it. Keep in mind those who are in prison, as though you were in prison with them; and those who are being badly treated, since you too are in the one body (Heb 13:1-3). Of such welcoming is the kingdom of Heaven, wherein is found our own perfection in God.

A medieval legend provides us with a beautiful example of this welcoming of forgiveness. Jesus and the disciples had gathered in Heaven to re-enact the last supper. They waited around the table while one place remained vacant. Then Judas walked in. Jesus went over to him and greeted him warmly. "Welcome, my brother. We have been waiting for you."

Regardless of the actions of others — "good" or "bad" — we respond the same: expressions of love or calls for love elicit the same response in ourselves: love. As Paul wrote to the Corinthians: "Let everything you do be done in love" (1 Co 16:14). We all live in this love, but do not know it. To remember is to obey the words of him whom God sent to remind us. John said: "But when anyone does obey what he [Jesus] has said, God's love comes to perfection in him. We can be sure that we are in God only when the one who claims to be living in him is living the same kind of life as Christ lived. . . . Anyone who claims to be in the light but hates his brothers is still in the dark" (1 Jn 2:5f, 9).

These "Persecutors" in whom we perceive darkness and who elicit darkness in ourselves become Heaven's gifts, for they offer us the opportunity of looking past the darkness to the light of Christ that is our true reality. Thus we may paraphrase the beatitude: "Happy those who are given the opportunity of being persecuted, for if they learn their lessons of forgiveness, theirs is the kingdom of Heaven."

The Question of Divorce

It has also been said: Anyone who divorces his wife must give her a writ of dismissal. But I say this to you: everyone who divorces his wife, except for the case of fornication, makes her an adulteress; and anyone who marries a divorced woman commits adultery (Mt 5:31f).

This teaching is amplified later in the gospel: "What God has united, man must not divide." (Mt 19:6).

Some forms of Christianity have traditionally taught that because of these words it was against the law of God for any marriage to end in divorce. Woe to those who did divorce for, in the name of God, they were ostracized and even excommunicated from His church. Rather than undoing sin and guilt — Jesus' only purpose — this teaching became an instrument of reinforcing it.

Forbidding anything makes it real, giving it a power it cannot have. Since there is not a marital partner who at one time or another has not had thoughts — conscious or unconscious — of ending the marriage, guilt over this "sinful thought" is unavoidable and becomes built into the relationship. Thus, the man who came to teach us about God's mercy and love has his words become the means of teaching His punishment, meted out by others in the name of His justice. The Course emphasizes that justice split off from love is not justice, which can only be known through forgiveness. Although we can never really know why Jesus gave this teaching, if he gave it at all, we do know that he could never have intended it to add to people's pain.

What has occurred is another unfortunate example of emphasizing form, ignoring the underlying content. Well-meaning people, therefore, believed they were complying with God's law by controlling their behavior, without realizing that it was their thoughts that needed correction. Like the Pharisees, they self-righteously believed that their problems were solved, while the real problem of their guilt remained, though no longer perceived. Successfully denied, this guilt became projected, often in judging another for what they secretly believed to be their sins.

God did not create a world of form, but one of spirit. Since marriage is a form, it cannot have been created by God and therefore He could not forbid its dissolution. To believe otherwise is to give a meaning to form it does not have, elevating it to the stature of the sacred or divine. This serves the ego's basic aim of having us see truth in the world of form (the right side of Table 2), obscuring truth's real source which is the mind (the left side). This mind is the home of the Holy Spirit, whose function is to reinterpret the world we made real, correcting our wrong-minded thinking that we may come to remember the world of reality that God created.

These teachings of Jesus are better understood as referring to the underlying spiritual principle that God has united all people in the creation, and no illusory belief in separation can divide our true reality as part of Christ, God's one Son. We must not divide whom God has united because we *cannot*. The Course's version of this scriptural passage, as we have seen earlier, is: "Whom God has joined as one, the ego cannot put asunder" (text, p. 332).

Regardless of our ego attempts to destroy or obscure the love that God gave when He created us, this love in reality can never be changed or undone. This is the principle of Atonement that denies the seeming reality of the separation. St. Paul's hymn to God's love is particularly appropriate here:

> *Nothing therefore can come between us and the love of Christ, even if we are troubled or worried, or being persecuted, or lacking food or clothes, or being threatened or being attacked. . . . For I*

am certain of this: neither death nor life, no angel no prince, nothing that exists, nothing still to come, not any power, or height or depth, not any created thing can ever come between us and the love of God made visible in Christ Jesus our Lord (Rm 8:35, 38f).

This love of God is made visible to us in seeing Christ in our partner, and this love is always present, regardless of our decision to overlook it. We can never be separated from it, and to believe we can is to affirm a reality that contradicts God's loving Will. In this sense, then, we have merely reproduced the sin of Adam by contradicting God, reinforcing our guilt because of what we believe we have done.

The counterpart to God's joining in Heaven is the Holy Spirit's joining on earth to serve His purpose of forgiveness. This joining affords both people the opportunity of minimizing the ego's special love so that the love of Christ becomes their only purpose and reality. Thus, its meaning extends beyond the laws of marriage to include all relationships, ranging from the most superficial to the lifelong. His love has already blessed and ensured the success of all relationships. Yet we remain free as to *when* we will accept His blessing and His purpose of forgiveness.

Once the ego has convinced us that the problem lies in the physical relationship and not in the *minds* of the people joined in the relationship, it does not care whether the uncomfortable physical relationship is terminated or merely suffered through. Either way the ego emerges triumphant since the underlying guilt is hidden beneath the anger or self-pitying innocence.

When a relationship is "broken up" by the ego, it has succeeded in making a decoy or smokescreen which enables us to believe that our problem lies in the other or in the relationship, anywhere but in ourselves. Thus, our basic problem of guilt is "protected" by externalizing it onto the relationship. This leads to the magical belief that by terminating the relationship (either through divorce or other means), one has terminated the problem. This is why in so many instances people jump from relationship to relationship, always seeking the "perfect relationship" that will end their problems. In seeking peace and happiness in someone else, they never come to recognize that their only hope for peace lies in their relationship with God. On the other hand, we can protect our guilt by *remaining* in a relationship that the Holy Spirit would have us leave, masochistically "enjoying" being the innocent victim, or else self-righteously believing that such suffering and pain is the sacrifice demanded by God for our salvation.

Whatever the path chosen by the ego, the purpose of the Holy Spirit is denied and it is in this denial that guilt is found, not in the specific form that is chosen for the ego's purpose. Regardless of this form of the ego's resolution to guilt, it is not a sin to be punished but a mistake to be corrected through the forgiveness that comes from the Holy Spirit. He sees in our partner the help to learn the truth of God's love, but if we are unable to learn the lesson at this time, He will provide other opportunities until we finally learn what God has ensured we will.

Thus, whatever guilt is not undone in a relationship will return again, and this is the real message of Jesus' teachings on divorce. It is also the message of the parable of "The Return of the Unclean Spirit" (Mt 12:43-45), where we find a clear warning of the consequences of not completing the process of forgiveness. An unclean spirit leaving a man will return if its home in him is unoccupied and, in fact, will return with "seven other spirits more evil than itself." Seven symbolized perfection for Jews, so Jesus' meaning is that the "evil" will be total, with the man "being worse than he was before." It is not enough to expel the unclean spirit of our guilt by simply removing our projections from another. Like the evil spirit which "wanders through waterless country looking for a place to rest," so does guilt continually search for a home. "Its [fear's] messengers steal guiltily away in hungry search of guilt. . . . No little shred of guilt escapes their hungry eyes" (text, p. 382). And if another projected object will not do, the guilt will return to its original home within our minds, greatly strengthened by the desire for attack — if not others, then ourselves. Jesus is teaching us here that guilt must be replaced in our minds by the love of

God, for only then is its source in the sin of separation undone entirely. As the text explains:

> *Sometimes a sin can be repeated over and over, with obviously distressing results, but without the loss of its appeal. And suddenly, you change its status from a sin to a mistake. Now you will not repeat it; you will merely stop and let it go, unless the guilt remains. For then you will but change the form of sin, granting that it was an error, but keeping it uncorrectable. This is not really a change in your perception, for it is sin that calls for punishment, not error (text, p. 377).*

In summary, by asking us not to divide what God has joined, Jesus asks that we learn our lessons of forgiveness so that we have joy to the full, changing our minds, not the external forms. Turning away from this opportunity to forgive will merely delay our learning. This "sin" against love is not punished by God, but by our own guilt and fear which become reinforced. Jesus gave us this principle as a guide to help us learn our lessons, not to incur still further guilt through our difficulties with the lessons. Turning away from love can never bring us peace, and the Holy Spirit has provided the opportunities in our various relationships that we may retrace our ego's steps of separation, and return to the love that unites us all as one family in God. When we find the lesson too difficult to learn, Jesus patiently waits with us until we are ready to take the next step. It is through the gentle love we feel from Him that we know we are forgiven, and in that forgiveness we eventually find the strength to extend this forgiving love from Jesus to others and to ourselves.

Forgiveness as the Expression of God's Love

Chapter 18 in Matthew's gospel may be called the Forgiveness chapter, for the entire chapter contains Jesus' instructions to the disciples on forgiveness, especially as it pertains to God's love. As the Course states: "Forgiveness is an earthly form of love, which as it is in Heaven has no form" (workbook, p. 344). Each of the chapter's sections urges Jesus' followers to extend the love of God to the people through their acts of forgiveness. Through our forgiveness here we teach and remember the love of God in Heaven.

The disciples are first told that they must become like little children, otherwise they can never enter God's kingdom (vv. 1-4). As in similar exhortations, Jesus is not issuing a warning or command. As he explains in the Course: " 'Except ye become as little children' means that unless you fully recognize your complete dependence on God, you cannot know the real power of the Son in his true relationship with the Father" (text, p. 10). Since guilt makes God into an enemy, recognizing our dependency on Him, which we have denied, can only occur when our inherent guiltlessness as God's children is accepted. At this point, we are able to identify with our invulnerability as spirit, the prerequisite for forgiveness. This quotation of Jesus does not refer to the so-called "innocence" of children. As we have seen, children are born into the world with the same fully developed egos we experience as adults. The perceived "innocence" is nothing more than the projection of the innocence that we feel has been lost in the infancy of the ego's existence, when the separation occurred.

The next teaching (vv. 5-10) asks us to extend this love from within ourselves to others, not to exclude any of these "little ones"; to do so is to exclude an unforgiven part of ourselves, which precludes our acceptance of Jesus. As he says: "Anyone who welcomes a little child . . . in my name welcomes me" (v. 5). If we are an "obstacle" to the "little ones," as expressed through our unforgiveness, we are the ones who will suffer. To attack another is to attack ourselves, and there is no more viciously punishing agent in this world than our guilt, for the ego is merciless in its attacks.

The parable of "The Lost Sheep" (vv. 12-14) explains the principle underlying these teaching: the Father's great love for us. God is like a shepherd of a hundred sheep who, on discovering one of them is lost, leaves the ninety-nine to search for the stray and then rejoices when it is found. "It is never the will of your Father in heaven that one of these little ones should be lost" (v. 14). The emphasis is on the disciples' persistence to extend God's love to all the ones entrusted to them by Jesus; that we should love one another as the Father loves us, a love born in forgiveness and mercy.

What follows (vv. 15-18) is perhaps the single most important teaching on forgiveness that Jesus left us. Succinctly and powerfully stated, it is one of the very few teachings found in almost identical form in the synoptics and John's gospel, where it is told to the disciples in Jesus' resurrection appearance in the upper room, and which we shall consider again in Part III. Matthew cites the teaching twice, in Chapter 16 to Peter and to the disciples here in Chapter 18: "Whatever you bind on earth shall be considered bound in heaven; whatever you loose on earth shall be considered loosed in heaven" (v. 18).

This statement can best be understood in light of the principles of cause and effect we discussed in Chapter 2. When we do not forgive others (bind their sins), we are reinforcing their own guilt over what they believe they have done. By our unforgiveness or defensiveness we demonstrate the effect of their sinfulness, which was its cause, reinforcing the reality of their belief in sin and guilt. In addition to their guilt we are reinforcing our own. The sin and guilt we fail to forgive in others remain in us as well, for our projections of anger cannot remove them from ourselves, since "ideas leave not their source."

On the other hand, by responding with defenselessness and forgiveness to others' attacks (loosing their sins), we demonstrate that these "sins" have had no effect and therefore cannot be a cause. Thus, they do not exist (are forgiven). In this way, we witness to God's love for them as well as for ourselves. When we truly forgive, the guilt in our *minds* over our sins against God and others is undone. It has been demonstrated that nothing has come between us and the "forgiveness" of our Father. Our sin has been powerless against God's love, which our forgiveness has manifested. St. Paul's words to the Colossians summarize this principle nicely: "God loves you, and you should be clothed in sincere compassion, in kindness and humility, gentleness and patience. Bear with one another; forgive each other as soon as a quarrel begins. The Lord has forgiven you; now you must do the same. Over all these clothes, to keep them together and complete them, put on love" (Col 3:12-14).

In vv. 19f Jesus gives the disciples one of his very few instructions on prayer: "I tell you solemnly once again, if two of you on earth agree to ask anything at all, it will be granted to you by my Father in heaven. For where two or three meet in my name, I shall be there with them." Prayer without forgiveness is an impossibility, for the guilt that unforgiveness protects is enough to prevent our accepting Heaven's response of love and peace. By uniting with another in forgiveness, we are undoing the belief in separation that is the basis of all guilt. We unite with each other in Jesus' name since he is the symbol of total forgiveness. In his name our guilt is undone and his presence, once concealed behind the veils of guilt and fear, is made visible. To hold on to our grievances is to retain the cloud of guilt that hides Jesus; joining with another removes it. As Jesus states in the Course: "For in your new [holy] relationship am I made welcome. And where I am made welcome, there I am" (text, p. 383). The barriers of guilt we placed in our mind between ourselves and the power of God are removed. What remains, then, is our own will identified with God's, now allowed ego-free expression in the world. As is stated in the Course: "Two minds with one intent become so strong that what they will becomes the Will of God" (workbook, p. 339).

Peter then approaches his Master and asks how often he must forgive his brother; as often as seven? Jesus answers: "Not seven, I tell you, but seventy-seven times" (v. 22). In some other translations, the number is given as seventy times seven, but its meaning remains the same: forgiveness of an infinite amount. Jesus amplified his answer to Peter with the parable of "The Unforgiving Debtor" (vv. 23-35).

A king has cancelled a debt of 10,000 talents, a fantastic sum owed to him by a penniless servant, for which the king would have been justified to sell him and his family. After being absolved of the debt, the servant meets another servant who owes him the paltry sum of a hundred denarii. Unlike his master, however, he insists on payment, throwing the man into prison when he cannot pay. The other servants complain to the king who reminds the unforgiving servant of the mercy accorded him: "I cancelled all that debt of yours when you appealed to me. Were you not bound, then, to have pity on your fellow servant just as I had pity on you?" (vv. 32f)

The message is clear. As we are forgiven by God, so must we forgive others. God asks us to share His forgiveness and, unless we do share it, we shall not have it for ourselves. In reality, it is not that God withholds his love from us, but rather that we would not be able to accept it as long as we hold on to our guilt by not forgiving others. This same principle was expressed in the Sermon on the Mount in our need to be reconciled with another first before we can approach God's altar (Mt 5:23f). The blasphemy against the Holy Spirit which can never be forgiven (Lk 12:10) may be understood in the same way. The "unforgivable sin" is unforgiveness. This sin can never be forgiven by the Holy Spirit because our guilt, maintained by unforgiveness, would prevent us from accepting His forgiving love. Only our own practice of forgiveness can undo an unforgiveness, for only then are we made open to God's love for us. Retaining our guilt through retaining grievances is really a decision against God's love, and thus He cannot "forgive" us because He does not go against our free will. Fear (or guilt) *can* obscure perfect love, although it cannot cast it out.

Therefore, Jesus urges us to forgive from our heart, that we may receive and know the forgiveness of God. As John says: "If we cannot be condemned by our own conscience, we need not be afraid in God's presence" (1 Jn 3:21). God does not ask us to love as He does, for His mercy is infinite and His love perfect. In fact, Jesus emphasizes the enormous contrast between the love of Heaven and earth in his choice of the amounts owed in the parable: the equivalents of about seven million dollars to twelve dollars. We are asked by the Holy Spirit only to reflect Heaven's love through our willingness to forgive.

Perhaps the most famous of all Jesus' references to forgiveness is in the Lord's Prayer, where we are told to forgive others as we entreat God to forgive us (Mt 6:12).

There is an interesting parallel to this in the hauntingly beautiful Kol Nidre prayer that ushers in Yom Kippur, the most sacred day in the Jewish liturgical calendar. The prayer was composed in the Middle Ages during the time of great Christian persecution, when Jewish people were coerced into confessing Christian faith under threat of their lives. However, they retained their own belief and continued to practice their Jewish faith under cover. The prayer begs God's forgiveness for this presumed blasphemy against Him, stating that their Christian vows ("Kol Nidre" means "all vows") be declared null and void. What is interesting is that only those vows were thought invalid that involved one's relationship with God. Those sins against one's neighbor could not be redressed except by undoing them directly with another.

The same principle underlies Jesus' teaching on judgment: "Do not judge, and you will not be judged; because the judgments you give are the judgments you will get, and the amount you measure out is the amount you will be given" (Mt 7:1f). When we judge others we are really judging ourselves. St. Paul recognized this as well: "If you pass judgment you have no excuse. In judging others you condemn yourself, since you behave no differently from those you judge" (Rm 2:1).

The decision to attack another is really the decision to hold on to our guilt through the dynamic of projection. Thus, it is not so much the judgment we shall receive from the outside that is the warning here, but the judgment we would make against ourselves by attacking another, reinforcing our own guilt. This is always the ego's hidden motive: to retain our guilt by projecting it onto others. As the Course teaches: " 'Judge not that ye be not judged' . . . means that if you judge the reality of others you will be unable to avoid judging your own" (text, pp. 41f). Jesus' words, as elsewhere, should not be taken as a threat of God's punishment or vengeance, but rather as a caution on the threat of punishment and vengeance we incur upon ourselves, which reinforces the belief in our own sinfulness. Of such is *not* the kingdom of Heaven. As the Course adds: "Judge not because you cannot, not because you are a miserable sinner too" (text, p. 500).

This, too, is the meaning of the Golden Rule (Mt 7:12), that we should treat others as we would have them treat us. The Rule holds because in our own minds others *will* treat us as we have treated them. Our guilt demands that belief, regardless of what is or is not in the other person's mind. If we attack others, we are asking that they attack us in return. On the other hand, if we forgive, extending God's love, it is that forgiveness we will receive. Paraphrasing the Course's second lesson of the Holy Spirit: to have forgiveness, teach forgiveness to learn it (text, p. 100). What we give *is* what we receive; what we ask for *is* our return. "Miracles are teaching devices for demonstrating it is as blessed to give as to receive" (text, p. 2). As the beatitude says: "Happy the merciful: they shall have mercy shown them" (Mt 5:7).

Love for Sinners and the Poor ("Anawim")

The two commandments Jesus left us in Matthew 22:34-40 — based on the Old Testament texts: to love God (Dt 6:5) and our neighbor as ourselves (Lv 19:18) — depend upon forgiveness for their realization, since love is impossible where there is unforgiveness. To love our neighbor as ourself is to perceive no differences or separation between us. This separation always reflects our belief in sin, maintained by projecting our guilt over the separation from our Creator. As our sin against God is expressed in our sins against each other, so does God's love reflect itself in our forgiveness of each other. For this reason, Jesus taught that the second commandment is like the first.

We find this theme reiterated in the Johannine writings. In the Last Discourses, Jesus states: "I give you a new commandment: love one another; just as I have loved you, you also must love one another" (Jn 13:34; cf. Jn 14:15; 15:9, 12, 17). In the first epistle, John writes: "Let us love one another since love comes from God. . . . Since God has loved us so much, we too should love one another. No one has ever seen God; but as long as we love one another God will live in us and His love will be made complete in us" (1 Jn 4:7, 11f). Finally, "Anyone who says, 'I love God,' and hates his brother, is a liar, since a man who does not love the brother that he can see cannot love God, whom he has never seen. So this is the commandment that he has given us, that anyone who loves God must also love his brother" (1 Jn 4:20f). St. Paul echoes the same message to the Romans: "Love each other as much as brothers should, and have a profound respect for each other" (Rm 12:10); "Avoid getting into debt, except the debt of mutual love. If you love your fellow men you have carried out your obligations. All the commandments . . . are summed up in this single command: You must love your neighbor as yourself. Love is the one thing that cannot hurt your neighbor; that is why it is the answer to every one of the commandments" (Rm 13:8-10).

Therefore, because he is the living embodiment of God's love Jesus can say that "in so far as you did this to one of the least of these brothers of mine, you did it to me" (Mt 25:40); what we do to each other we *do* do to Jesus, because the veil of guilt we place between ourselves and another is the same veil we place between ourselves and him. Guilt will always be projected, and thus protected. It will ultimately prevent pure love from being expressed to anyone, and the love withheld from our neighbor is withheld from ourselves and God. The love and forgiveness that is shared and extended is given also to ourselves and God.

Our need for each other is our need for forgiveness. As St. Paul wrote: "Together we love or together we die" (2 Co 7:3). Alone we remain imprisoned in our life of sin; joined together in Jesus' name we step out of darkness into light. This is one of the central themes of the Course, where it is said, for example: "You cannot enter God's Presence . . . alone" (text, p. 185); "The ark of peace is entered two by two" (text, p. 404); and "[The journey] is a way you go together, not alone" (text, p. 605).

The essential relationship between forgiveness and love is highlighted in the parable of "The Two Debtors," told by Jesus in the episode with the sinful woman at the Pharisee's table (Lk 7:36-50). In this pericope, Jesus speaks of the relationship almost in quantifiable terms, implying this formula:

1) Guilt blocks the expression of love.
2) Forgiveness removes this block.

3) Therefore, the more forgiveness we express, the more love is freed; or, by the amount of love that is present we can ascertain how much forgiveness has occurred, for that is how much guilt has been removed.

In the scene at Simon the Pharisee's table, Jesus is reproached for allowing the sinful woman to wipe her tears from his feet with her hair, and then kiss and anoint them. Jesus replies with the parable of two debtors who are pardoned by their creditor, one for a debt of five hundred denarii, the other for fifty. Jesus asks which of the two will have more love for the creditor. The correct answer is the one who was pardoned more; since he received more forgiveness, he could express more love.

Love is not quantifiable of course, and cannot be measured like a pound of potatoes. However, Jesus is using this analogy to demonstrate the power of forgiveness, and it serves to explain Jesus' "attraction" to the so-called poor and sinful. This is the group known as "anawim," the Hebrew word which is the source of the word used in the second beatitude, frequently translated as "meek" or "lowly." We can understand this group to include all those who fear, which includes all of us. To say that Jesus loved any one particular group more than another is to ascribe to him the same ego attributes of special love we find in ourselves. Being the manifest expression of God's love, Jesus could only extend the all-inclusive love of his Father, who "knows no favorites." How, then, can we understand what seemed to be a preference for the "anawim," especially when compared with this statement from the Course: "Alone we are all lowly, but together we shine with brightness so intense that none of us can even think of it" (text, p. 248)? Special love would separate us from this light, while the all-inclusive love of God unites us with it and in it.

The answer to this question lies not in the seeming attraction of Jesus for these "lowly," but in their attraction for him. Jesus' love went out to all people, but only if this love could be accepted by them could it be expressed. His healing power, although never diminished since it came from God, could be blocked by the fear and guilt of those in need. We are told that he was unable to perform miracles in Nazareth because of the people's lack of faith in him (Mt 13:57f). Jesus criticized the Pharisees for their self-righteousness and belief that they were perfect. Denying their own guilt and fear behind the assertions that others were the sinners, this group experienced no need for healing. When the Pharisees protested their lack of (spiritual) blindness to Jesus, he retorted: "Blind? If you were, you would not be guilty, but since you say, 'We see,' your guilt remains" (Jn 9:41). It is the denial of their own guilt in attacking others that reinforces it in themselves.

The word "poor" or "anawim" has been misunderstood to be a material state, as we saw in Chapter 5. This mistake is based on the reversal of cause and effect, mind and the world, that was discussed in Chapter 3. Poverty is but another word for the "scarcity principle," the state of mind that believes in lack, one of the cornerstones of the ego's thought system. As the Course states: "Poverty is of the ego, and never of God" (text, p. 206). As always, the ego seeks to convince us that the problem lies external to us, and so poverty is projected onto the world where it is now seen and believed: "You have projected outward . . . and therefore you would have to perceive it this way" (text, p. 206). Once the projection is made real, the ego takes the process one step further by denying the fear and guilt associated with it and giving the projected poverty a positive value. This is the dynamic known as "reaction formation." The state of material poverty becomes idealized, strengthened by the belief that Jesus "loved the poor." Psychology witnessed the same phenomenon in the 1960's and 1970's. In reaction against the traditionally pessimistic psychiatric approach to psychosis, some "Third Force" psychologists began almost to proselytize for mental illness, writing of psychosis in quasi-mystical language and even suggesting that schizophrenics were our modern day saints. Such denial obscures the problem of our guilt still further, the ego's perennial goal.

Since we all have egos, otherwise we would not be in this world, we all must share in its poverty. The course states that "the poor are merely those who have invested wrongly, and they are poor indeed! Because they are in need it is given you to help them, since you are among them" (text, p. 205). The "poor" or "anawim" that Jesus "loved" were those who were painfully aware of their need for help and healing. They were the "little children" of Mt 18:3, depending totally on God for support. Openly asking this help from Jesus, they were able to receive it of him. And so he could help them.

This open recognition of our guilt, expressing our desire for forgiveness, is all Jesus requires of us. The rest is up to him. By repenting our sinfulness and bringing our guilt before him, as did the sinful woman in Luke 7, we are able to accept the forgiveness he holds out to us. This not only absolves us of our sin, but releases us to love. As Jesus explained to Simon the Pharisee: "Her sins, her many sins, must have been forgiven her, or she would not have shown such great love. It is the man who is forgiven little who shows little love" (Lk 7:47). If we have forgiven little, it is because we have defended our sin and guilt instead of bringing it to Heaven's light. This principle may help to account for the tremendous zeal of the converts who are aflame with the love of God. When the guilt of their preconversion lives is suddenly removed by the experience of God's mercy and love, converts are filled with overwhelming joy and gratitude that overflow to others.

Love for the "sinner" means love without judgment, and Jesus explains this in the following teaching to the "non-believers": "Do not keep judging according to appearances; let your judgment be according to what is right" (Jn 7:24). What is truly "right" is recognition of our identity in Christ, the place where Heaven's light shines as the light of the world. Right judgment sees all people as poor, since we all are afraid. We inherit the earth — the wealth of God's kingdom — when we "confess" our fear and need for help. Appearances, however, frequently conceal this identity in the cloud of guilt with which we surround ourselves, and so we fail to see ourselves as we really are. This veil of darkness is the ego's projection of sin and guilt, judging others as "sons of the devil" instead of children of light. If we continue to "judge according to appearances" we will maintain this belief, not only in our neighbor's darkness but in our own as well, since they are one and the same. By judging according to the light, however, both of us are freed to see ourselves in the Presence of God, and the darkness of our ego lives disappears. We live, not our ego, but Christ lives in us and as us (Ga 2:20).

Another instance of Jesus' forgiveness of sinners is the incident placed in John 8:2-11. It is a beautiful scene of forgiveness in which Jesus' response is contrasted with that of the people. A woman caught in the act of adultery is brought in full public view to be condemned, and the scribes and Pharisees ask Jesus his opinion on what should be done. The Law, they state, demands her to be stoned to death. In response to their rejection of the woman, Jesus says: "If there is one of you who has not sinned, let him be the first to throw a stone at her" (v. 7). We may understand this to mean that only if you are without sin can you truly judge as God would, for only then will your judgments be free from guilt. When thoughts of sin are present in us, we will inevitably see sin in our neighbor and judge against it. In this instance, it was not really the woman's adulterous actions that were condemned, but her personal "sinfulness" which mirrored the people's sense of their sinfulness, for which they felt guilty in their hearts. Their egos were "on the make" for one who could be the scapegoat for their sins, and the woman served this need nicely. Having sent out the ego's messengers, the people received its messages. As described in the Course:

> *The messengers of fear are harshly ordered to seek out guilt, and cherish every scrap of evil and of sin that they can find, losing none of them on pain of death, and laying them respectfully before their lord and master. . . . No little shred of guilt excapes their hungry eyes. And in their savage search for sin they pounce on any living thing they see, and carry it screaming to their master, to be devoured (text, p. 382).*

Their projection of this guilt was "justified" by the woman's adultery, but the real motivation was their need to see another, rather than themselves, as guilty and sinful.

Jesus shows us, however, that the only way to relate to the "sinner" with love, as our Father would, is to be free from sin ourselves. At that point, it becomes impossible to cast a stone at anyone. Our innocence attests to our brother's or sister's, allowing us to perceive only an expression of love or the call for it. Either way, our response is to love. We forgive our brother or sister by looking past the darkness of the "sinful action" to the light of purity shining in God's child. Thus we judge like God Himself, of whom the psalmist sings: "If I asked darkness to cover me, and light to become night around me, that darkness would not be dark to you, night would be as light as day" (Ps 139:11f). And so after the woman's accusers depart, Jesus looks to her and asks: "Has no one condemned you?" "No one, sir," she replies. "Neither do I condemn you," says Jesus, "go away and don't sin any more" (vv. 10f). I do not judge you, Jesus says, and now you must cease to judge yourself.

Forgiveness not only removes sin, but sickness as well. In Mark's gospel, a paralytic is brought to Jesus who heals him by saying: "My child, your sins are forgiven" (Mk 2:5), making the same equation between healing and forgiveness we find in the Course (e.g., manual, p. 53). In biblical times, sickness was understood to be a punishment for sins, a belief we now see comes from the guilt that demands punishment. Sickness was inevitably seen as this punishment, either for the person's sins or those of the parents — "(God punishes) the father's fault in the sons and in the grandsons to the third and fourth generation" (Ex 34:7).

In the story of the blind man in John 9:1-41, we are given further instruction into this meaning of forgiveness. The disciples approach Jesus, asking about the congenitally blind man: "Who sinned, this man or his parents, for him to have been born blind?"(v. 2). Jesus replies that no one had sinned, and corrects this erroneous belief that sickness is a punishment for sin. Rather, he teaches them, the man was born blind "so that the works of God might be displayed in him" (v. 3); that is, his blindness provides an opportunity for forgiveness to demonstrate the power of God's healing. The blind man's learning his lesson of forgiveness allowed the Holy Spirit to heal not only himself, but others through him. What had been a source of suffering and pain, when given over to God in faith ("Lord, I believe" v. 38), becomes a means of teaching God's love. The sick body is transformed into a true temple of the Holy Spirit, the man's faith being the instrument of this transformation. St. Peter exclaims in Acts: "Now you must repent and turn to God, so that your sins may be wiped out" (Ac 3:19). By turning to Jesus in faith, our sin, guilt and fear are undone, and we are healed. Sickness and suffering become loving opportunities for remembering the grace and comfort of God – "that the Lord may send the time of comfort" (Ac 3:20). We find light in the midst of darkness that we might see the God of truth and know He is in ourselves. Thus, through our gentle defenselessness, born of meekness and humility in seeking God's mercy, we inherit the peace that comes from finding God here on earth.

Chapter 8

FORGIVENESS: THE EXAMPLE

Jesus has remained the central figure in the hearts and minds of the Western world for two thousand years, not only for what he said and taught, but for who he was. It was written of Jesus that he taught with authority (Mt 7:29), and it was his authority, coming from God, that gave truth to what he taught. In the Course he says, in the context of himself: "Teaching is done in many ways, above all by example" (text, p. 75). We remember Jesus because he lived out perfectly and completely the very principles of forgiveness that he taught. We see this in his public ministry, culminating in his final days which began with the arrest in the Garden of Gethsemane and ending in his crucifixion and resurrection.

This chapter is divided into two principal sections. The first treats Jesus' ministry, with its focus on undoing guilt by extending God's love to all people. The second discusses the meaning of the crucifixion in terms of the principles of cause and effect we considered in Chapter 2, showing how indeed, in the words of the gospel, Jesus took away the sin of the world. In effect, this entire chapter may be seen as answering the question: "What does it mean to be in the presence of perfect love?"

The Public Ministry: The Universality of Love

The universal vision of Jesus that loved all God's people equally typified the years of his ministry. Most scripture scholars agree that it was this all-inclusive love for people, regardless of their station or personal history, that more than anything else enraged the authorities and turned them against him. Remembering the dynamics of the ego helps us understand Jesus' "new way" of loving, as well as the reaction this "new way" produced in others.

St. Paul provides the key to understanding Jesus' unique capacity to love by stating he was sinless (2 Co 5:21). Without sin there can be no guilt; without guilt there can be no projection. Without guilt's demand to see others as separate from us, we are free to affirm our inherent unity in the Sonship of God, what St. Paul called the body of Christ. Jesus' lack of ego enabled him to have no special relationships. In his perception, none of his brothers or sisters was special for, as he writes in the Course, "All my brothers are special" (text, p. 10).

Certainly Jesus was closer to some people than to others. He related differently to the multitudes, the "seventy-two" who were sent out, the women who faithfully remained with him, his band of disciples, Peter, James and John who shared in the transfiguration and watch at Gethsemane, and finally to John alone, the "beloved disciple" who seemed to enjoy a unique intimacy with his Lord. Despite these levels of intimacy, however, Jesus loved them all the same. His love expressed itself differently because people's needs differed, as did their capacity to accept this love. As the Course would say: many forms, one content.

As long as we feel guilt, there will be a need to find suitable objects for projection, which are maintained through our rationalizations. This allows us to project in seeming innocence. Our need to believe that there are sinners is our need to see our own particular form of sinfulness in someone else so that we can be free of it. Lacking this sin or guilt, Jesus also lacked the need to project. His Father's love thus could freely extend through him and embrace all people as one.

An important aspect of Jewish practice was the carefully defined rules and rituals for separating the clean from the unclean. The book of Leviticus, particularly Chapters Eleven through Fifteen, extensively discusses these definitions and procedures. These unclean forms included certain foods, animals, diseases such as leprosy, the dead, and various expressions of sexual impurities. The projections are named, described, and then excluded. Of the leper it is written, for example: "A man infected with leprosy must wear his clothing torn and his hair disordered; he must shield his upper lip and cry, 'Unclean, unclean.' As long as the disease lasts he must be unclean; and therefore he must live apart: he must live outside the camp" (Lv 13:45f). In the book of Numbers we are given a similar procedure from the mouth of God concerning the unclean: "Order the sons of Israel to put out of the camp all lepers, and all who suffer from a discharge, or who have become unclean by touching a corpse. Man or woman, you must put them out and forbid them the camp. The sons of Israel must not defile in this way the camp where I dwell among them" (Nb 5:2f).

To be sure, many of these laws were prompted by health considerations as well as symbolically expressing internal purification. Despite this, however, one can discern in what was essentially a psychologically naive people a strong unconscious need to project guilt's impurities onto externals, and then to exclude them from their presence.

By the time of Jesus, these practices were rigorously enforced by the ruling parties. This group, usually referred to in the gospels as the "Pharisees," was criticized by Jesus for their smugness and self-righteousness. Their confidence in securing a place in Heaven by meeting the requirements of the Law expressed the unconscious belief that they had finally disposed of their guilt. It was not the self-righteousness as such that Jesus challenged, but the projection of guilt. It was this challenge the people found so threatening.

From the ego's point of view, they were right to be threatened. The message of love Jesus taught was unequivocal, and he repeatedly demonstrated it by going out among all the people, embracing one and all as brother and sister, children of one Father. Those judged as social outcasts Jesus loved and healed: one of the tax collectors became his disciple (Matthew); he ate at the same table with the rich and sinners; he healed the son of the Roman centurion; he touched and healed the leper; he befriended the adulterous woman and women in general; he revealed himself to the hated Samaritans; he healed the hemorrhaging woman of her impurity and the epileptic demoniac of his disorder; and he raised the dead. In each of these encounters, it was as if Jesus were saying: "The way I love you is the way God loves you. No matter what your seeming sin or apparent impurity, it cannot come between you and your Father's love. Therefore you are healed, and forgiven for what you never did."

This love sets no conditions and has no limits, in contrast to the special love described in Chapter 1. It is the love described by St. Paul in his famous hymn:

> *Love is always patient and kind; it is never jealous; love is never boastful or conceited; it is never rude or selfish; it does not take offense, and is not resentful. Love takes no pleasure in other people's sins but delights in the truth; it is always ready to excuse, to trust, to hope, and to endure whatever comes. Love does not come to an end (1 Co 13:4-8).*

Jesus was repeatedly demonstrating, in as many different situations as possible, that nothing that we do or believe we are — however unpleasant, repugnant or immoral — can alter our fundamental relationship with God. Nothing in this world can separate us from our Creator's love for us, or ours for Him. The circumstances that *seemed* to separate us were merely our own ego projections. These ultimately are powerless against God's love and cannot change how He sees us. As the prophet Habbakuk exclaimed to God: "Your eyes are too pure to rest on wickedness, you cannot look at tyranny" (Hab 1:13).

Here we see the truly radical nature of Jesus' message: forgiveness and love applied equally and without exception to all of God's children. It is based upon the perception that all are equal members of the Sonship of God, and a mistaken belief about anyone's place in this Sonship is to be corrected. Since this mistaken belief is based on fear and guilt, the correction can only be love and forgiveness.

Jesus could not see one form of this ego illusion as greater or lesser than any other. In the vision of Heaven, there can be no gradations of illusions or mistakes. Something either is or it is not. This is the corollary to the first principle stated in the Course: "There is no order of difficulty in miracles" (text, p. 1). Truth is true; all else is only a mistake which, when brought to truth, is gently corrected, not judged against and punished.

The danger to the ego is obvious, since its entire thought system is based upon judgment. If there is no one unto whom we can project our guilt, we have no option except to confront it in ourselves. This is the step we seek to avoid at almost any price, and the structures of our world support this avoidance by reinforcing the belief that the problems lie outside us. We are taught to separate our projected forms of uncleanliness through rituals, practices and justified anger. Those who challenge this system of projection place themselves in potential danger, at least as the world sees it. The Course describes the process in this way:

> *Much of the ego's strange behavior is directly attributable to its definition of guilt. To the ego,* the guiltless are guilty. *Those who do not attack are its "enemies" because, by not valuing its interpretation of salvation, they are in an excellent position to let it go. . . . the crucifixion is the symbol of the ego. When it was confronted with the real guiltlessness of God's Son [in Jesus] it did attempt to kill him, and the reason it gave was that guiltlessness is blasphemous to God. To the ego,* the ego *is God, and guiltlessness must be interpreted as the final guilt that fully justifies murder (text, p. 224).*

The ego's terror of confronting its guilt suddenly flashes to the surface of our consciousness, and it seeks to destroy what threatens it. Into this ego's den of panic and fury Jesus continued to walk with his message of forgiveness. In so doing, he met with the only response the ego can give: the wish to destroy what is so threatening to it. Jesus *had* to be destroyed by the people. If *all* sins are forgiven in *all* people, there is no guilt: no guilt, no ego.

Thus, the ego's fear quickly turns to anger, directed at the person representing the threat, who now must be killed. We see the people's angry response growing as Jesus's love for sinners and disregard for custom become increasingly manifest. After Jesus healed on the sabbath, against Jewish law, John writes: "It was because he did things like this . . . [that they] began to persecute Jesus" (Jn 5:16). Jesus' reply to their criticism, "My Father goes on working, and so do I" (Jn 5:17), only made the people "more intent on killing him" (Jn 5:18).

When Jesus came to Jerusalem to celebrate the feast of Tabernacles (Succoth), the people said of him: "Isn't this the man they want to kill?" (Jn 7:25), and later in the scene

John reports that "some would have liked to arrest him" (Jn 7:44). At the feast of Dedication (Channukah), the people "fetched stones to stone him" (Jn 10:31), and others wished to arrest him once again (Jn 10:39). In his last visit to Jerusalem, the week before his death at Passover, the people came to the home of Lazarus whom Jesus had raised from the dead, not only to kill Jesus but now Lazarus as well. These murmurings against Jesus culminated in the crucifixion, certainly the most powerful form of his message of forgiveness.

Crucifixion and Resurrection

We may summarize the purpose of Jesus' mission as being to teach the basic principle of the Atonement: the separation from God never truly happened. Appearances to the contrary, we remain as God created us — one in spirit with Him and with all creation. The crucifixion and resurrection were Jesus' ultimate means of delivering this message, and the final demonstration that all the other lessons he taught were true.

1. The Message of the Crucifixion

Jesus is the name of the man who first awoke from the dream of separation, seeing "the face of Christ in all his brothers and [who] remembered God" (manual, p. 83). Because of this, the Holy Spirit "established Jesus as the leader in carrying out His plan since he was the first to complete his own part perfectly" (manual, p. 85). Jesus "set . . . in motion" the *process* of the Atonement that was given to the Holy Spirit as a *principle*. The Atonement was established by his resurrection, which can be defined as the awakening from the dream of death, of which the crucifixion is the most prominent symbol.

To accept the Atonement for ourselves, our one responsibility, is to accept the fundamental unreality of the separation. We remain forever as God created us, never having left our Father's house. Accepting the Atonement is, in effect, the "metanoia" or change of mind that Jesus urged for his followers. It is the shift in perception that sees forgiveness instead of sin, knows life instead of death, and identifies with the kingdom of God instead of the kingdom of the ego. Accepting the Atonement enables us to recognize that our sin against our Father could never have been in reality, and therefore has already been undone. Thus, there is no basis for our guilt and we have no need to protect it through the various illusions we have adopted in our self-defense.

The pain and suffering we experience, culminating in death, entered this world through the "sin" of separation. Death itself remains the most powerful witness to our post-separation dream. James nicely summarizes this dynamic: ". . . desire conceives and gives birth to sin, and when sin is fully grown, it too has a child, and the child is death" (Jm 1:15). Our wish (or thought) to be separated causes our sin, which in turn causes death. Restated, death is the inevitable effect of sin, which is itself the effect of our belief in its reality.

The undoing of this basic ego belief constituted Jesus' mission in word and deed. It was a lesson to be witnessed at a certain time and place in history, and learned throughout the rest of time — a lesson Jesus taught once in his earthly life and teaches forever in his risen life. His was the mission that fulfilled Isaiah's words: "On this mountain he [God] will remove the mourning veil covering all peoples, and the shroud enwrapping all nations, he will destroy Death for ever. The Lord . . . will wipe away the tears from every cheek; he will take away his people's shame everywhere on earth" (Is 25:7f).

Jesus undid the belief in separation, or sin, by demonstrating that its effects did not exist. Reviewing the two characteristics of the law of cause and effect discussed in Chapter 2, we see that 1) cause and effect are mutually dependent: without one the other cannot be, and 2) if anything exists it must be a cause: if it is not causative, it cannot exist. Thus, if the effects of sin are not there they could not have been caused. If sin is not a cause it cannot exist. Jesus took the most powerful witness to the seeming reality of sin, namely death, and by overcoming it in his resurrection, demonstrated conclusively that not being real, death's "cause," — sin — must also not be real. As John the Baptist exclaimed: "[Jesus is] the lamb of God that takes away the sin of the world" (Jn 1:29).

Stated another way, we can say that Jesus' purpose was to undo the belief in the reality of the victim-victimizer dichotomy, the center of the ego's defensive system against the unity of God and His creation. The basis of justice for the Semitic world at the time of Jesus was "an eye for an eye." This merely reinforced the cause-effect relationship between sin and suffering, teaching that a "victim has been wronged by a "victimizer." Jesus came to teach another lesson.

In the Course, Jesus states that "I am in charge of the process of Atonement, which I undertook to begin" (text, p. 6). Atonement corrects the error of separation, which holds that God was the victim of the Son's attack, who then became the victim of his Father's justified vengeance. Thus was sin, guilt and fear born, and they became the laws of this world. To the eyes of almost all who witnessed Jesus' crucifixion, not to mention those who followed, it did appear as if he were the ultimate victim of the ego's cruelty, suffering immeasurably at the hands of those whom he had only loved and healed. As Jesus writes in the Course: "I elected, for your sake and mine, to demonstrate that the most outrageous assault, as judged by the ego, does not matter. As the world judges these things, but not as God knows them, I was betrayed, abandoned, beaten, torn, and finally killed" (text, p. 86). In all of history, one cannot envision an individual more justified in identifying himself as an innocent victim of the cruel, ungrateful world. Moreover, traditional theology taught, as we shall consider in the following chapter, that Jesus was also the victim of his Father's vengeful need for reparation for the sins of the world.

However, Jesus did not share the world's evaluation of himself. Rather, he "offered a different interpretation of attack" (text, p. 85), and thus could teach that this "most outrageous assault" had no effect on him. He demonstrated this truth in his defenseless attitude and response during his maltreatment and, as his ultimate lesson, by overcoming death in his resurrection. Seeing the seeming attack as a call for love, Jesus could not see himself as a victim and thus did not see victimizers. In this way the errors of their misperceptions were undone, not being shared by him. In that instant salvation came into the world, for the belief in the separation of victim and victimizer no longer existed.

2. The Final Days: Invulnerability and Defenselessness

There is a statement from a source I could not trace that reads: "Forgiveness is the perfume that the trampled flower casts back upon the foot that crushed it." Peter writes of Jesus in his first letter: He "left an example for you to follow the way he took. He had not done anything wrong, and there had been no perjury in his mouth. He was insulted and did not retaliate with insults; when he was tortured, he made no threats but he put his trust in the righteous judge" (1 P 2:21-23).

Both statements summarize Jesus' example of forgiveness. In the gospel of John, Jesus says that "a man can have no greater love than to lay down his life for his friends" (Jn 15:13). By itself, this is not unique; thousands throughout history have done likewise. What is unique about Jesus was not his death, nor even its seeming cruelty, but the *manner* in which he died; in fact, the way in which Jesus responded from the moment of his arrest to the time of his death on Calvary. It has been said that Jesus did not only teach us how to live, but how to die. In his invulnerability and defenselessness, Jesus left us the clearest example of forgiveness, even in the face of one's own death.

When Jesus was arrested in the Garden of Gethsemane, Peter immediately went to the defense of his Master. Drawing his sword, Peter struck one of the arresting soldiers and cut off his ear. In his perception, Jesus was in danger and needed physical protection. However, Jesus was teaching a new perception: a world in which people could not really be endangered because of who they were. Their healed minds held the strength of Heaven, and the protection of God went with them. Thus, Jesus answers Peter: "Put your sword back, for all who draw the sword will die by the sword. Or do you think that I cannot appeal to my Father who would promptly send more than twelve legions of angels to my defense?" (Mt 26:52f). In Luke's gospel, it is further stated that Jesus touched the soldier Peter had wounded and healed him, undoing Peter's error.

Throughout the psychological and physical abuse Jesus endured during his final days, he never once raised a hand or spoke a word in his defense. He did not interfere with what was being done to him. Aware of his real security, Jesus remained silent when he was brought before Pilate and asked to defend himself. An incredulous Pilate asked Jesus: "Do you not hear how many charges they have brought against you?"(Mt 27:13). Matthew continues his narrative: "But to the governor's complete amazement, he offered no reply to any of the charges" (Mt 27:14). As the soldiers continued to mock and scourge him, Jesus did not speak. He was the perfect example of his own injunction to "turn the other cheek." As he writes in the Course: "You cannot be hurt, and do not want to show your brother anything except your wholeness. Show him that he cannot hurt you and hold nothing against him, or you hold it against yourself. This is the meaning of 'turning the other cheek' " (text, p. 75). Jesus went through these final hours without anger, hurt or vindictiveness of any kind. Due to his own sinlessness he could not see attack. Thus, there was no need to defend himself or to project blame or responsibility onto others. His absolute trust in God, his certainty of who he was, made any defense unnecessary and even irrelevant.

The climax to all Jesus' lessons in defenselessness and forgiveness was the crucifixion, certainly the most tempting of all situations to become defensive and angry. Moreover, it was certainly within Jesus' power to save himself. The onlookers taunted him, saying to each other: "He saved others . . . he cannot save himself. . . . He puts his trust in God; now let God rescue him if he wants him" (Mt 27:42f). However, it was precisely *because* he trusted God that Jesus could remain on the cross, unafraid of death. While his body and person could be attacked and injured, his true identity in God remained unassailed, beyond all harm.

As he hung from the cross, perceived by others to be suffering and in the throes of death, Jesus rested in the secure love of God. Looking down upon the jeering crowd clamoring for his murder, Jesus could see only their need for help, not their hate. He recognized that their actions arose from fear of his message of truth and of his Father who sent him. They did not know what they were doing to themselves. Their rage and taunts became transformed in his most loving perception into calls for help, and anger became impossible. Emptied of all the human limitations that would have separated him from the people he loved, Jesus called to his Father on their behalf: "Father forgive them; they do not know what they are doing" (Lk 23:34). This plea for forgiveness of the people before him came out of that love, through a vision of all people united in the Father, unseparated by the fear and guilt that would belie the fundamental truth of the unity of creation. In this single act of love was his message epitomized. In that single instant was the world changed. The light of forgiveness had come at last into the world of darkness.

3. Forgiveness of Specialness

We left the disciples, two chapters ago, huddled in terror and guilt in the upper room, fearfully awaiting whatever calamitous retribution God held in store for them. Huddled together in darkness, they feared the light.

The ego's expectation of what would happen in the event Jesus *should* appear is expressed in the following joke, which fortunately for all of us is not true: On Easter morning, John sees the risen Jesus and races madly back to tell the others: "Do I have news for you. Some of it is good; some bad. The good news is that Jesus has risen from the dead, just as he said. The bad news is that he wants to know where you guys were."

The ego's guilt could expect nothing else except an angry response from the "sinned-against" Jesus. In fact, an angry Jesus, hurt by the betrayal and abandonment of his closest friends and followers, all of whom had sworn never to leave him, would have been the normal reaction of almost any other person in such a situation. If Jesus had been in his ego frame of mind, identifying with his body and the attacking bodies of his accusers, he could not have avoided experiencing physical and psychological suffering, and thus be forced by the ego's laws to project the cause of this suffering onto others. As we have seen, the greatest temptation for the ego is the wish to make others guilty for our suffering, to make them responsible for the misery that we have really brought on ourselves by our ego decisions. Because Jesus knew that nothing was being done to him, that he was merely the target of the projections of others calling out for help, he was free from this temptation. He was not this piece of crucified flesh hanging in humiliation from the cross, as he was seen by the world, but the Son of God in glory: the Christ as God created Him. This was the message of salvation he came to teach and demonstrate.

Thus, in the midst of the disciples trembling with remorse and apprehension, "Jesus came and stood among them. He said to them, 'Peace be with you,' and showed them his hands and his side" (Jn 20:20a). What greater gift could a loving brother bestow upon those who are his own than this greeting of peace, when all within them is conflict and confusion?

In those four simple words that yet speak volumes — "Peace be with you" — Jesus says to his disciples and to all of us: "My love for you before your seeming sins is the same now, and will be forever. Your sins were nothing but a passing cloud that concealed the sun for a little while. But now the cloud is gone, having had no effect at all on the sun, and you can see again. Whatever your guilt, however beyond forgiveness your perceived wretchedness, despite the fear that our relationship was beyond reparation — my love for you has never changed. Your sins have been forgiven, for my love, coming from the Father, is everlasting." As St. Paul wrote, himself the recipient of Jesus' forgiveness: "Nothing therefore . . . can ever come between us and the love of God made visible in Christ Jesus our Lord" (Rm 8:35, 39).

In all the world there is no greater joy than to know that our sins have been forgiven. As the psalmist says: "Happy the man whose fault is forgiven, whose sin is blotted out; happy the man whom Yahweh accuses of no guilt" (Ps 32:1f). Every form of unhappiness — depression, pain, fear, anxiety, sense of loss — comes from our guilt: the belief we have sinned and must pay for it through suffering. This burden of guilt weighs heavily, but we become so accustomed to it that we scarcely notice its oppressive shadow upon our lives. This cloud of guilt obscures the light of Heaven and we walk the world of darkened shadows, like Plato's prisoners, adjusting our eyes to survive, forgetting what it is to be in the sun.

Suddenly the light appears in our midst, and the darkness is dispelled. Sin disappears back into its own nothingness as the light of Heaven is restored to us, and we see clearly. This sudden re-emergence of light is our joy in knowing that despite our guilt, we remain secure in the Father's love.

Thus, the evangelist continues: "The disciples were filled with joy when they saw the Lord, and he said to them again, 'Peace be with you'" (Jn 20:20b, 21a). Joy resulting from forgiveness is not the joy that comes from meeting our individual ego needs, where the "good feeling" is really the ego's joy in having successfully defended itself, through specialness, against the threat of God. Real joy, like its counterpart, peace, comes only from our release from the chains of the ego. Forgiveness, our one true need, makes this joy in us complete. As the vision of forgiveness is described in the Course: "Nothing that you remember that made your heart sing with joy has ever brought you even a little part of the happiness this sight will bring you" (text, p. 328).

This freedom from guilt and pain was Jesus' gift to his disciples and to the whole world. He led us all through the ego's valley of the shadow of suffering and death to the joy, peace and light that is on the other side. Each of us, in our own way, is continually confronted by the experience of identifying with either the victim or the victimizer in our egos, and Jesus is the perfect model for this journey through the illusions of attack, suffering and death.

How tempting it is, as we suffer, to say before one who seems to be attacking or accusing us: "Behold me, brother, at your hand I die" (text, p. 526). In this way our innocence is seemingly guaranteed, forever established in the sin of others, sealed by the guilt which we seek to impose on them. Beneath our face of "innocence," the Course teaches, lies the face that accuses the world: "I am the thing you made of me, and as you look on me, you stand condemned because of what I am" (text p. 611). As long as any guilt remains within us, any trace of belief in our sinfulness, projection is impossible to avoid, however subtle its form of expression may be. The guilt experienced by others is thus reinforced by the guilt we seek to project from ourselves onto them, binding us all in chains of fear and hate.

How filled with guilt the majority of the people must have been who watched the crucified murder of this innocent man, or who fled with horror from this witness to their sin!

How easy it must have been to have had this belief in their own sinfulness reinforced by the events on Calvary!

How much these people must have looked for and even demanded the condemnation they believed was deservedly coming to them from the lips of this man, expecting to be condemned with every breath he was taking!

How, in fact, could they have avoided projecting their guilt onto him — seeing in his forgiving eyes of innocence the stern stare of judgment — unable to accept that their sins had, in truth, been forgiven them?

How unbearable it would have been to have heard the message of salvation and love proclaimed in his every action!

And, finally, in his resurrection appearances, how seemingly impossible it would have been to have understood fully the ultimate message that redeems the world, and answers the question posed at the beginning of this chapter: To be in the presence of perfect love is to stand beneath the cross of guilt and suffering, tempted either to project our guilt onto others or to harbor its despair within . . . and then hear the holiest words ever spoken: "Behold me, brothers, at your hands I live, and I live forever. Do not be afraid, but be at peace and filled with joy. All your sins have been forgiven you!"

Chapter 9

THE MISUNDERSTANDING OF THE CRUCIFIXION

Jesus came to deliver the message of forgiveness for what had *not* been done, and through his very life, death and resurrection he put this message of salvation into action. It was a lesson of love, whose fruits were to be unity, peace, and freedom from suffering for all people. When these fruits do not seem to follow, as often through Christian history they have not, we can conclude that we have misunderstood and not learned the lesson.

Distorting the Present

It should come as no surprise that the crucifixion was misunderstood. Its message so radically departed from all the world believed it would have required an almost ego-free person to have understood its full implications. It is part of our ego nature to attempt to understand present events in terms of the past. We have already explored this almost universal tendency in the first chapter of this book. If we could ever be completely open to the present — the full expression of what the Course calls the "holy instant" — the past would disappear, and with it our entire investment in the ego. To guard against what for it would be catastrophe, the ego continually counsels us to interpret the present in terms of the past, ensuring that nothing changes. The present, hence the future, will merely reflect what has already been, and the ego rests forever safe in the web of guilt and fear that is its identity.

Because of our tendency to cling to the known, the Course urges:

> *Simply do this; be still, and lay aside all thoughts of what you are and what God is; all concepts you have learned about the world; all images you hold about yourself. Empty your mind of everything it thinks is either true or false, or good or bad, of every thought it judges worthy, and all the ideas*

> *of which it is ashamed. Hold onto nothing. Do not bring with you one thought the past has taught, nor one belief you ever learned before from anything. Forget this world, forget this course, and come with wholly empty hands unto your God (workbook, p. 350).*

Jesus came to teach us we were wrong about everything we ever believed about our world, ourselves, God, and our relationship to Him. His teaching culminated in the crucifixion, which summarized in one single act all that he had taught and demonstrated. If the world had had ears to listen, this is the prayer it would have "heard" from Jesus' heart, asking us to join with him that our Father's Will be done.

> *Father, we do not know the way to You. But we have called, and You have answered us. We will not interfere. Salvation's ways are not our own, for they belong to You. And it is unto You we look for them. Our hands are open to receive Your gifts. We have no thoughts we think apart from You, and cherish no beliefs of what we are, or Who created us. Yours is the way that we would find and follow. And we ask but that Your Will, which is our own as well, be done in us and in the world, that it become a part of Heaven now. Amen (workbook, p. 350).*

When Jesus arose that first Easter morning, the crucifixion, with its apparent sufferings, had to be seen in a different light. How could someone who was killed be alive? This was the paradox of the cross with which the world was confronted: how could there be love in the face of hate, strength when all that appeared was weakness, life when there was only death? We cannot admit as being equally true, belonging to the same order of reality, the perception that Jesus suffered and died, at the same time we believe in his risen life. These two orders of "reality" cannot coexist, since they rest on premises that are mutually exclusive. One is based on the reality of the ego's thought system, which we have seen is a "package deal." If one aspect of the system is accepted as true, all of it must be. Central to the ego's world is the body, and if it is accorded reality so then is pain, suffering and death. The resurrection, on the other hand, belongs to the Holy Spirit's thought system, which knows only that "what is false is false, and what is true has never changed" (workbook, p. 445). Truth is spirit and eternal life; the ego and death are false. There is no compromise. Confronted with the two thought systems, one must go; the other remains.

It was inevitable, then, that the disciples' egos would interfere with their understanding of the crucifixion. Their genuine love and devotion to Jesus would not allow them totally to deny their experience of him, before or after his crucifixion, but their unconscious guilt demanded that if Jesus did in fact live on in his resurrection, at least his message of forgiveness could be changed. Thus, the ego's compromise with truth: "If you can't lick him, join him," but join with him on the ego's terms. While on one level perpetuating the memory of the one sent by God to save the world, on another it sought to distort his message of unity by preaching separation and division. The disciples' special relationship with Jesus dictated the projection of their guilt onto the savior-idol who walked across the screen of their lives. Becoming now a symbol of guilt — the fate of all special love objects — Jesus' message of salvation would have become this as well, the exact opposite of what he intended. In this way the ego emerged triumphant, for whether people accepted Jesus or not, only a very small handful truly lived what he taught. Thus was the ego's religion of guilt maintained, and this chapter will explore how and why this came about. We begin with the concept of atonement: *what* is atoned for, and *how* this is accomplished.

Atonement with Sacrifice

Guilt demands punishment. On the deepest level of the ego's thought system, this punishment will always come from God, since it is God we believe we have attacked. Our God of love has turned into a vengeful God whose punishment is to be feared: "The attraction of guilt produces fear of love . . ." (text, p. 382). As long as our belief in sin is maintained, so must our fear of God be maintained as well.

The connection is indissoluble. Uncompromising in its demands that sin must always be punished, the ego is yet willing to make bargains, offering us "respite" from its harsh meting out of punishment. These bargains are almost literally bargains with the "devil," similar to Faust's, for we are merely buying time before the inevitable outcome of our death at the hands of God becomes due.

We have seen how the ego's reversal of cause and effect leads us to believe that our suffering is external to our minds. On a deeper level, however, the ego whispers in our ears that the suffering is coming to us because we were bad. The ego's desire for vengeance causes it to be on the lookout to reinterpret all things as punishments it would have us learn (the ego's version of workbook lesson #193). All suffering, pain, sickness and death are interpreted as the deserved effects of our sinfulness, which is their cause. By suffering, therefore, we pay back to the object of our sin what is its just due. In our society, we see this principle at work in the penal system. People found guilty of crime against the state must be punished so that society is compensated for what was done against it, a process we call justice. Our suffering *atones* for our sins, which our guilt demands. In such manner, we are reconciled with the victimized or aggrieved party. Atonement makes amends or establishes reparation for our misdeeds, and we are cleansed and forgiven.

A more socially acceptable form of atonement that the ego also holds dear is that of sacrifice. People harboring unconscious guilt feelings often expiate these feelings through acts of self-denial. Here, as we saw when discussing the dynamics of sickness, people unconsciously feel that they will "beat God to the punch," taking the punishment into their hands as it were, so that He will not do so. In this way, they atone for their sins by suffering for the good of others or themselves, sacrificing their time, money, effort, etc., that others may find happiness or peace. What is essential here is not the "acts" of helping others, but the underlying ego dynamic of sacrifice. This manifests itself in other forms, too, such as those who always seem to hurt themselves, unconsciously bringing about suffering through sickness, personal injury, inability to earn or retain money, and destruction or abuse of personal property. One prominent example of such destruction is automobiles. As cars are a principal means of getting around in our modern world, they easily become symbols of the ego or extensions of our ego selves, as seen in dreams, for example. Cars thus become vulnerable to our unconscious attempts to act out against ourselves by having accidents, leaving them in states of disrepair, etc. In its most extreme form, self-sacrifice becomes martyrdom, which we shall examine more closely below.

It is clear that within this thought system God demands sacrifice. "How fearful, then, has God become to you, and how great a sacrifice do you believe His Love demands! For total love would demand total sacrifice" (text, p. 303). This belief in striking a bargain with God so that His love can be secured is the core of all special relationships, wherein we believe we can only receive love when we give up something. "Suffering and sacrifice are the gifts with which the ego would 'bless' all unions. And those who are united at its altar accept suffering and sacrifice as the price of union" (text, p. 296). Sacrifice as salvation from guilt is one of the key concepts in the ego's logic. "Sacrifice is so essential to your thought system that salvation apart from sacrifice means nothing to you. Your confusion of sacrifice and love is so profound that you cannot conceive of love without sacrifice" (text, p. 302). This clearly contradicts God's statement in the book of Hosea: "What I want is love, not sacrifice" (Ho 6:6).

We turn now to how this belief in salvation *through* sacrifice and suffering manifested itself in the Judaic tradition, later forming the theoretical foundation for the Christian understanding of Jesus' crucifixion.

The Suffering Servant

Since the ego is always on the lookout to point an accusing causal finger at catastrophe, world calamities such as the Great Flood were inevitably understood as the direct result or effect of people's sinfulness. Belief in this causal connection, of course, is not restricted to Judaeo-Christianity, nor is the connection between sacrifice and salvation, but we shall confine our discussion to the Judaeo-Christian tradition as this is the context reflected in *A Course in Miracles.*

The Biblical account of the Great Flood, geologically thought to be an actual prehistoric fact, is understood in this way: "Yahweh saw that the wickedness of man was great on the earth . . . [and He] said to Noah, 'The end has come for all things of flesh. . . . I mean to bring a flood, and send the waters over the earth, to destroy all flesh on it . . . everything on earth shall perish' " (Gn 6:5, 13, 17). The Flood, then, is the punishment visited by God as just retribution for sin.

During the period immediately preceding the Babylonian Exile and destruction of the Temple, the prophet Jeremiah wrote on behalf of God: "You may ask yourself, 'Why has all this happened to me?' Because of your great wickedness. . . . I will scatter you like chaff driven by the desert wind. This is your share, the wage of your apostacy. This comes from me . . . because you have forgotten me and put your trust in a Delusion" (Jr 13:22, 24f).

Although on one level our belief in sin *will* lead to suffering because of our guilt, it is not true that suffering is a punishment brought on by God. The prototype for this belief is the expulsion of Adam and Eve from the Garden of Eden, where God punishes the "sinners" by banishing them from Paradise. What actually occurred is that Adam and Eve's guilt became projected onto an avenging God, who was then made to seek retribution to maintain the balance of the scales of justice. These scales always demand that someone must be sacrificed that truth be vindicated. Within this perspective, the suffering of the people is their just due for the sin they believe they have committed: the turning away from the living God within, now seen as having turned away from them. "The House of Israel," spoke Ezekiel, "was exiled for their sin in behaving so treacherously to me. . . . They all perished by the sword. I treated them as their filthy sins deserved and hid my face from them" (Ezk 39:23f).

The key principle in this view of suffering becomes clear: whether it was the plight of the world undergoing the horrors of the Great Flood, the collective suffering of the Children of Israel during the Exile, or the seemingly unjust, personal calamities of a Job, external affliction was seen to be the effect of people's internal state of sin. In the minds of most people, this belief is unconscious; however, the prophets saw their function as bringing this sin-punishment connection clearly before the eyes of the people, so that their guilt would be uppermost in their minds. The prophets hoped that out of fear of punishment at the hands of their wrathful Father the people would turn from their paths of wickedness back to Him.

We have seen how this dynamic reinforces the belief in the reality of sin. If we are punished, it can only be because we have sinned. The interpretation of God's punishment strengthens the belief in the reality of the separation, since the fear of God logically and inevitably follows from it. We see this ego dynamic subtly at work in the following attempt to interpret salvation: the Suffering Servant.

During the Babylonian Exile of the 6th century, B.C., the prophets taught that the people's fate, including the destruction of the Temple, was the result of their sin. Yet a cry of hope arose in the voice of Deutero Isaiah through his four Servant Songs (Is 42, 49, 50, 53). These songs were based on the premise that suffering was punishment from God, yet it was redemptive because God was offering His people salvation through the vicarious sufferings of His Servant, thus re-establishing the covenant of love between them. This is the story of the Servant:

The Servant's mission was to "bring true justice to the nations" (42:1b); to be the "light of the nations, to open the eyes of the blind, to free captives from prison, and those who live in darkness from the dungeon" (42:6f); to be the instrument through whom God's "salvation may reach to the ends of the earth" (49:6).

How this was to be accomplished was also explicitly stated in these songs. The Servant is to be the instrument of salvation through his own suffering and death: he will be "a thing despised and rejected by men, a man of sorrows and familiar with suffering, a man to make people screen their faces" (53:3); his sufferings will really be our own

(53:4); and through taking people's faults upon himself he will "justify many" (53:11b). He will offer "his life in atonement" (53:10a); and through this act peace will be brought to the world and its wounds healed (53:5).

Throughout it all, the Servant is defenseless: "For my part, I made no resistance neither did I turn away. I offered my back to those who struck me, my cheeks to those who tore at my beard; I did not cover my face against insult and spittle" (50:5f). The description continues in the third person: "Harshly dealt with, he bore it humbly, he never opened his mouth, like a lamb that is led to the slaughterhouse, like a sheep that is dumb before its shearers never opening its mouth" (53:7).

The Servant is able to maintain this attitude of defenselessness because he knows that the Lord, his God, is coming to his help (50:7, 9), that his "vindicator is here at hand" (50:8). And so the Servant of God "will prosper, he shall be lifted up, exalted, rise to great heights" (52:13); "his soul's anguish over he shall see the light and be content" (53:11a); "he shall have a long life," and through him what God wishes will be done (53:10b).

It is clear from this description how this "plan for salvation" reinforces the very problem — guilt — it is attempting to undo. This plan is based on sacrifice; that one whom God "upholds," whom God considers "my chosen one in whom my soul delights" (42:1a), is the one selected to suffer in atonement for the sins of the people. He himself has not sinned, but through his sufferings and torturous death the sins of others will be erased: "Yet he was pierced through for our faults, crushed for our sins. On him lies a punishment that brings us peace, and through his wounds we are healed. . . . Yahweh burdened him with the sins of all of us" (53:5f).

We have seen how defenses do what they would defend. The very fact that a plan such as this is needed reinforces the guilt and sin it was meant to take away. Moreover, the image of God that it rests upon reproduces the image of God that the ego's system demands: a God who seeks retribution and punishment as expiation for sin, demanding suffering and even death as the price He would exact to appease His bloodthirsty need for vengeance. In the above example, sacrifice is the governing principle of salvation, and the fact that it is God's chosen, His innocent servant who must be sacrificed, lends even greater power to the ego's plan. How can a "sinful" person *not* feel guilty knowing that another, untainted by sin, has suffered because of him? Imagine what this does to the God of love. He has become transformed into a Father at war with His children, hellbent on their bloodied destruction that peace be restored. Quoting again from the Course's third law of chaos:

> *See how the fear of God is reinforced by this . . . principle. Now it becomes impossible to turn to Him for help in misery. For now He has become the "enemy" Who caused it, to Whom appeal is useless. . . . There can be no release and no escape. Atonement thus becomes a myth, and vengeance, not forgiveness, is the will of God. From where all this begins, there is no sight of help that can succeed. Only destruction can be the outcome. And God Himself seems to be siding with it, to overcome His Son (text, p. 456).*

Rather than undo the *cause* of all suffering — our belief in the reality of the separation — this plan of salvation makes it even stronger. The sufferings of God's Servant reinforce our belief in sin; otherwise God would not have had to demand retribution. The Servant's very suffering makes us even guiltier, for we know someone else has been sacrificed because of what we have done. The strengthening of the guilt-attack cycle we discussed in the first chapter must be the result. The greater our guilt, the greater is the need for the ego to "save" us from it, which in this case comes through the attack on one who is explicitly innocent. Our guilt is reinforced and so the cycle continues. This is why the history of the Jewish people, as recorded throughout the Old and New Testaments, is a recurring story of sin, guilt and punishment. Nothing ever changed. Atonement became identified with suffering and sacrifice, and thus identified with the reality of our sinfulness and guilt.

Given the Jewish people's understanding of God's plan

for salvation, it is not difficult to see how the Jewish followers of Jesus would have viewed his crucifixion and death. He became God's Suffering Servant, and in his "suffering, victimized and dying body" the people saw their own salvation. The Jesus who truly lived in God's guiltless present was perceived through the guiltridden eyes of the past, and in him these eyes saw the fulfillment of Isaiah's guilt-reinforcing plan of salvation. Thus were sacrifice, guilt and punishment enthroned upon God's altar, and true forgiveness and atonement wrapped within the blood-stained body they saw on the cross and then placed in a sepulchre, symbol of hatred and death.

As Jesus states in the Course:

> *If the crucifixion is seen from an upside-down point of view, it does appear as if God permitted and even encouraged one of His Sons to suffer because he was good. This particularly unfortunate interpretation, which arose out of projection, has led many people to be bitterly afraid of God. Such anti-religious concepts enter into many religions. Yet the real Christian should pause and ask, "How could this be?" Is it likely that God Himself would be capable of the kind of thinking which His Own words have clearly stated is unworthy of His Son? . . . It is so essential that all such thinking be dispelled that we must be sure that nothing of this kind remains in your mind. I was not "punished" because you were bad. The wholly benign lesson the Atonement teaches is lost if it is tainted with this kind of distortion in any form. . . . God does not believe in retribution. His Mind does not create that way. He does not hold your "evil" deeds against you. Is it likely that he would hold them against me? (text, p. 32).*

In summary, this perception of the crucifixion makes our sin real and our guilt justified, forever beyond the forgiving love of God. There is, psychologically speaking, no possible way to admit the truth of this sin and at the same time be free from it. Perceiving a world of suffering, pain and death, we must also perceive guilt and fear. As a defense we project this guilt, for belief in suffering demands that others be responsible and punished for their sin. If they are not punished, then we alone must suffer the consequences of our guilt. Once suffering, regardless of its form, is made real, someone must pay the price. Ultimately and inevitably, God Himself is seen as the author of this suffering, and His nature is changed from a God of love to a God of fear, hatred, vengeance, and even murder.

When we apply this idea to Jesus' crucifixion, we can see the same dynamics at work. If we believe that Jesus suffered *because* of our sins — that he, an innocent man, was punished by God and died *because* we were bad — it would be impossible for us not to be even guiltier. We then could not help but project this guilt onto others, seeing them as responsible for the death we unconsciously believe we brought about. Nor could we help projecting onto Jesus, and even onto God, a judgment that would punish us for our sins. Thus, we are unable to learn that our sins are forgiven — the lesson Jesus came to teach us — and have learned instead that salvation is sacrifice. As the Course concludes:

> *Be very sure that you recognize how utterly impossible this assumption* [*of God's vengeance*] *is, and how entirely it arises from projection. . . . Sacrifice is a notion totally unknown to God. It arises solely from fear, and frightened people can be vicious. Sacrificing in any way is a violation of my injunction that you should be merciful even as your Father in Heaven is merciful. It has been hard for many Christians to realize that this applies to themselves. Good teachers never terrorize their students. To terrorize is to attack, and this results in rejection of what the teacher offers. The result is learning failure (text, pp. 32f).*

Reinforcement of Guilt: Martyrdom and Persecution

The ego's plan of salvation thus called for the projection of our guilt onto Jesus, the innocent lamb of God who is punished instead of ourselves. In this "mystery of salvation," our sins are magically removed from us by his suffering. He became the ransom that God demanded for them, and now that His blood-avenging need has been satisfied, we are vicariously healed through Jesus' death and absolved from our sin: he was killed so we do not have to be.

Since the ego teaches that suffering is how we atone for our sins, the more *we* suffer, the freer we become of Jesus' bloodstains that are proof of our crime; we would have paid our debt to him through our own blood. Moreover, if indeed Jesus died because of us, then what greater atonement could we perform than to identify with his death, glorifying in a death of our own that would be so similar to his?

There is a statue of the crucified Jesus that states to the onlooker: "This is what I have done for you. What have you done for me?" Can a person standing beneath this statue and reading these words feel anything except guilt? Is there any person on earth who would feel that he or she has done more for Jesus than he has done for us? In such manner, the ego's commitment to Jesus is based upon guilt, hardly love.

Our guilt over Jesus' apparent sufferings — because of our sin — would inevitably lead us to identify with that suffering. People who would "take up their cross and follow Jesus" would feel that the greatest thing they could do for the savior they believe suffered and died for them is to suffer for him. This is the basis for the tradition of martyrdom, wherein sincere Christians believed that they could become closer to Jesus by identifying with *his* suffering and martyrdom. As St. Paul wrote to the Philippians: "All I want is to know Christ and the power of his resurrection and to share his sufferings by reproducing the pattern of his death" (Ph 3:10). Paul received his wish, being executed in Rome as a martyr in 67 A.D. Tradition also taught that Peter was martyred. Because he believed he was not as worthy as Jesus, he went his Master one step further by being crucified upside down.

It was in part out of the need to sacrifice and suffer that the tradition of Christian asceticism arose. Central to this tradition was the mistake we examined in Part I of projecting the problem of the ego onto the body, attempting to resolve it there. The source of sin was transferred from the mind to the flesh, where it was attacked and vanquished. When suffering is glorified in this way, the body is made real and guilt can only be reinforced.

The ego is not finished, however. Not only does it revel in the projection of suffering onto our bodies, but it also seeks other people's bodies to project onto in an attempt to avoid responsibility for our own decision to be separate. From this need arose what is the saddest part of Christianity's history: its need to find scapegoats to be persecuted and punished. The guilt that the apostles felt as a result of their special relationship with Jesus found the logical target for projection in the Jews who did not believe in Jesus, and who were persecuting them for their beliefs. As a leading scripture scholar stated it: the Jews kicked the followers of Jesus out of the synagogue, and they in turn kicked the Jews out of the kingdom. One could not imagine a less auspicious way of beginning to teach Jesus' message of forgiveness and love. As he stated in the Course:

> *The Apostles often misunderstood it [the crucifixion], and for the same reason that anyone misunderstands it. Their own imperfect love made them vulnerable to projection, and out of their own fear they spoke of the "wrath of God" as His retaliatory weapon. Nor could they speak of the crucifixion entirely without anger, because their sense of guilt had made them angry. . . . As you read the teachings of the Apostles, remember that I told them myself that there was much they would understand later, because they were not wholly ready to follow me at the time. I do not want you to allow any fear into the thought system toward which I am guiding you. I do not call for martyrs but for teachers. No one is punished for sins, and the Sons of God are not sinners. Any concept of punishment involves the projection of blame, and reinforces the idea that blame is justified. The result is a lesson in blame, for all behavior teaches the beliefs that motivate it (text, pp. 87f).*

This pattern of blaming others quickly accelerated. The early Christians soon turned on each other, in addition to the non-believers, and the unity of Jesus' kingdom became divided and subdivided as each little group began vying with the others as to which was the true church of Jesus. Once such competitiveness enters, of course, there can be no true church of Jesus. The tradition of persecution that began immediately upon the death of Jesus continued throughout the centuries that followed. Christians sought to punish others for the sins they, the "righteous ones," unconsciously believed *they* had committed. Two thousand years of persecutions have made us all painfully aware of the results of this process of projection: the ego's vicious circle of guilt leading to attack, strengthening the guilt, and on and on.

The tragedy of this history heightened still further when this hatred, persecution and murder were done in the name of the Prince of Peace. The ego's unconscious demand to project its guilt — shared by all of us — did not allow these otherwise reasonable men and women to recognize the illogic, not to mention insanity, of their position. We should never underestimate the power of denial with its need to keep the truth away from us. The Course summarizes this point: "It is unwise to accept any concept if you have to invert a whole frame of reference in order to justify it. This procedure is painful in its minor applications and genuinely tragic on a wider scale. Persecution frequently results in an attempt to 'justify' the terrible misperception that God Himself persecuted His Own Son on behalf of salvation" (text, p. 32).

The persecuting Christian institutions during their two thousand year history merely reflected the same need to persecute that is found in each of us, and we should be wary of adopting a holier-than-thou attitude when considering this history. As Jesus forgave those who seemed to be persecuting him, so must we say, and mean, to those *we* believe persecute ourselves or others: "Father, forgive them; they do not know what they are doing," counting ourselves among them. Only in this way can we find the forgiveness of Jesus' love.

The Unreality of Death

There was a more specific misreading of Jesus' message that we can address as well. By making suffering and sacrifice real, hence the body, death too became real, and the clear message of the resurrection was denied. As Jesus summarizes his teaching lesson in the Course: "There is no death because the Son of God is like his Father. Nothing you can do can change Eternal Love. Forget your dreams of sin and guilt, and come with me instead to share the resurrection of God's Son" (manual, p. 84).

There is perhaps no more heavily invested reality in the ego's world than death. It is the great symbol of the ego for it makes God into an avenging Father who demands death as the price for our sinfulness. It is

> *the central dream from which all illusions stem. . . . It is the one fixed, unchangeable belief of the world that all things in it are born only to die. . . . The grimness of the symbol is enough to show it cannot coexist with God. . . . If death is real for anything, there is no life. Death denies life. But if there is reality in life, death is denied. No compromise in this is possible. There is either a God of fear or One of Love. . . . [God] did not make death because He did not make fear (manual, p. 63).*

The common association made in our culture between death and tragedy is the witness fo this false association we have made among physical death, pain, and punishment by God. Even if punishment by God is not a conscious belief, as it most frequently is not, it remains the ego's bottom line.

The logical extension of this belief in an avenging God is the belief in hell, which

> *is inescapable to those who identify with the ego. Their nightmares and their fears are all associated with it. The ego teaches that hell is in the future, for this is what all its teaching is directed to. Hell is its goal. For although the ego aims at death and dissolution as an end, it does not believe it. The goal of death, which it craves for you, leaves it*

> *unsatisfied. No one who follows the ego's teaching is without the fear of death (text, p. 280).*

All who wander in this world in guilt must fear death, for guilt must always be punished: ". . . the belief in guilt must lead to the belief in hell, and always does. The only way in which the ego allows the fear of hell to be experienced is to bring hell here, but always as a foretaste of the future. For no one who considers himself as deserving of hell can believe that punishment will end in peace" (text, p. 281). This fear of death, as the Course teaches, is merely the cover over its attraction. The ego's attraction to guilt, suffering and pain finds its ultimate fruition in death, the most compelling witness to the reality of its own existence.

We live in a culture dominated by thoughts of protection for our body, culminating in the fear of its own demise. We fear death because we believe we will be separated from those we "love" and need, or we fear it for ourselves, defending against the secret fear that we will be punished for our sins. Thus, the ego will always cling to death, for it means *its* life, and we can see how Western religions and culture have over-emphasized the body's death. It has been made into a religion, replete with funereal and mourning rituals that seek to comfort us against a pain that can never truly be comforted, now that death has been made real. Once the material world has been accorded reality, it is indeed a sad event when something occurs that seems to mean the body's end. Yet, all we have really done is fall into the ego's trap of "making the error real," and then defending ourselves against it.

Imagine, then, Jesus' wonderful gift in demonstrating that death is not what it seems at all. In the inspiring words of St. Paul, Jesus showed us that death is not to be feared: "Death is swallowed up in victory. Death, where is your victory? Death, where is your sting? . . . So let us thank God for giving us the victory through our Lord Jesus Christ" (1 Co 15:54f, 57). Death is merely a belief, and in his resurrection Jesus proved that belief to be an illusion. As he states in the Course: "What better way to teach the first and fundamental principle in a course on miracles than by showing you the one that seems to be the hardest can be accomplished first?" (text, p. 389). This "hardest" was the overcoming of death — but even more to the point, it was the exercise of forgiveness in the face of one's own murder.

Jesus taught us another way of looking at death, just as he taught us another way of looking at the body, which merely serves the purpose given it by the mind. To a mind believing in guilt the body will serve as an instrument of separation, with death being the ultimate witness to the belief that truth is illusion, and illusion truth. To the Holy Spirit, however, the body serves a different purpose, for it becomes an instrument wherein we learn and teach His lessons of forgiveness. Death, then, is the quiet laying down of the body after it has served this holy purpose. We are asked to use the body "to bring the Word of God to those who have it not . . . [for then] the body becomes holy. Because it is holy it cannot be sick, nor can it die. When its usefulness is done it is laid by, and that is all" (manual, p. 31). The 19th century Indian saint, Ramakrishna, taught similarly that death is merely going from one room into another.

The story is told of the Buddha that when asked by his disciples who he was — "Are you the Buddha, the Great Teacher, the Enlightened One, etc.?" — merely replied: "I am none of these. I am awake." Jesus, too, was awake. He awoke from the dream of death — the meaning of resurrection — because he came to the one realization that we all must come to: only spirit is real, and it can never die. All other illusions fall away in light of this truth. Through Jesus' forgiving act of salvation, everyone gained — not only the ones who believed in him, but all who would come to learn the lesson he came to teach. The perfect love Jesus witnessed to is the perfect love that lives in us, the love that waits patiently for the ego's veil to be undone. This is the veil that Matthew tells us was rent at the moment of Jesus' death (Mt 27:51), symbolizing the veil of guilt and fear that had kept us separated from our God and from each other. Through this one all-loving act, the true justice and love of God's Servant was restored to all people. This love-without-sacrifice is the real message of the crucifixion.

Chapter 10

FAITH IN THE GOD OF LOVE

As we go through the ego's hell by confronting our own guilt and fear, we would be unable to tolerate the resulting anxiety and terror were it not for God's ever present help. The third beatitude teaches, "Happy those who mourn: they shall be comforted" (Mt 5:5). Indeed, as our ego mourns its own demise, we will need God's loving comfort more than ever. This comfort is God's Holy Spirit, the Comforter Jesus promised to send to us (Jn 14:16). Yet our guilt demands that God be cruel, quick to punish, and unwilling to forgive because of our sin against Him, let alone be the One who will comfort us. This fear of a punitive Father holds our guilt securely intact. Moreover, it prevents going to God in our need since we are convinced His merciless unforgiveness will destroy us. We saw illustrations of this dynamic in the preceding chapter where people projected their own perceived guilt onto a God who sought to punish if not destroy them for their sins against Him.

From the ego's point of view, our fear of God is the perfect defense as it keeps away from us the one Person who can extinguish it. We are therefore thrown back onto our ego to save us, and we have already examined the disastrous consequences this has for us as individuals, not to mention its effect on the world. In this context, then, we can better understand the importance of the central message Jesus came to announce, and which is the theme of this chapter: God is love, and there is no power in our minds or in the world that can truly separate us from this love. If God is love and does not condemn us, then our guilt is illusory and the ego's thought system must crumble. Whatever we believed we had done in our faithlessness had no effects, could not be a cause, and therefore could not exist. As St. Paul wrote: "We may be unfaithful, but he is always faithful, for he cannot disown his own self" (2 Tm 2:13). This Self is not only God's, but ours: the Self He created in His own image and likeness. Thus, throughout Jesus' gospel we can hear him saying to us: "The way I love you is the way the Father loves you. See His love in me and know His forgiveness for what was never truly done. The separation from God was merely a bad dream."

God's Love for Us

We cannot turn to God for help until our concept of Him can shift. To do otherwise would be insane. No one in need turns to one he believes will destroy him. It is imperative we make this shift, and turning to the gospels we see the importance Jesus placed in correcting our misperceptions of our Creator. Nowhere is this teaching more clearly enunciated than in the parables.

As scripture scholars have pointed out, many of the parables were directed towards Jesus' critics who objected to his demonstration of love for all people, "saint" and "sinner" alike. Jesus' purpose was to show, through his own loving actions, how his Father acts. He stood as God's representative, for in him people would see the perfect embodiment of the Father's love that embraced all people as one, equal members of His family. These parables can be seen as an explanation of Jesus' message of God's universal love and forgiveness.

Chapter Fifteen of Luke's gospel presents three parables of God's mercy, given by Jesus as answer to the complaints of the scribes and Pharisees that he welcomed sinners and ate with them. In the twin parables of "The Lost Sheep" (vv. 4-7) and "The Lost Drachma" (vv. 8-10), Jesus depicts the great joy in Heaven over the return of one sinner, one of the lost ones. The shepherd leaves his ninety-nine sheep to search for the one who is lost, and upon finding it will "joyfully take it on his shoulders and then, when he got home, call together his friends and neighbors . . . [and say:] 'Rejoice with me . . . I have found my sheep that was lost' " (vv. 5f). Similarly, a woman finding her lost drachma after a thorough search will call in her friends and neighbors to rejoice with her. The parables' point is underscored by Jesus: "In the same way, I tell you, there is rejoicing among the angels of God over one repentant sinner"(v. 10). The

Course reflects this same thought in describing our homecoming: "and how great will be the joy in Heaven when you join the mighty chorus to the Love of God!" (text, p. 511).

God's mercy is infinite and all-inclusive; no one is excluded from His kingdom, and He continually strives to find those who are lost (the "sinners"). Thus, He rejoices when a repentant sinner returns and can accept his Father's forgiveness. The Course metaphorically speaks of God's weeping "at the 'sacrifice' of His children who believe they are lost to Him" (text, p. 82), and that "God is lonely without His Sons" (text, p. 19). God, of course, cannot weep or be lonely, but these references reflect both His love for us and the Holy Spirit's desire that we return to our Father and be free from the pain of believing we are still separate from Him.

This portrait of God's forgiving love in the parable of "The Prodigal Son"(vv. 11-32) is perhaps the most famous of all, and should more properly be entitled "The Father's Love." The parable is in two parts. The first (vv. 11-24), similar to the two previous parables, shows the Father's rejoicing over the return of the sinning son. Whatever sins committed by the son in the far country, squandering his father's money, are instantly forgiven the moment the son returns home. It is as if nothing had happened, and in terms of the father's love for his son, nothing *did* happen for his love remained unbroken. The son's "confession" — "Father, I have sinned against heaven and against you; I no longer deserve to be called your son" (v. 21) — is met with forgiving love by the father who calls for a celebration: "This son of mine was dead and has come back to life; he was lost and is found" (v. 24). This is what God is like, Jesus is telling us: eagerly waiting for our coming to our senses (v. 17). When we do, He embraces us totally in His love and forgiveness.

The second half of the parable (25-32) extends the message, and more pointedly. The eldest son, who has faithfully remained home during the younger brother's debauchery, resents the father's forgiveness: "Look, all these years I have slaved for you and never once disobeyed your orders, yet you never offered me so much as a kid for me to celebrate with my friends. But, for this son of yours, when he comes back after swallowing up your property . . . you kill the calf we have been fattening"(vv. 29f). By his standards of justice he has been offended, for his brother had done less and received more. But that is not how God's justice operates, Jesus tells us. Our Father does not love us less because He gives to another. The father answers his angry son: "My son, you are with me always, and all I have is yours. But it was only right we should celebrate and rejoice, because your brother here was dead and come to life; he was lost and is found" (vv. 31f).

The attitude of the eldest son is an example of the special love discussed in Chapter 1. The distortion introduced by the ego holds that love is quantifiable, so that if another receives love, someone else has less of it. Jesus teaches that the love of Heaven is not limited but infinite. As with the miracle of the loaves and fishes, there is love for everyone. It embraces both "sinner" and "saint"; the son who has sinned against his father as well as the son who has remained faithful. God's love need not be earned and cannot be bargained for. Since it is always present it need merely be accepted. The parable is thus addressed to those who believe they deserve God's love more than others because of their good works or essential goodness. Self-righteously proclaiming their superiority, this group complains about Jesus' love for those who in their eyes do not deserve it. The parable calls upon them to decide otherwise and love as the Father loves.

This same point is made in the parable of "The Vineyard Laborers" (Mt 20:1-16), which was also originally meant for Jesus' critics. Here, workers are paid the same wage, regardless of how many hours of work they put in. The wage was a fair one, based on a full day's employment, yet those who worked all day complained to the landowner about the seeming injustice: "The men who came last . . . have done only one hour, and you have treated them the same as us, though we have done a heavy day's work in all the heat" (v. 12). But, the owner replied, "My friend, I am not being unjust to you; did we not agree on one denarius? Take your earnings and go. I choose to pay the last comer as much as I pay you. Have I no right to do what I like with my own? Why be envious because I am generous?"(vv. 13-15).

Regardless of what we might do or not do to deserve God's love, His love is constant, merciful and compassionate to the children He loves, who still dream of His punishing anger. All of us share equally in God's kingdom because we are His beloved children. As the Course suggests: "When you are afraid, be still and know that God is real, and you are His beloved Son in whom He is well pleased" (text, p. 49). Nothing else is required of us. Jesus' commandment that we love one another as he loves us (Jn 15:12) is the commandment to imitate this unconditional love, given freely to all people, regardless of their response. We live always in the grace of God's freely given love. What Jesus taught during his earthly life is what he teaches now in the Course: "Spirit is in a state of grace forever. Your reality is only spirit. Therefore you are in a state of grace forever" (text, p. 7).

The Availability of God's Love

God's loving help in times of need is always available if we choose to accept it. This is the message of parallel parables in Luke. "The Importunate Friend" (Lk 11:5-8) seeking bread succeeds through his persistence in rousing his friend from sleep: ". . . if the man does not get up and give it to him for friendship's sake, persistence will be enough to make him get up and give his friend all he wants" (v. 8). The parable is placed in the context of prayer for it is preceded by Luke's version of the Lord's Prayer, and is followed by Jesus' assurance of God's faithful response to our prayers: "Ask and it will be given you; search, and you will always find; knock and the door will be opened to you. For the one who asks always receives; the one who searches always finds" (Lk 11:9f). "The Importunate Widow" (Lk 18:1-8) is also about prayer: "Then he told them a parable about the need to pray continually and never lose heart" (v. 1). The parable tells of the widow's persistence with the unscrupulous judge who in exasperation grants what is coming to her: "Maybe I have neither fear of God nor respect for man, but since she keeps pestering me I must give this widow her just rights, or she will persist in coming and worry me to death" (vv. 4f).

The parables contrast the inconvenienced friend and judge, respectively, with God. Both men eventually accede to the persistent requests, and Jesus is saying to us: If these two grant the requests made upon them, how much more will your Heavenly Father grant what you ask of Him? For "what father among you would hand his son a stone when he asked for bread? Or hand him a snake instead of a fish? Or hand him a scorpion if he asked for an egg? If you, then, who are evil know how to give your children what is good, how much more will the heavenly Father give the Holy Spirit to those who ask Him!" (Lk 11:11-13).

The question actually posed by the two parables is: "Can you imagine someone refusing this request?" Jesus' answer is: "Of course not!" God will give us even more than we ask, before we ask. As Jesus taught in the Sermon on the Mount: We should pray in secret, and God "who is in that secret place . . . [and] sees all that is done in secret will reward you. . . . Your Father knows what you need before you ask him" (Mt 6:6-8).

Therefore, all God needs from us is our persistent efforts and faith in Him, that "we may pray continually and never lose heart" (Lk 18:1). In Chapter 5, we discussed the real meaning of prayer. Since God did not create this material world, which only exists in our deluded minds as miscreative thoughts, He can never grant our requests for material things; His love is not material. On the contrary, what our Father knows we need is the healing of our mind, for which purpose He gave us His Holy Spirit, now made manifest through Jesus. When it appears as if God is delayed in His response of help, it is because we have asked for the wrong things, and God does not answer with illusions which would only exacerbate the fear underlying the request. As the Course says of the corrective value of the Atonement: ". . . if it [the Atonement] is used truly, it will inevitably be expressed in whatever way is most helpful to the receiver. This means that a miracle, to attain its full efficacy, must be expressed in a language that the recipient can understand without fear. . . . The whole aim of the miracle is to raise the level of communication, not to lower it by increasing fear" (text, pp. 20f). The delaying agent is our unconscious ego, which continually searches for forms of punishment to prove our guilt.

The expression of faith in God's help reflects the desire to let go of our ego. Only when we do this can we accept the help of Jesus that is *already* present in our mind, where the problem is. God never lets a call for help go unanswered, because His love *is* the answer. Our concern is only with keeping faith in ourselves and others; to choose God instead of the ego. As Jesus emphasized in the closing line of the second parable: "But when the Son of Man comes, will he find any faith on earth?" (Lk 18:8). Without this faith in Jesus' voice to speak for our right-minded decision, we will never know the love of God he represents. In the words of St. Paul: ". . . what matters is faith that makes its power felt through love" (Ga 5:6).

Our persistent prayer is not for God's sake but for our own, since it reflects our freedom to choose. God is not testing our patience, as might be inferred from the parables, but rather he waits upon our coming to Him without the ego's resistance. When we do ask, it is unthinkable that our loving Father would not meet our need. Our egos tell us He would turn away, but Jesus teaches that He would merely stand with already opened arms and meet our need for guilt's release with His loving providence.

God's mercy is continually being extended, despite our guilt's denial that He would ever come to our assistance. This is the meaning of "The Barren Fig Tree" (Lk 13:6-9). The owner of a fig tree that has been barren for three years asks the gardener to cut the tree down, since it would seem hopeless for there to be any yield. Yet the gardener asks for one more opportunity: "Sir . . . leave it one more year and give me time to dig around it and manure it: it may bear fruit next year; if not, then you can cut it down" (vv. 8f). The manuring of fig trees was a rare occurrence in Palestine at that time, so Jesus is emphasizing the extent of God's love for us: He would stop at nothing in order to reach us, that we might bear the fruits of peace and joy that He would have us bear.

We must, however, make the choice ourselves. When we choose to turn to God, His mercy is there beyond measure. In Thomas Merton's lovely phrase, God is "mercy within mercy within mercy." We see this in the parable of "The Two Sons" (Mt 21:28-32): one who refuses to work in his father's vineyard and then changes his mind; the other who first agrees and then reneges. It is the repentant son who does the father's will, and thus he is the one Jesus says enters the Father's kingdom. This parable is another example of Jesus explaining his gospel: at the moment a person returns to God — the moment of metanoia — all is forgiven and the ego's past disappears. "This holy instant is salvation come" (workbook, p. 404), the Course teaches, for "in the holy instant, free of the past, you see that love is in you, and you have no need to look without and snatch love guiltily from where you thought it was" (text, p. 292).

Luke (23:39-43) provides a perfect illustration of this principle in the account of the two thieves hanging on the cross alongside Jesus. The "bad thief" ridicules Jesus, projecting onto him his self-hatred for his sinful past: "Are you not the Christ? . . . Save yourself and us as well" (v. 39). The "good thief," on the other hand, recognizes Jesus' innocence and the injustice done to him. He rebukes the other: "Have you no fear of God at all? . . . You got the same sentence as he did, but in our case we deserved it: we are paying for what we did. But this man has done nothing wrong" (40f). Looking out at Jesus, he says: "Remember me when you come into your kingdom" (v. 42). He could not have said this were he himself not repentant, looking out from his own forgiveness to see the innocence of Jesus. His turning to Jesus is enough to ensure God's forgiveness, allowing Jesus to say: "Indeed, I promise you . . . today you will be with me in paradise" (v. 43); i.e., through your desire for forgiveness, you can accept your union with me in our Father's love. This is Jesus' continual message which his loving hands hold out to us, awaiting our desire for it. Bringing the sins and mistakes of the past into God's loving Presence is sufficient to allow His light to dissolve them. Thus does guilt, brought to forgiveness, disappear; and what remains is the love of God. As the Course says: "[Forgiveness] does not countenance illusions, but collects them lightly, with a little laugh, and gently lays them at the feet of truth. And there they disappear entirely" (workbook, pp. 242f).

God's love has no limitations, extending to all people for our Father has no favorites. This is the theme of "The Good Samaritan" (Lk 10:29-37). The parable speaks of a traveler beaten up by robbers and left half dead. Three other travelers approach him; the first two, a priest and a Levite, pass him by. The third, a Samaritan, is "moved with compassion" and ministers to him. The parable was given by Jesus in response to a lawyer's question regarding the commandment to love our neighbor as ourself. His question — "And who is my neighbor?" — really related to the limits on this love; i.e., who could be excluded from being our neighbor? Jewish thought at the time of Jesus placed certain limits on the obligation to love. The Pharisees did not have to love the non-Pharisee; the "sons of darkness" were excluded from the love of the Essenes (a contemporary Jewish monastic community), who thought of themselves as the "sons of light"; according to a contemporary rabbinic saying, heretics, informers and renegades were to be pushed into a ditch and not pulled out; and we learn from Mt 5:43 that it was a belief at that time that one need not love one's enemy.

The key to Jesus' answer to the lawyer is the traveler from Samaria. Samaritans were hated figures among the Jewish people, and vice versa. This traveler, then, was the least likely person to stop and aid the beaten Jew. This is Jesus' point: Who is our neighbor? All people, regardless of who they are or what they have done. Our responsibility to each other has no boundaries or limitations, since we *are* each other, all part of the one family of God. To exclude a single person, regardless of the reason, is to exclude part of ourselves since we share the same identity in Christ. By the law of projection, what we exclude in others is what we have excluded from ourselves, and Jesus would have "not one spot of darkness still remain(s) to hide the face of Christ from anyone" (text, p. 622). By choosing the hated Samaritan as the doer of the good deed, Jesus was emphasizing this principle. Even though the beaten man was an "enemy," the Samaritan transcended this division to apply the universal law of love: "You shall love your neighbor as yourself," and all people are our neighbors. This is how God loves, and so this is how we should love: poor or rich, sick or well, friend or enemy.

Trusting God

When we have changed our image of God to the loving and providing Father He is, we become psychologically free to turn to Him. Confidently we place our trust in Him, calling God, as did Jesus, "Abba, Father." Jesus left numerous teachings on this trust or faith.

Trusting God, we need never be concerned about our life and what we are to eat, nor about our body and how to clothe it (Mt 6:25). We would then be like the birds in the sky or the lilies of the field, which do not hoard food or worry what the next day will bring. Yet they are fed and taken care of. How much more, then, will our heavenly Father take care of us! Therefore, Jesus says to us: "Do not worry; do not say, 'What are we to eat? What are we to drink? How are we to be clothed? . . .' Your Heavenly Father knows you need them all. Set your hearts on his kingdom first, and on his righteousness, and all those other things will be given you as well" (Mt 6:31, 33f). As St. Paul said, writing to the Corinthians out of his own experience of God's providence: "There is no limit to the blessings which God can send you — He will make sure that you will always have all you need for yourselves in every possible circumstance, and still have something to spare for all sorts of good works" (2 Co 9:8).

We have already discussed how abundance does not apply to the things of the world. Trusting God does not mean trusting that our material needs will be met by Him. Knowing such gifts are fundamentally illusory, God could never give them to us. The Course teaches that "things but represent the thoughts that make them" (workbook, p. 345). Material poverty, when identified as a problem, can only result from a belief in spiritual poverty (the scarcity principle). Our Heavenly Father, through His Spirit, recognizes the need for correcting this belief, which *is* the problem. When our ego thoughts are forgiven, there will be no further projection of scarcity and our material world will flow naturally and happily from these forgiving thoughts. "Forgiveness turns the world of sin into a world of glory, wonderful to see. Each flower shines in light, and every bird sings of the joy of Heaven. There is no sadness and there is no parting here, for everything is totally forgiven. . . . Forgiveness brings no little miracles to lay before the gate of Heaven. Here the Son of God Himself comes to receive each gift that brings him nearer to his home" (text, p. 510). These gifts are not those the world treasures, but the gifts of God:

> *Count, then the silver miracles and golden dreams of happiness as all the treasures you would keep within the storehouse of the world. The door is open, not to thieves, but to your starving brothers, who mistook for gold the shining of a pebble, and who stored a heap of snow that shone like silver. . . . The door is open, that all those may come who would no longer starve, and would enjoy the feast of plenty set before them there. And they will meet with your invited Guests* [*the Holy Spirit and Christ*] *the miracle has asked to come to you. . . . The Guests have brought unlimited supply with Them. . . . And in their sharing there can be no gap in which abundance falters and grows thin (text, pp. 554f).*

Therefore we trust the God who will heal our minds, and then, indeed, all else will be given us for we would have removed the blocks of unforgiveness that precluded the natural flow of a happy world extending from a happy thought. Jesus urges us to believe his words, for only then can we find peace: "Everyone who listens to these words of mine and acts on them will be like a sensible man who built his house on rock. Rain came down, floods rose, gales blew and hurled themselves against the house, and it did not fall: it was founded on rock" (Mt 7:24f). God is the only foundation that can withstand the turbulences of our world. As the Course writes of the ego: "Do not try to make this impoverished house stand. Its weakness is your strength. Only God could make a home that is worthy of His creations. . . . [this] home will stand forever, and is ready for you when you choose to enter it" (text, p. 50). If we can bring our problems to this foundation, which Jesus represents, we are relieved of them: "Come to me, all you who labor and are overburdened, and I will give you rest. Shoulder my yoke and learn from me, for I am gentle and humble in heart, and you will find rest for your souls.Yes, my yoke is easy and my burden light" (Mt 11:28-30). Our faith in God should be like that of little children, whose dependence on their parents is total, trusting that they will protect them. This is how we should be, for "it is to such as these that the kingdom of heaven belongs" (Mt 19:14b).

We walk the world of fear with our guilt, seemingly trapped in this ego prison of misery, suffering and death. In this house of death, it is impossible to escape despair and we ask, along with the disciples: "Who can be saved, then?" (Mt 19:25b) and how can it be done? In gratitude we hear Jesus' answer: "For men, this is impossible; for God everything is possible" (Mt 19:26f).

As we live midst the violence of the world that mirrors the violence in our minds, we are comforted by the reassurance of Jesus' words to us: "Do not be afraid of those who kill the body but cannot kill the soul. . . . Can you not buy two sparrows for a penny? And yet not one falls to the ground without your Father knowing. Why, every hair on your head has been counted. So there is no need to be afraid; you are worth more than hundreds of sparrows" (Mt 10:28-30). If we are attacked, accused or even imprisoned, "Do not worry about how to speak or what to say; what you are to say will be given to you when the time comes; because it is not you who will be speaking; the Spirit of your Father will be speaking in you" (Mt 10:19f). We will never be alone because the Comforter of God protects us regardless of seeming danger. Our faith in Him affirms that nothing in this world has the power to come between us and God's peace; His love for us made manifest in Jesus.

In another of the scriptural citations in the Sermon on the Mount, Jesus cautions against the ego's interpretation of this faith (Mt 5:33-37). When we are frightened and feel endangered by external conditions, we can easily be tempted into calling for help on a God of magic who will take care of our external problems, obviating the need to deal with the real problems in our mind — as the cliché states: "God will do it for us." Believing in a God of magic reflects the ego's shift of a loving Father into a punishing one. Through the dynamic of reaction formation, we defend ourselves against this negative image of God by constructing special love idols of Him, seeing in them the ideal provider of what we believe we need, denying the unconscious belief that He will deprive and punish us. Thus Jesus teaches us not to make any oaths, neither to idols of God nor to ones we made of our ego selves: "Do not swear at all, either by Heaven, since that is God's throne; or by the earth, since that is his footstool; or by Jerusalem, since that is the city of the great king. Do not swear by your own head either, since you cannot turn a single hair white or black"(vv. 34-36).

Truth needs no defense or affirmation in swearing by it. This merely reflects the weakness of our faith and then defends against it. Such defense, as we have seen, strengthens the underlying problem by reinforcing our belief in its reality. True faith is in the God who lives within us, beyond our projections. Since problems exist only in our minds, it is God's strength in our mind that protects us. By calling upon the Holy Spirit, we call on the Voice of the One who speaks for who we really are, and who alone can bring us the power, protection and safety of Heaven. Jesus exhorts us further: "All you need say is 'Yes' if you mean yes, 'No' if you mean no" (v. 37). Our simple Yes to God is all that is required; if the Spirit says we should do something, we should do it; and if He says No, we refrain. Anything more comes from our ego, which does not have the power to do or know anything at all ("It cannot turn a single hair white or black"). James amplifies this teaching when he adds to Jesus' words on not swearing: "Otherwise you make yourselves liable to judgment" (Jm 5:12). To swear by the ego, even in God's name, merely reinforces the guilt of the ego's usurping God's power, trying to control Him. This guilt then judges against our identity as God's beloved child.

Thus, when we feel pain or mourn a perceived loss, we

will be comforted by God if we truly turn to Him. "What worry can beset the one who gives his future to the loving Hands of God? What can he suffer? What can cause him pain, or bring experience of loss to him? What can he fear? And what can he regard except with love? For he who has escaped all fear of future pain has found his way to present peace, and certainty of care the world can never threaten" (workbook, p. 361). If, on the other hand, the God we turn to is a projection of our ego, the comfort will be illusory and short-lived, a subtle form of attack that will quickly turn to guilt and increased suffering.

Only the true and living God in our hearts can bring us rest unto our souls; for only He corrects the problem at its source: our "sin" of having turned from Him. Jesus is teaching us not to use prayer as magic — praying for what we do not have or believe we need — nor as a spectacle to impress others (Mt 6:5f). Rather, our prayer must be based on faith in what we have but do not see. We pray for forgiveness, that we may receive what we have already been given and accept the reality that already is.

Jesus has given us the perfect example of this prayer, exemplifying the principle he gave to his disciples: "Everything you ask for and pray for, believe that you have it already, and it will be yours. And when you stand in prayer, forgive whatever you have against anybody . . . " (Mk 11:24f). *Before* the miracle of raising Lazarus from the dead, Jesus thanked his Father: "Father, I thank you for hearing my prayer. I knew indeed that you always hear me, but I speak for the sake of all these who stand around me, so that they may believe it was you who sent me" (Jn 11:42). When told of the death of Jairus' daughter, Jesus tells the grief-stricken man: "Do not be afraid, only have faith and she will be safe" (Lk 8:50). When Jesus went into the girl's house, she arose at his call. It was Jesus' absolute faith in his Father that allowed him to perform his many "signs and wonders," not to mention *the* sign and wonder of his final days. This faith becomes the model and inspiration for us as we are "busy with . . . [our] Father's affairs" (Lk 2:49b). As Jesus told his disciples: "I tell you most solemnly, whoever believes in me will perform the same works as I do myself, he will perform even greater works" (Jn 14:12).

In the gospel, Jesus continually implores the disciples to have faith in him, for only then will they know the One who sent him. At the Last Supper, Jesus says: "Do not let your hearts be troubled. Trust in God still, and trust in me" (Jn 14:1). In preparing them for the difficulties that would follow after his death, Jesus said: "I have told you all this so that your faith may not be shaken" (Jn 16:1). In Luke's account of the Last Supper, Jesus singles out Simon Peter and says to him: "I have prayed for you, Simon, that your faith may not fail, and once you have recovered, you in your turn must strengthen your brothers" (Lk 22:32).

Repeatedly in the four gospels Jesus tells his followers not to be afraid. Whether it is fear of a raging storm, persecutions, insults, illness, another's lack of faith, not having enough material goods to survive or meet future needs, Peter's fear of walking on water, or the disciples' fear at his transfiguration or resurrection appearances, Jesus is calmly reassuring them that their hearts need not be troubled nor afraid (Jn 14:27), for he is ever present and will never leave them to face their difficulties alone.

Similarly, Jesus emphasizes the importance of faith in healing. The Holy Spirit cannot heal without this faith; with it, there is nothing He cannot do, no illness or fear that cannot be undone. Even death can be overcome. Where Jesus finds faith he can heal; where he does not, he is unable to. As Matthew comments about Jesus' unacceptance in Nazareth: "And he did not work many miracles there because of their lack of faith" (Mt 13:58). The disciples were specifically told they could not cast out the demon from the epileptic demoniac due to the absence of faith. But "if your faith were the size of a mustard seed you could say to this mountain 'Move from here to there,' and it would move; nothing would be impossible for you" (Mt 17:20). When Peter became afraid of walking on the water and began to sink, Jesus exclaimed as he held him: "Man of little faith . . . why did you doubt?" (Mt 14:31).

Thus, Jesus can say to those whom he healed: "Your faith has restored you to health" (Mt 9:22); or "Your faith deserves it, so let this [healing of blindness] be done for you" (Mt 9:29). As Jesus said to the disciples of John the Baptist: "Happy is the man who does not lose faith in me" (Mt 11:6). Happy *is* the man, because he has restored to himself the source of all happiness: God.

With this faith, everything we ask for we will receive (Mt 21:22). But Jesus does not ask that our faith be perfect: if it were, we would not have needed his perfect faith. He asks only that we be willing to draw upon him, using his strength to bolster what we perceive to be our weakness. In reality, however, it is what the Course refers to as "the little willingness"; our part which allows Jesus to do his. As the father of the healed epileptic exclaimed to Jesus: "I do have faith. Help the little faith I have!" (Mk 9:24).

Trusting What is Unseen

No spiritual path is without its valleys of the shadow of death, the dark night of the soul we considered in Chapter 5. The ego dynamics of guilt and fear have helped us understand the nature of this dark night, when the individual confronts the overwhelming nothingness of self, along with the seeming absence of God's grace or comfort. It is a period of spiritual aridity and darkness, where all seems meaningless and hopeless, and death the only solution.

In the midst of the trials and tribulations that confront us in the recurring dark nights of our journey to God, Jesus assures us that God will comfort us. What seems to be failure is merely a thin veil concealing the success that God will bring about. This possibility of failure was the reality faced by the disciples as they slowly watched the disintegration of their dreams for the Messianic kingdom: there was Jesus unwelcome in his own village, greeted with ridicule and anger by the Jewish leaders, and disaffection and rejection by many of his own followers, the growing animosity and plotting against him, culminating in the devastating events of that Passover in Jerusalem. Jesus offered many teachings to assist the disciples' understanding of what was happening and would happen, and we shall consider these now.

Perhaps preparing the disciples for his own death and resurrection, Jesus entered into a discussion with the Sadducees concerning resurrection, which that group denied. The discussion closes with Jesus' assertion about his Father: "He is God, not of the dead, but of the living. You are very much mistaken" (Mk 12:27). The Sadducees' mistake was in not recognizing the power of God at work in situations that appear hopeless; they took the surface appearance to be reality.

When circumstances seem to move against us, it is because we are looking at events through our own eyes, rather than the eyes of faith. What to human eyes seems totally senseless or hopeless is really the working through of God's plan for our happiness through forgiveness. As the Course says: ". . . you cannot distinguish between advance and retreat. Some of your greatest advances you have judged as failures, and some of your deepest retreats you have evaluated as success" (text, p. 357). To meet this discouragement Jesus gave the people several parables, which he explained later to his disciples that they might be given the "secret of the kingdom of God" (Mk 4:11).

In the parable of "The Seed Growing By Itself" (Mk 4:26-29), Jesus teaches what the kingdom of God is like: "A man throws seed on the land. Night and day while he sleeps, when he is awake, the seed is sprouting and growing; how, he does not know. Of its own accord, the land produces first the shoot, then the ear, then the full grain in the ear. And when the crop is ready, he loses no time; he starts to reap because the harvest has come." Of ourselves, Jesus tells us, we can do nothing. God does it all. Though our part is merely to plant the seed, Jesus is certainly not advocating quietism. Planting the seed symbolizes our decision to trust in God's providence and to follow in the path He appoints for us. As James wrote: "Be patient, brothers. . . . Think of a farmer: how patiently he waits for the precious fruit of the ground until it has had the autumn rains and the spring rains! You too have to be patient; do not lose heart . . ." (Jm 5:7f). The real work is God's, and we need not understand it. We say "Yes" and follow His guidance, knowing that what we have begun, He will finish. As Paul wrote to the Philippians: "I am quite certain that the One who began this good work in you will see that it is finished . . ." (Ph

1:6). The beginnings carry with them the promise of God's fulfillment.

This theme of the need for patience and the inability to carry out the work that belongs to God is seen in parallel parables in Matthew 13. "The Darnel" (Mt 13:24-30) and "The Dragnet" (Mt 13:47-50) both deal with the eschatological (the "Final Things") problem of separating the good from the bad. The first parable treats the problem of darnel (chaff) having been sown among the wheat so that they are mixed together, while the second deals with a large net cast into the sea catching both good and bad fish alike. Jesus' listeners are urged to let God do the separating. If we attempt to do this on our own, before it is time, we would make numerous mistakes. Rather, we should patiently wait and trust that God will do this work.

Though the parables aim at the expected "Final Judgment," we may also understand them to speak of the need to separate out what is of the ego from what is of God, since our lives are a mixture of both. We might be able to see the problem, but would not know how to proceed. Therefore, the man cautions his servants who wish to uproot the darnel: Do not do that, "because when you weed out the darnel you might pull up the wheat with it. Let them both grow until harvest; and at harvest time I shall say to the reapers: first collect the darnel and tie it in bundles to be burned, then gather the wheat into my barn" (vv. 29f). We do not know our own fear and cannot judge what is in our best interests. If we wait patiently, however, God will take care of us. We need not be concerned about the ego elements in our lives, or the darkness they seem to bring. God asks only that we do our best, and leave to Him the working with our ego selves. In the end He will separate it out, leaving only the Self He knows and loves as His own.

The littleness of our beginnings contrasted with the magnitude of God's completion — our ego vs. God — is the theme of the parables of "The Mustard Seed" (Mt 13:31f) and "The Yeast" (Mt 13:33). What seems tiny and insignificant in human eyes is in reality the opposite. The "smallest of all the seeds" becomes "the biggest shrub of all . . . a tree so that the birds of the air come and shelter in its branches" (v.

32); or yeast leavens three measures of flour. The "littlest" is really the greatest, because it contains the power and the grandeur of God. However stubborn our personal egos may be, God can yet do great things through us. Within, a wonderful and powerful Child is being nourished. This is the Christ in us, of whom the Course writes:

> *Christ is reborn as but a little Child each time a wanderer would leave his home. For he must learn that what he would protect is but this Child, Who comes defenseless and Who is protected by defenselessness. . . . Christ has called you friend and brother. He has even come to ask your help in letting Him go home today, completed and completely. He has come as does a little child, who must beseech his father for protection and for love. He rules the universe, and yet He asks unceasingly that you return with Him, and take illusions as your gods no more (workbook, pp. 332f).*

Thus, Jesus asks that we have faith in the Nourisher of this Child within. The reason we may doubt, as he told the Sadducees, is the we "understand neither the scriptures nor the power of God"(Mk 12:24). In the words of the Course, we do not understand the difference between grandeur and grandiosity: "Grandeur is of God, and only of Him. Therefore it is in you. . . . Grandiosity is always a cover for despair. It is without hope because it is not real. . . . Yet your grandeur is not delusional because you did not make it. . . . [God] would have you replace the ego's belief in littleness with His Own exalted Answer to what you are, so that you can cease to question it and know it for what it is" (text, pp. 165-67).

The insignificance of the present moment, with its seeming failures, contains within it the seeds of triumph. What *seems* is not always what *is*. Jesus' teachings echo the hope and faith of the twenty-second psalm, whose opening lines, the gospels tell us, fell from his lips as he hung on the cross: "And about the ninth hour, Jesus cried out in a loud voice, 'Eli, Eli, lama sabachthani?' that is, 'My God, my God, why have you deserted me?'" (Mt 27:46) This psalm begins with the pained groanings of hopeless despair, and ends with the glorification of the God who has come in the midst of this darkness. "For he has not despised or disdained the poor man in his poverty, has not hidden his face from him, but has answered him when he called" (Ps 22:24). Thus does our Father always answer in the midst of our travails, illuminating the hopelessness of our darkness with His shining light. Above all, Jesus is asking us, we should take God's love seriously, for nothing is more certain than His loving mercy for His children.

Therefore, despite how things seem, there is God's own Voice in our minds, speaking to us His comforting words of love: "Know that I am with you always; yes, to the end of time" (Mt 28:20). When our guilt becomes intolerable to bear and we seem to have lost all that once was meaningful, in the midst of the poverty of our mourning for what we once believed was so real, God comes to us in His loving mercy, bearing witness to the consoling words of the beatitude: "Happy those who mourn: they shall be comforted" (Mt 5:5).

Chapter 11
THE POWER OF DECISION

Part I emphasized that forgiveness is a decision we must make. Where we had chosen to project our guilt onto others, now we need make another choice to correct our faulty one. As the Course says: "In this world the only remaining freedom is the freedom of choice; always between two choices or two voices" (manual, p. 75). A recurrent theme of Jesus' gospel is this power of our decision. Jesus holds two choices before us — to follow him to the kingdom of heaven, or to listen to the ego's invitation to the kingdom of this world. Jesus helps us choose, but we must make the choice ourselves. It is the same decision he made, which is encapsulated in the temptations in the wilderness. This scene introduces this chapter.

The Decision of Jesus

The three synoptic gospels (Matthew, Mark and Luke) are in accord in placing the devil's temptation of Jesus after his baptism by John the Baptist, and immediately before the beginning of his public ministry. The baptism signals Jesus' internal readiness to begin his Father's work after the "hidden years" of preparation, while the temptations reflect his decision to choose only his Father's Will.

In Satan's three temptations (Mt 4:1-11), we see clearly the choice that is placed before Jesus; the choice we labeled in Chapter 5 as between magic and the miracle. He is tempted to misuse the power of God in his mind: to change stones into bread; to hurl himself from a high place to demonstrate God's protection of him; and to gain power over all the world's kingdoms by worshipping the devil. The devil is the symbol of the ego, the power we believe we have to oppose God — the separation — projected outside ourselves.[1]

[1] *The pre-Freudian world of Biblical times could not have understood this dynamic of projection. Thus, it could never have seen that something that appeared to be outside — an "evil force" — was really nothing but thoughts of guilt and fear. We who belong to a more sophisticated psychological age can readily understand this*

Jesus himself confronts the same choice that is presented to us: to choose between God and Mammon, Heavenly and worldly power. As Jesus says in the Course: "I could not understand their [body and the ego] importance to you if I had not once been tempted to believe in them myself" (text, p. 51). It is significant that the evangelists placed this encounter with the "devil" before the beginning of Jesus' public ministry, highlighting the place our decision holds in the spiritual life. Before we can do the work the Holy Spirit asks of us, we must first decide who is our master. Without such a decision we will continually distort God's power, magically using it on behalf of the ego. This "moment of decision" occurs during the period between the phases of our life discussed in Chapter 4, the "mid-life crisis" that we all must confront. Choosing to ignore it leads to an inner deadness never recognized for what it truly is.

The fourth beatitude says: "Happy those who hunger and thirst for what is right; they shall be satisfied" (Mt 5:6). When once we emulate Jesus and choose to seek God's righteousness, we have His promise that in our seeking we will be found. St. Augustine wrote that to seek God is already to have found Him; for only if we had some experience of God would we be seeking Him. Thus, we desire the God we have known but forgotten, and whom we choose to know again. As St. Paul wrote so perceptively about himself and all of us: "I cannot understand my own behavior. I fail to carry out the things I want to do, and I find myself doing the very things I hate. . . . Instead of doing the good things I want to do, I carry out the sinful things I do not want" (Rm 7:15, 19). Understanding the dynamics of the ego helps account for this otherwise paradoxical phenomenon of running away from what we truly want.

This recurring non-acceptance of God and His peace necessitates the ongoing decision we must make along our pathway Home. These decisions occur on different levels. It is made once, and that sets into motion a process wherein

dynamic. Moreover, we can recognize that positing a power in opposition to God is to limit Him. This reflects the mistaken idea of "original sin" that there can be a power in the world other than God. This was the error that Jesus came to correct.

we reinforce this decision, choosing again and again as we live through our days: "Each day, each hour and minute, even every second, you are deciding between the crucifixion and the resurrection; between the ego and the Holy Spirit" (text, p. 255). Every subsequent decision for God reaffirms that first instant when we said: "Help, Father. There must be another way to live." These ongoing decisions serve to carry us further along the journey which, in Jesus' eyes, has already been completed: "It is a journey without distance to a goal that has never changed" (text, p. 139). His faith in us extends from the Father's faith in him: the knowledge that we remain united in His love, despite our wanderings through far countries. "God has ordained I cannot call in vain, and in His certainty I rest content. For you *will* hear, and you *will* choose again. And in this choice is everyone made free" (text, p. 621). The Course reinterprets the Matthean statement: "Many are called, but few are chosen" (Mt 22:14) to read: "'All are called but few choose to listen.' Therefore, they do not choose right. The 'chosen ones' are merely those who choose right sooner" (text, p. 39). This chapter will consider the gospels's urgings to accept Jesus' call, and the power of our minds to make such a choice.

The Urgency to Decide

Once this "Yes" to God is spoken, a whole series of events follows that prepares us for the work we are to do in God's name, for ourselves and for others. These events constitute the "opportunities for forgiveness" we have discussed in Part I. Each step that leads us closer to Jesus is expressed in a decision whether to follow his lead or that of the ego. As he taught in the Sermon on the Mount: "No one can be the slave of two masters. . . . You cannot be the slave both of God and of money" (Mt 6:24). Scripture sometimes formulates this choice as a conflict between darkness and light, or flesh and spirit. In the Course, it is said: "You see the flesh or recognize the spirit. There is no compromise between the two" (text, p. 614). We find this contrast particularly emphasized in the Johannine and Pauline writings. In his nocturnal visit to Jesus, for example, Nicodemus is taught the difference between these two worlds: "Unless a man is born through water and the spirit, he cannot enter the kingdom of God: what is born of the flesh is flesh; what is born of the Spirit is spirit" (Jn 3:5f). This theme is reiterated when Jesus tells his followers: "It is the spirit that gives life, the flesh has nothing to offer" (Jn 6:63). Later in the gospel, Jesus says: "I am the light of the world; anyone who follows me will not be walking in the dark; he will have the light of life" (Jn 8:12).

St. Paul echoes these thoughts in this passage: "The night is almost over, it will be daylight soon — let us give up all things we prefer to do under cover of the dark; let us arm ourselves and appear in the light" (Rm 13:12). To the Ephesians, he writes: "You must give up your old way of life; you must put aside your old self, which gets corrupted by following illusory desires. Your mind must be renewed by a spiritual revolution so that you can put on the new self that has been created in God's way, in the goodness and holiness of the truth" (Ep 4:22-24).

From the beginning of his ministry, Jesus highlights this theme: "The time has come . . . and the kingdom of God is close at hand. Repent and believe the Good News" (Mk 1:15). Repentance in this context can be understood as the change of mind the Greek gospel calls "metanoia," the change that corrects our previous decision to identify with the ego, accepting instead God's merciful love as mediated through Jesus. This theme runs through all the gospels, and the urgency of this message for the early church lay in the belief that the "parousia" or return of Jesus was immanent. If people did not choose now, all was lost. On a deeper level, however, we can understand the same urgency in choosing to identify with Jesus' kingdom of forgiveness and love, or else remaining bound in the hell of our guilt and fear. For us, the parousia is not a *deus ex machina* magically descending to heal the world, but our inner acceptance of forgiveness that will herald Jesus' "return" to our healed minds.

In no other aspect of the gospels is this theme of decision presented with such persistent clarity than in the parables. There are a series of five parables in the gospel of Matthew which, among many others in the synoptics, contain this theme of the need to choose. They, in the main, express concern that the people would be unprepared for Jesus' return.

In the parable of "The Burglar" (Mt 24:42 : 44), we are exhorted to "stay awake, because you do not know the day when your master is coming." If the householder knew the time the burglar would arrive, he would have been prepared for him. Since we do not know when Jesus, here symbolized by the burglar, will appear we must "stand ready." Similarly, in the parable of "The Conscientious Steward" (Mt 24:45-51) the servant must always be mindful of his master's orders, lest the master return unexpectedly and find him negligent. We are to remain faithful to what God has entrusted to us and be free from temptation to hear the ego's voice.

In the famous parable of "The Ten Bridesmaids" (Mt 25:1-13), Jesus urges us to be wise and prepared, to keep our lamps filled with oil in case the bridegroom returns when we are not expecting him. Our choices must continually be reaffirmed; a decision made once but now abandoned counts for nothing. The light of the world, which shines within us, must be kept lit if we are to join with the great light that *is* the kingdom.

The parable of "The Talents" (Mt 25:14-30) emphasizes the importance of keeping faithful to what God has entrusted to us, the function He has given us on behalf of the kingdom. Each of us has certain gifts — the five, two and one talents respectively. Jesus urges that we be as the first two servants who, upon the master's return, had doubled their money. However, woe to the fearful and insecure servant who, lacking faith, buries his one talent in the soil, preventing its increase: "for to everyone who has will be given more, and he will have more than enough; but from the man who has not, even what he has will be taken away" (v. 29). This is not meant as a threat, but as a caution: the love we receive from God must be shared with others, thus increasing its presence in the world. If we block the extension of God's gift, what we have will be lost to us. Love increases when it is given away; if it is not shared because of fear, this fear will always prevent our acceptance of God's love.

The final parable in the series is "The Last Judgment" (Mt 25:31-46), whose theme of helping the needy derives from Isaiah 58:6f and Ezekiel 18:5-9. Here, as in the other parables, we find the note of urgency to decide, and Jesus tells us we will be saved by our good deeds. As he said to his disciples at the Last Supper: "By this love you have for one another, everyone will know that you are my disciples" (Jn 13:35). This love impels us to take care of those in need —the hungry, thirsty, lonely, naked, sick and imprisoned. However, we have seen that our definition of the needy and poor must expand to include all people. Poverty is of the ego, which is the impoverished state of mind that believes that we have separated ourselves from God's abundance.

It is not our sins of commission that are the issue here but those of omission: failing to go out to those in need and distress. We go out to these brothers and sisters, not only to meet their needs for forgiveness but to meet our own as well. In giving others the love of God we give it to ourselves, realizing we are not separate from them. This joining undoes the ego's belief in separation, the source of all guilt and fear. To hasten the coming of the kingdom we must join with our brothers and sisters. Because "ideas leave not their source," what we do to Jesus and others we do to ourselves. As Jesus writes in the Course, based on Mt 25:40 and reflecting our oneness in Christ: "If what you did to my brother you do to me, and if you do everything for yourself because we are part of you, everything we do belongs to you as well" (text, p. 162).

Another parable that illustrates the importance Jesus placed on choice is "The Rich Man and Lazarus" (Lk 16:19-31). In the story, a rich and a poor man die; the rich man goes to hell while the other, Lazarus, is with Abraham in Heaven. The suffering man pleads with the patriarch that he find comfort, but is told that the gulf is too great between Heaven and hell to allow any contact between them. The man then asks Abraham to send Lazarus back to earth to warn his five brothers so they do not end up where he is. However, Abraham replies that not even such a sign would help: If they will not listen either to Moses or to the prophets, they will not be convinced even if someone should rise from the dead" (v. 31).

The meaning of the parable lies in this final sentence,

and it is aimed as a warning to those who, like the five remaining brothers, live a selfish and materialistic existence, believing that death is the end of life, a life that embodies the hedonistic value of the verse from Isaiah (22:13): "Let us eat and drink, for tomorrow we may be dead." To those who are like the five brothers God's appeal cannot be heard. Not even the greatest sign — a resurrection — would affect them. Therefore, they must first *decide* to accept God's word. Demanding an external sign as proof of God is really believing in magic, since we must instead choose the miracle that reflects our internal shift. The Course instructs: "The use of miracles as spectacles to induce belief is a misunderstanding of their purpose" (text, p. 1). Thus Jesus taught elsewhere: "Why does this generation demand a sign? I tell you solemnly, no sign shall be given to this generation" (Mk8:12). No sign will be given because it would not be the loving or helpful thing to do, reinforcing, as it were, the belief in magic which ultimately reinforces the belief in the separation.

Similarly,the rich man's request cannot be granted, not because God is unwilling, but because the brothers' fear would prevent their acceptance of God's truth, even if it were as clear as rising from the dead. Lazarus, on the other hand, received his reward because of his defenseless humility in choosing God's help. His very name reflects this desire: "Lazarus" means "God's help" in Aramaic. The parable thus urges us to repent and turn our minds back to God, for only then can Jesus truly help us.

Honoring the Power of Our Mind

At the same time the gospel emphasizes the importance of our decision, it emphasizes the power of our mind. The "power of Heaven and earth" that belongs to Jesus he offers us, once we choose to share our life and mind with him. As he says in the Course: It was only my decision that gave me all power in Heaven and earth. My only gift to you is to help you make the same decision. . . . I am your model for decision. By deciding for God I showed you that this decision can be made, and that you can make it. . . . [The Holy Spirit] teaches you how to keep me as your model for your thought . . . " (text, p. 71). This is St. Paul's prayer as well: "In your minds you must be the same as Christ Jesus" (Ph 2:5). Because we can choose to be "for him" or "against him," our mind becomes the most powerful instrument in this world. It has the potential of allying itself with God —the only true power — or turning away from Him, thereby holding this power in abeyance.

When we identify with the power of Heaven that Jesus offers, there is nothing we cannot do, no obstacles we cannot overcome. Our faith in this power can even move mountains. As Jesus said: "Believe in the light and you will become sons of light" (Jn 12:36). Our minds are this world's most powerful instrument — literally making up our world — and thus to believe in something will make it real for us. When we choose to deny this power of light by seeing our minds as separate from God, we affirm the reality of the separation and at the same time deny ourselves the peace, joy and well-being that is our natural inheritance of abundance as God's children. Pain and suffering are the inevitable result of such a choice, and through projection we see this suffering coming from outside us, rather than from our own decision.

Our basic problem is the decision to see ourselves separated from God and thus unloved by Him, not what the world would identify as problems. It is this decision that must be changed. The correction for this error must occur in the place where it was made: in our minds, not in the world. "You must change your mind, not your behavior," the Course urges, for "correction belongs only at the level where change is possible" (text, p. 25). The healing Spirit of God does not operate in a vacuum, but only through ourselves.

In discussing fear, Jesus states in the course:

> *Fear cannot be controlled by me, but it can be self-controlled. . . . The correction of fear is your responsibility. when you ask for release from fear, you are implying that it is not. You should ask, instead, for help in the conditions that have brought the fear about. These conditions always entail a willingness to be separate. . . . If I intervened between your thoughts and their results [fear], I*

would be tampering with a basic law of cause and effect; the most fundamental law there is. I would hardly help you if I depreciated the power of your own thinking (text, pp. 25,27).

One cannot undo fear by reducing or underestimating the power of the mind. If the power of our mind which chose mistakenly is not honored and respected, then we are denying that very mind the power to correct itself through the Holy Spirit. We would have successfully denied the only means for our salvation — our power of decision — its efficacy to save us.

In the book of Revelation, Jesus says he stands at the door and knocks, waiting for us to open it if we choose (Rv 3:20). He does not break the door down nor impose his will on our own, but stands patiently, reminding us of what we truly want. Jesus cannot and does not choose for us.

A concrete example of this principle is given in Jesus' encounter with the rich young man (Mk 10:17-22). The man approached Jesus, asking how he might attain eternal life. Jesus first tells him he must obey the commandments, which the man assures him he has. Jesus recognizes his desire and "looked steadily at him and loved him" (v. 21a). Mark's account of this episode is noteworthy as it is the only place in the three synoptic gospels where it is stated that Jesus loved anyone. This is all the more interesting in light of what follows: Jesus responds with an additional condition: "There is one thing you lack. Go and sell everything you own and give the money to the poor, and . . . follow me" (v. 21b). Yet the man cannot do it. His attachment to worldly possessions was too great: "His face fell at these words and he went away sad" (v. 22).

Our emphasis here is on Jesus' reaction. Surely he could have kept the young man with him. Jesus knew he was making the "wrong" decision, i.e., he could not find the peace of eternal life until he did what was asked. Yet Jesus also knew the fear in the man's heart, a fear that would have been greatly intensified had he disposed of his wealth while still believing he needed its security. It would seem,moreover, that Jesus recognized his fear from the beginning, as he first gave him the "easier" answer. It was the young man's desire for more that led Jesus to respond with the condition he could not meet. If Jesus had exercised his authority, inevitably placing the fear of God in him, the man's fear would only have increased. Reinforcing the young man's guilt would have gained Jesus nothing but the man's hidden resentment. Love is always gentle and kind, never seeking to impose power over anyone. As the Course says of the Holy Spirit: His Voice "does not command because it is incapable of arrogance. It does not demand, because it does not seek control. It does not overcome, because it does not attack. It merely reminds. . . . [It] is always quiet, because it speaks of peace" (text, p. 70). If the rich, young man could not freely choose to follow Jesus, he could not truly follow him at all. Jesus' love was so great that he fully respected the man's freedom. Thus, he could allow him to walk off all the while looking at him with love, patiently waiting, we can assume, the day when he *would* be able to accept the love Jesus offered and release his special relationship with his possessions, the ego's substitute for the love of God.

It is tempting for those in positions of authority to exercise control over those who look up to them, especially when the authorities are convinced of the correctness of their own position. This is particularly true in situations involving therapy or spiritual direction. Therapists or counselors are cast in the role of expert or God, and are often expected to have all the answers to the other's problems. Our need to have an expert tell us what to do often dovetails with the other's need to be an expert, forming a special relationship based on mutual need satisfaction. Moreover, the therapist's usurping another's freedom not only incurs guilt on the therapist's part, but also depreciates the patient's power to choose and change his or her mind.

This same dynamic can be observed in many other forms. Parents often impose their learning on their children, not allowing them the freedom and possibility to learn on their own. The expediency of the moment can take precedence over the greater benefit of allowing children to learn from their own mistakes. Fanatics — be they political or religious — seek to convert others to their belief system, mistaking the form of belief for the content of love that alone can transcend the seeming differences within the world. History has provided many examples of well meaning groups becoming part of the same corruption, hatred and division their message of truth was meant to correct.

This lesson was powerfully brought home to me in one of my first experiences with a psychiatric patient. While still an undergraduate, I participated in a special program in a mental hospital. A group of us were assigned several patients to meet with over the summer months. One of those assigned to me was Frank, who had been hospitalized for many years. Frank believed he was an agent of the F.B.I., and was plotting to overthrow the hospital and kill the director. With the naive idealism of youth, I was determined to break through this thought system and convince Frank of the errors in his thinking.

Our first meetings went well as I remained non-directive, basically accepting all that was said. Frank seemed to trust me and increasingly revealed the details of his delusional system. One day, I decided it was time to "move in" on the problem. I began pressuring Frank to see the correctness of my position as opposed to his, relentless in my determination that he see things my way. Then a striking thing happened. A strange look suddenly came across Frank's face. As he began to speak it was as if another voice were speaking, which said: "Watch it, Frank, he's getting too close." With that, Frank walked away and never acknowledged my presence again. That "voice" was right; Frank should not have trusted me, and he did well in not having anything more to do with me. My eagerness to be helpful belied my own underlying fear, lack of faith, and disrespect for his freedom to have his defenses. Jesus would have treated him differently.

PART III: APOSTLESHIP

INTRODUCTION

Having made a decision to follow Jesus and learn his lessons of forgiveness, we are sent out into the world to be about our Father's business of forgiveness. We can properly be called apostles or teachers of God: those who are sent to others to learn the lessons they now will teach. The beatitude "Happy the peacemakers: they shall be called Sons of God" (Mt 5:9) is the one to which all the others lead. It reflects the apostle's work in the world of bringing Jesus' peace to those who believe they are without it, remembering for themselves their natural inheritance as their Father's children.

It is impossible to bring peace without also having it. When one is truly at peace it must extend to others, for such is the law of extension. Therefore, the way we become peacemakers is to be at peace ourselves. The focus is always on what we *are*, not on what we *do*. However, what reinforces the belief of what we are is teaching it. The Course states as the second lesson of the Holy Spirit: "To have peace, teach peace to learn it" (text, p. 98). In the teacher's manual we read: "To teach *is* to learn, so that teacher and learner are the same. . . . To teach is to demonstrate. . . . From your demonstrations others learn, and so do you. . . . You cannot give to someone else, but only to yourself, and this you learn through teaching" (manual, p. 1). We all walk salvation's road together: learning forgiveness as we teach it, and having been forgiven, continuing to forgive. The prayer popularly attributed to St. Francis can well be called the apostle's prayer:

Lord, make me an instrument of your peace.
Where there is hatred, let me sow love.
Where there is injury, pardon.
Where there is doubt, faith.
Where there is despair, hope.
Where there is darkness, light.
Where there is sadness, joy.
O Divine Master, grant that I may not so much
seek
To be consoled, as to console.

To be understood, as to understand.
To be loved, as to love; for
It is in giving, that we receive.
It is in pardoning, that we are pardoned.
It is in dying, that we are born to eternal life.

As apostles of Jesus, we teach others the forgiveness he has taught us. Immediately following his greeting of peace to the apostles gathered in the upper room, giving them a direct experience of forgiveness, Jesus sends them to others to share in this blessing of absolution from sin and undoing of guilt: "As the Father sent me, so am I sending you" (Jn 20:21b). Jesus gives them the Holy Spirit, the interior presence of God's Voice which will guide, protect and comfort them: "Receive the Holy Spirit. For those whose sins you forgive, they are forgiven; for those whose sins you retain, they are retained" (Jn 20:23). Sent out into the world, the apostles have as their special assignment to teach the forgiveness of sins they have just experienced.

An apostle, therefore, is a messenger, sent by Jesus to deliver this single message that does save the world. The Course emphasizes the crucial difference between Heaven's messengers and the world's": "The messages that they deliver are intended first for them. And it is only as they can accept them for themselves that they become able to bring them further, and to give them everywhere that they were meant to be" (workbook, pp. 281f). The same message of forgiveness we bring and demonstrate to others is what we need to hear and learn. As we bring Jesus to others, we strengthen his presence in ourselves and thus we learn the truth of his promise to be with us always, until the end of time (Mt 28:20).

In one sense, the preceding chapters on forgiveness, faith and decision contain many important teachings on what it means to be a disciple of Jesus and, therefore, what it means to be an apostle. Thus, this part is limited to those teachings of Jesus that relate more specifically to the stage of apostleship when we have decided to follow Jesus' path and live our lives accordingly. We also shall consider some of the pitfalls that may arise on this path.

Rejection and Persecution

An observation frequently noted by students of *A Course in Miracles,* echoing the experience of followers of any spiritual path, is the anger that is frequently expressed by people when in the presence of defenselessness. We have already discussed this phenomenon in the case of Jesus, whose pure example of forgiveness — in thought, word and deed —brought out even more forcefully the ego reactions of those around him. His apostles have experienced this ever since, for similar reasons. This reaction is seen not only among strangers, but even among one's own people. Thus, we see Jesus' unacceptance in his own village of Nazareth, where his relatives were "convinced he was out of his mind" (Mk 3:21). Jesus comments later: "A prophet is only despised in his own country, among his own relations and in his own house" (Mk 6:4).

There are several passages in the gospels where Jesus warns his disciples of just this persecution because of him. We already have quoted from the famous final beatitudes: "Happy those who are persecuted in the cause of right: theirs is the kingdom of heaven. Happy are you when people abuse you and persecute you and speak all kinds of calumny against you on my account. Rejoice and be glad, for your reward will be great in heaven; this is how they persecuted the prophets before you" (Mt 5:10-12).

The warning continues later in the same gospel: "If they have called the master of the house Beelzebub, what will they not say of his household?" (Mt 10:25). Moreover, "Beware of men: they will hand you over to Sanhedrins and scourge you in their synagogues. You will be dragged before governors and kings for my sake, to bear witness before them and the pagans. . . . Brother will betray brother to death, and the father his child; children will rise against their parents and have them put to death. You will be hated by all men on account of my name" (Mt 10:17f, 21f).

Later, Jesus warns them: "They will hand you over to be tortured and put to death; and you will be hated by all the nations on account of my name. And then many will fall away; men will betray one another and hate one another" (Mt 24:9f). Finally, at the Last Supper he warns the disciples: "If the world hates you, remember that it hated me before you" (Jn 15:18), and: "they will expel you from the synagogues, and indeed the hour is coming when anyone who kills you will think he is doing a holy duty for God" (Jn 16:2).

As we have observed, scripture scholarship has established that much of the four gospels as we know them, including the passages just quoted, were actually the words of the early church. In the years and decades that followed Jesus' death the followers of Jesus, now known as Christians, experienced great persecutions and sufferings at the hands of those who saw them as political and religious threats. In addition, they experienced divisions within their own ranks. They "spiritualized" their sufferings, seeing themselves as innocent victims of the unjustified attacks of unbelievers, infidels and pagans, and placing the justification for their belief — now understood as the price of discipleship — in the mouth of Jesus, the greatest "Victim" of all. Their sufferings, as we saw in Chapter 9, became identified with his. Thus was their salvation ensured, and the damnation of their persecutors sealed in the words of Jesus himself.

We have discussed the expected ego reactions when teaching the truths that Jesus taught and lived, but how *he* interprets these differently. The ego's perception of innocence suffering at the hands of evil is transformed into an opportunity for forgiveness and healing. When people or groups of people would disagree or object, Jesus asks us not to take the objection or seeming attack personally but rather to "turn the other cheek," defenselessly witnessing to the inherent truth of his message of forgiveness. Thus, he urges his disciples: "Keep this carefully in mind: you are not to prepare your defense, because I myself shall give you an eloquence and a wisdom that none of your opponents will be able to resist or contradict" (Lk 21:14f). This eloquence could only be the defenselessness and forgiveness that Jesus himself exhibited at the end of his life. It is the gentle yet powerful eloquence that says: "Your seeming sins against me have had no effect, and so they cannot be real. Thus are all your sins forgiven, and mine along with yours."

Knowing Jesus' love, we know we are forgiven: our

guilt is gone, and so is our fear. Thus, Jesus counsels us: "Do not be afraid of those who kill the body but cannot kill the soul" (Mt 10:28); and comforts our fear: "You will be hated by all men on account of my name, but not a hair of your head will be lost. Your endurance will win you your lives" (Lk 21:17-19). These words have been cited in defense of martyrdom, glorifying a fate that seems to mimic Jesus', but in light of the Course's principles of forgiveness we can understand them to be comforting words that teach us there is nothing to fear, as "the Son of God needs no defense against the truth of his reality" (workbook, p. 249). We are not bodies, and so regardless of what happens to our physical self, we remain forever safe in our Father's love. This is the truly radical nature of Jesus' message: the vision of an inherently illusory world that is the only basis for genuine forgiveness.

Finally, we cite Jesus' instructions to his disciples when they find rejection as they travel from town to town, certainly not an uncommon occurrence: "and if anyone does not welcome you or listen to what you have to say, as you walk out of the house or town shake the dust from your feet" (Mt 10:14). He certainly is not counseling us to "wipe our hands" of those who disagree, but is asking us to walk away with no investment in feeling hurt — identifying as the victim — or angry —becoming the victimizer. Rather, we shake the dust of the *ego* from our feet, holding on only to the vision of forgiveness that Jesus has given us. We recognize that another's way may not be ours, and that our responsibility is only to remain faithful to the way Jesus has given us. In the Course, Jesus cautions us against the "spiritual specialness" of seeing the Course as the *only* way to God, a caution which could be applied to his two thousand year old gospel as well: Rather, he says, *A Course in Miracles* is only "a special form of the universal course. . . . [of which] there are many thousands of other forms, all with the same outcome" (manual, p. 3). Whenever we are tempted to judge another's path, or to take another's criticism personally, we can hear Jesus gently reminding us: "do not take another's path as your own; but neither should you judge it." Into a world of fear, upheld by the justified belief in a We-They perception, Jesus sends his apostles to bring another message, which is learned as it is taught. Recall the statement from the Course, cited earlier, that Jesus calls for teachers, not martyrs: teaching peace and forgiveness is his kind purpose of "persecution," correcting the glorified suffering of martyrdom that is the ego's.

"Render unto Caesar"

To value nothing in this world is not to deny a value to this world. Rather, it is to place that value in the context of God and our journey to His kingdom. The value of the things of this world lies in their capacity to be Jesus' instrument of leading us to the Father. Independent of that goal they are meaningless, and we are merely foolish to pursue these special relationships as ends in their own right.

However, this does not mean that it is "evil" or "unholy" to be involved with material things. It is a temptation for those on the spiritual path to be judgmental and critical towards those whose values seem rooted in this world. Those who judge look to the outside of the cup rather than the inside. It could only be their own imperfect self that would look critically on anyone, seeing in them the projection of their own guilt and self-judgment. People cling to the things of this world out of fear, not evil, believing that God could not love them, let alone provide for them. Therefore, they put their trust in their own power and the power of this world, reflecting their belief in the scarcity principle.

As St. Paul said to the Romans: "Do not model yourselves on the behavior of the world around you, but let your behavior change, modeled by your new mind. This is the only way to discover the will of God and know what is good, what it is that God wants, what is the perfect thing to do" (Rm 12:2). Though we should reflect the loving gentleness of Jesus in our actions, we should nonetheless be independent of the influences of the world, letting ourselves be subject only to the influence of the Holy Spirit.

One particularly unfortunate temptation is to become involved in disputes regarding the externals of religious life or observance, forgetting the unity of our life in the Person to whom the rituals are meant to point. St.Paul was emphatic on this issue. As he tells Timothy:

> *Instead of giving in to your impulses like a young man, fasten your attention on holiness, faith, love and peace, in union with all those who call on the Lord with pure minds. Avoid those futile and silly speculations, understanding that they only give rise to quarrels; and a servant of the Lord is not to engage in quarrels, but has to be kind to everyone, a good teacher, and patient. He has to be gentle when he corrects people who dispute what he says, never forgetting that God may give them a change of mind so that they recognize the truth and come to their senses . . . (2 Tm 2:22-26).*

In discussing a similar dispute over the externals of religious life, this time regarding the use of food, St. Paul says to the Corinthians in a passage reminiscent of his message to the Romans we quoted earlier: "Food, of course, cannot bring us in touch with God: we lose nothing if we refuse to eat, we gain nothing if we eat" (1 Co 8:8). Moreover, "If an unbeliever invites you to his house, go if you want to, and eat whatever is put in front of you, without asking questions just to satisfy conscience. . . . Whatever you eat, whatever you drink, whatever you do at all, do it for the glory of God" (1 Co 10:27, 31).

To oppose a misplaced emphasis on externals is to make the same mistake as the one who is emphasizing the externals, as it focuses on what divides, rather than on what unites us. What results is merely fear matching up with fear: the attack-defense cycle discussin in Chapter 1. If we can truly see all people as our brothers and sisters, we are fulfilling our function as Jesus' apostle of loving as he did. Valuing the things of this world is seen as a cry for the love people do not believe is deserved. We cannot minister to this need by opposing them, but only through joining in their seeming need, gently leading them to another way of relating to the world. This was the same principle underlying Jesus' life: living in the ego's world, even unto death, leading us to the world beyond death which is our true home.

The Course elaborates on this principle:

> *Suppose a brother insists on having you do something you think you do not want to do. His very insistence should tell you that he believes salvation lies in it. If you insist on refusing and experience a quick response of opposition, you are believing that your salvation lies in* not *doing it. You, then, are making the same mistake he is, and are making his error real to both of you. Insistence means investment, and what you invest in is always related to your notion of salvation. . . . Whenever you become angry with a brother, for whatever reason, you are believing that the ego is to be saved, and to be saved by attack. If he attacks, you are agreeing with this belief; and if you attack, you are reinforcing it. . . .* Recognize what does not matter, *and if your brothers ask you for something "Outrageous," do it* because *it does not matter. Refuse, and your opposition establishes that it does matter to you. . . . He is asking for salvation, as you are. . . . No "outrageous" requests can be made of one who recognizes what is valuable and wants to accept nothing else. Salvation is for the mind, and it is attained through peace. This is the only thing that can be saved and the only way to save it. Any response other than love arises from a confusion about the "what" and the "how" of salvation, and this is the only answer (text, pp. 205f).*

The popular phrase "When in Rome do as the Romans do" expresses the same idea, which St. Paul understood when he spoke to the Corinthians: "So though I am not a slave of any man I have made myself the slave of everyone so as to win as many as I could. . . . I made myself all things to all men in order too save some at any cost" (1 Co 9:19, 22). To the Colossians he said words that could benefit the cause of any would-be proselytizer, let alone make the listener's situation easier and more bearable: "Be tactful with those who are not Christians and be sure you make the best use of your time with them. Talk to them agreeably and with a flavor of wit, and try to fit your answers to the needs of each one" (Col 4:5f).

If we would be messengers of Jesus, we must be able to speak the language of those to whom we are sent.[1] The Course emphasizes that "if you would be heard by those who suffer, you must speak their language. If you would be a savior, you must understand what needs to be escaped" (manual, p. 61). If, for example, we are sent to Russia to deliver the message of Jesus, our first task would be to learn Russian. Similarly, to teach the rulers of the world who the true Ruler is, we must first join with them within their particular structure. Otherwise, our words and message would be dismissed, if not attacked outright. We unite within their form so that we may teach the lesson of the Spirit that is beyond all form. Forms separate and divide; Spirit unites. We should not appear to be different for then we are perceived as a threat, and the underlying fear, the fundamental problem, becomes reinforced. As the Course counsels: "You do not change appearance, though you smile more frequently. Your forehead is serene; your eyes are quiet. . . . You walk this path as others walk, nor do you seem to be distinct from them, although you are indeed. Thus can you serve them while you serve yourself, and set their footsteps on the way that God has opened up to you, and them through you. Illusion still appears to cling to you, that you may reach them. Yet it has stepped back" (workbook, p. 284). Jesus left us many teachings and examples of this important principle.

In the Sermon on the Mount, he tells the people to do their good works in secret, without fanfare: "Be careful not to parade your good deeds before men to attract their notice . . . when you give alms, do not have it trumpeted before you . . . your almsgiving must be secret" (Mt 6:1f, 4). Regarding fasting, Jesus says: "When you fast, put oil on

[1]*In its original inspiration, the idea of "speaking in tongues" (see Ac 2:1-13), was probably an injunction to communicate to people in their own language, or "to fit . . . answers to the needs of each one." It makes no sense to speak in a way that no one, or only specially gifted ones, can understand. This phenomenon may well reflect people's unconscious conflict of wishing to communicate and not communicate at the same time, the basic conflict between spirit and ego.*

your head and wash your face, so that no one will know you are fasting except your Father who sees all that is done in secret; and your Father . . . will reward you" (Mt 6:17f). Later in his ministry, Jesus sets the example of not fasting at all (Mt 9:14-18), contrasting his followers with the Pharisees and the disciples of John the Baptist. When Jesus and the disciples come to Capernaum and are asked to pay the temple tax of half a shekel, even though as natives they were exempt from the tax, Jesus replied: "[We are] exempt. However, so as not to offend these people, go to the lake and cast a hook; take the first fish that bites, open its mouth and there you will find a shekel; take it and give it to them for me and for you" (Mt 17:27).

Asked to heal, Jesus frequently adopted the healing practices of the time. These included, for example, the belief in the healing properties of spittle. Thus, in healing the blind man in John 9:1-41, Jesus "spat on the ground, made a paste with the spittle, [and] put this over the eyes of the blind man" (v. 6). In Mark 8:22-26, he heals a blind man by placing his spittle directly on the man's eyes, and a man with a speech impediment is healed by Jesus: touching "his tongue with spittle" (Mk 7:33). Jesus certainly did not need to do these things to heal, but it demonstrated the principle of doing the "outrageous" things *in* the world, yet retaining the awareness that the Source of healing is not *of* it. We obey the laws of the world because we know we are relly obedient to the laws of God. Thus, Jesus addresses the people and his disciples: "The scribes and the Pharisees occupy the chair of Moses. You must therefore do what they tell you and listen to what they say; but do not be guided by what they do: since they do not practice what they preach" (Mt 23:1-3). We should respect others' paths, but do not necessarily have to agree with them. The Course urges: "You are not making use of this course if you insist on using means which have served others well, neglecting what was made for *you*" (text, p. 363).

The Pharisees hoped to trap Jesus in an act of civil disobedience, and asked if it were permissible to pay taxes to Caesar. Jesus' reply, however, caught them off guard. Being told that it was Caesar's head and name that appeared on the coin, he said: "Give back to Caesar what belongs to Caesar — and to God what belongs to God" (Mt 22:21).

St. Paul set the norms for our conduct according to this principle:

> *You must all obey the governing authorities. . . . Good behavior is not afraid of magistrates; only criminals have anything to fear. If you want to live without being afraid of authority, you must live honestly and authority may even honor you. The state is there to serve God for your benefit. If you break the law, however, you may well have fear: the bearing of the sword has its significance. . . . You must obey, therefore, not only because you are afraid of being punished, but also for conscience's sake. This is also the reason why you must pay taxes, since all government officials are God's officers (Rm 13:1, 3-6).*

This does not mean supporting what our governments do or do not do; nor should it imply for us a specific course of action or non-action. The principle refers to an attitude that does not judge or condemn, but seeks only to do what Jesus asks. It means that if we wish to be instruments of correction, we must act in love. We join with our brothers and sisters in spirit, which is impossible once our motivation is to set ourselves in opposition to them. As we saw earlier, an ego is always wrong, but a Son of God — our true identity — is always right, and it is this "rightness" in spirit with which we identify.

The question, if we may again paraphrase Hamlet, is not: to act, or not to act (regarding tax or draft laws, supporting government policy, etc.). Rather the issue is which voice we choose to listen to — the ego or the Holy Spirit —and this has nothing to do with the *form* of our response. Perhaps we would be told to act differently from others, or to refrain from certain societal or legal demands; or perhaps our guidance would be to "remain the same," for by our willingness to comply with social demands we communicate the message of unity. What is essential is the purpose for our actions or non-actions. The form by itself means nothing. Thus, Jesus gives a "footnote" to the quotation cited earlier from the Course, when he says: "I have said that if a brother asks a foolish thing of you to do it. But be certain that this does not mean to do a foolish thing that would hurt either him or you, for what would hurt one would hurt the other" (text, p. 308). There is only one Person who knows what would truly hurt, and thus there is only one Person who knows what we should do. He is the one we should ask.

"The Jonah Complex"

As we set out on the spiritual path, filled with the love of God and the desire to bring that love to all those to whom we are sent, it seems as if there is nothing that can ever deter us from our newly found purpose, or tempt us to give away this "priceless pearl" we at last have found. For a period of time this may certainly be so. But we should never underestimate the power of the ego, or the extent of our underlying fear of truly stepping out into the light. As we have seen, we will continually be tempted to return to the darkness of our ego for safety and security.

There has probably not been a single person who, after hearing God's call, has not at some point or another become frightened, believing that He made a mistake. This fear is understandable from the perspective of the ego, which *is* afraid, and this fear often reflects itself in a desire to run in the other direction, as far from God as possible. The classic response belonged to the prophet Johah who, upon hearing God's word to warn Niniveh of its wickedness, literally ran from God and took the first boat he could out of Joppa.

In our hearts, each of us — partially identified with our ego — fears our function *because* it is of God. Coming to our rescue, the ego offers us a means whereby we can be "safe" from this threat. In Part I we saw how the ego keeps us from the real problem in our mind by convincing us that the problem lies elsewhere. To fulfill its purpose of riveting our attention away from our guilt, the ego sets up an endless series of pseudo-problems or smoke screens to decoy us from where we should really look. It makes an unreal problem seem real, which leads us to devote our time, energy and effort towards its resolution. As long as we remain convinced of the reality of this unreal problem we continue to seek its solution, while the real problem of our fear of God remains protected. This process is particularly frustrating since a non-problem can have no solution. If the seeming problem *is* solved, another will quickly arise to take its place.

One of the more famous of the biblical examples is Moses. His fear of what God was calling him to do —leading the Children of Israel in His name — manifested itself in his fear of speaking. Moses' speech impediment may be understood as the ego's subtle way of expressing its own fear and desire to obstruct the Will of God. God tells Moses: "I send you to Pharaoh to bring the sons of Israel, my people, out of Egypt" (Ex 3:10). Moses objects: "Who am I to go to Pharaoh? . . ." (Ex 3:11). But God replies: "I shall be with you" (Ex 3:12). This is not enough, nor are the signs that God provides for Moses as reassurance. He protests still further: "But, my Lord, never in my life have I been a man of eloquence. . . . I am a slow speaker and not able to speak well" (Ex 4:10). God answers him: "Who gave man his mouth. . . . Who makes him dumb or deaf, gives him sight or leaves him blind? Is it not I, Yahweh? Now go, I shall help you to speak and tell you what to say" (Ex 4:11f). Even this assurance does not suffice and Moses objects again, after which God finally agrees to let Moses's brother Aaron be the mouthpiece through whom He shall speak.

Moses' fear of his function and of the God who gave it to him reflected itself in his speech problem, which was the smoke screen, letting the ego off the hook. By resolving that pseudo-problem, through Aaron, the fundamental problem of Moses' fear could never be resolved for it was buried in his unconscious. Throughout the Exodus story, in fact, we see repeated instances of Moses' fear of totally submitting his will to his Creator. This fear is ultimately "punished" by his not being able to cross over the river Jordan into the Promised Land. This punishment seems to be God's reaction to the incident at Meribah, where Moses draws water for the parched people by angrily striking the rock twice, in apparent distrust of God's power and detracting from His miracle. Thus, this avenging God says to Moses: "Because you did not believe that I could proclaim my holiness in the eyes of the sons of Israel, you shall not lead this assembly into the land I am giving them" (Nb 20:12). This punishment, of course, could not be God's, but reflects the ego's need to punish guilt.

The same process is seen in the book of Jonah. The prophet's flight from God lands him in the belly of the whale. *That* becomes the problem which must be solved. Though Jonah is thrown ashore and, like Moses, fulfills his prophetic function, his underlying fear is never healed. Despite the success of his mission — the conversion of the people of Nineveh — Jonah is not happy. He rages at God for having spared the people, and then becomes angry because God destroys the castor oil plant that had given him shade, defending himself against God's questioning: "I have every right to be angry, to the point of death" (Jon 4:9b). Not at peace with God, he is not at peace with himself.

As apostles, we all have specific functions to fulfill —whatever their form — which our forgiveness makes possible. We must be wary that our egos do not divert us with problems that are not really problems at all. Concerns with illness, money, safety, special hate or special love relationships, are all ego attempts to distract and "protect" us from the work we are to do in God's name. Recognizing these pseudo-problems for what they are, calling on God to help us through the temptation of making the unreal real, allows the true reality of our life and purpose to manifest itself again. Seeing through the darkened web of illusion the ego has woven, we catch glimpses of the light of our function which is held out to us. The errors drop away, replaced by the light of truth that has never ceased to shine. Thus we all are speeded along the road that leads to God.

Another form taken by the "Jonah complex," in Abraham Maslow's phrase, is attempting to attack our self or our function. As we draw nearer to the light we find ourselves,as St. Augustine observed so perceptively, plunged back into darkness. This darkness often comes in the form of attacking ourselves, frequently a part of our physical or psychological body that comes to symbolize our function. Moses, for example, afraid to speak God's words to his people, developed a speech impediment. Jonah, who feared the light of God's message to Nineveh, whose sins represented his own, ended up enveloped in the darkness of the whale. These "ego-attacks" can be subtle or obvious, and often fall under the category of psychosomatic illness where our bodily symptoms reflect the symbolic character of the form of guilt we are experiencing.

There are two other temptations that "protect" us from our function, as our ego "rears its ugly head." The first of these is the temptation to leave our particular situation —families, friends, occupations — and follow a new path. Although it is certainly true that Jesus may indeed ask this of us as part of our own particular Atonement plan, as he did of the disciples, it is more often the case that we are asked to remain just where we are. The real call from Jesus is for the change of mind that allows us to choose him as our teacher, rather than the ego. An inherent part of the call is our saying "yes," not only to certain functions in the world, but more importantly, to undo our guilt through the lessons in forgiveness that are provided for us. Usually, this means remaining right where we are, at least at first, so that we can heal those relationships and situations where our guilt has been maintained.

That Jesus asks us to leave all behind and follow him is clear, but "leaving all behind" refers to an interior state. Any external changes would follow from what first changes inside. Discussing this very issue, the Course states: "Changes are required in the *minds* of God's teachers. . . . It is most unlikely that changes in attitudes would not be the first step in the newly-made teacher of God's training. . . . There are those who are called upon to change their life situation almost immediately, but these are generally special cases" (manual, p. 25). Therefore, the desire to leave situations or relationships behind is very often a subtle ego defense against the real meaning of the call, for it can mean an unwillingness to confront the manifestations of the ego in the relationships and situations at hand. Thus, it becomes an ego maneuver to move us away from the problem *and* the solution. It bids us take our life in our own hands, rather than trusting in the direction of Jesus.

St. Paul understood this problem very well. He emphatically told the Corinthians: "What each one has is what the Lord has given him and he should continue as he was when God's call reached him. This is the ruling I give in all the churches. If anyone had already been circumcised at the time of his call, he need not disguise it, and anyone who was uncircumcised at the time of his call need not be circumcised; because to be circumcised or uncircumcised means nothing: what does matter is to keep the commandments of God. Let everyone stay as he was at the time of his call" (1 Co 7:17-20).

The same situation holds, Paul continues, for those born slave or free, married or unmarried. Unless guided to change their situation, they should remain. To *insist* on a change, even on an unconscious level, places the emphasis in the wrong place, as we have seen in our discussion of Table 2. Salvation is not found in altering an existing external state, any more than it is found in maintaining it. Salvation is metanoia, letting go of our ego that we may identify with the Christ in us. Peace can come in no other way. Changing the outside of our lives without changing the inside is worthless, and even harmful, since it leads to the self-righteousness that prevents any change from occuring at all. We make whatever external changes are needed when told to do so by the Holy Spirit, and we can only be sure of whose voice we are hearing to the extent that we can be free of our guilt. Thus, once again, we see that our only true responsibility is practicing the lessons in forgiveness Jesus provides for us, so that our guilt may be undone. In this way, we become free to be about our Father's business.

Before we are able to put the new wine of Jesus' life into our lives, we must first change the wineskins: "People [do not] put new wine into old wineskins; if they do, the skins burst, the wine runs out, and the skins are lost. No, they put new wine into fresh skins and both are preserved" (Mt 9:17). Fresh skins are not put on from the outside, for these will merely be replications of the old. Rather, the old skins are made new by our forgiveness. The Holy Spirit takes our talents and abilities, changing their purpose, and thus nothing is ever wasted. This allows Him to transform our "old skins" for us. The Course instructs us: " . . . all dark cornerstones of unforgiveness [must be] removed. Otherwise the old thought system still has a basis for return" (manual, p. 25). We stay where we are at the time of the call so as to allow the Holy Spirit to transform us *where we are*. Only then can we be truly healed.

The second temptation we may encounter is becoming overly sensitive to even the slightest ego reactions we may have, exaggerating our mistakes. A mild twinge of annoyance in our voice is enough to make us feel intensely guilty; a momentary wave of fear passing over us "proves" our trust in God has been a sham. It seems as if the ego has won after all, and we are nothing more than spiritual frauds.

However, the truth is quite different. It may certainly be true that traces (and sometimes more than traces) of our ego survive, manifesting themselves from time to time. But to be totally ego-free is an unrealistic goal to say the least. To be totally beyond our ego would make it almost impossible to function in this world, not to mention render us virtually inaccessible to those who are still very much part of the world. In the words of the Course: "Do not despair, then, because of limitations. It is your function to escape from them, but not to be without them" (manual, p. 61). A more reasonable and practical goal would be to keep in communion with Jesus, that when our egos do rear their ugly heads we can turn to him for immediate correction. This calls for a constant vigilance and sensitivity to our deepest self, where the ego's foundation is found. As the gospel says: "You are the salt of the earth. But if salt becomes tasteless, what can make it salty again? It is good for nothing . . . " (Mt 5:13). Mark adds: "Have salt in yourselves and be at peace with one another" (Mk 9:50).

This sensitivity, however, can become a two-edged sword. On the one hand, it allows us to turn over to Jesus our ego temptations; but on the other, it causes us to react even to the slightest ego stirrings. What really happens is that things we would never have noticed before now stick out like sore thumbs, a situation where "the mind becomes increasingly sensitive to what it would once have regarded as very minor intrusions of discomfort" (text, pp. 18f).

Think of a white cloth. When it is dirty, an additional spot or two will go unnoticed and will cause no alarm or concern. But when the cloth is cleaned, even the slightest spec of dirt will show up glaringly. That is the situation we can find ourselves in. Our awareness of the peace that forgiveness brings has become so clear and desirable, the slightest deviation from this is jarring. In truth, contrary to the ego's interpretation of it, this is a sign of our spiritual advancement. As the Course has reminded us: "[we] cannot distinguish between advance and retreat" (text, p.357). We have become increasingly attracted to Heaven's light, and so even the slightest form of darkness —unforgiveness — is sufficient to cause us distress. This distress then motivates us to bring the darkness, however small, to Jesus' light that it can be dispelled. In doing so we are expressing our desire to be as perfect as he is, that all our brothers and sisters can be rejoined together with ourselves in the one Light of God. St. Paul's prayer to the Ephesians can be seen as a prayer for all apostles:

> *Out of his [the Father's] infinite glory, may he give you the power through his Spirit for your hidden self to grow strong, so that Christ may live in your hearts through faith, and then, planted in love and built on love, you will with all the saints have strength to grasp the breadth and the length, the height and the depth; until knowing the love of Christ, which is beyond all knowledge, you are filled with the utter fullness of God (Ep 3:16-19).*

Humility vs. Arrogance

The Course teaches that we "have a function in the world in its own terms. . . . Forgiveness represents (y)our function here. . . . we have indeed been given everything by God. Yet do we need forgiveness to perceive that this is so" (workbook, pp. 355f). If we can truly forgive, then we have undone all ego barriers that would prevent us from remembering our identity as God's children. As we forgive, we are able to hear the Holy Spirit's gentle Voice reminding us of what we have forgotten. Increasingly, our actions become guided by Him and Him alone, and we exemplify St. Augustine's principle: "Love and do what you will." If love is truly in our heart, then whatever we do will be in accordance with God's Will and we cannot help but function in the world as He would have us do.

The problem enters when we do not identify ourselves with this function of forgiveness, but instead see ourselves through the eyes of what we do. Thus, we believe that we are the ones doing the work, that our doing it reflects back upon us, and that the well-being of others depends upon us. Clearly, all we have done at this point is usurp a function that is not our own, and unconsciously set up a situation where we are in competition with the Holy Spirit, which is the reflection of the original error of separating from God. Forgiveness' importance thus lies in restoring to the Holy Spirit His proper function. Our function is merely to let Him do His: "I will step back and let Him lead the way" (workbook, p. 284). Thus we know who the Agent of healing and peace truly is.

Many years ago, the famous German conductor Erich Kleiber conducted "The Marriage of Figaro," a speciality of his, in Buenos Aires. The performance so moved the audience that they would not let him leave the stage, repeatedly calling him back through their applause. Finally, Kleiber returned with a copy of Mozart's score in his hand, holding it up to the audience as if to say: "I'm not the one you should applaud; it is the composer." That is how we should react as well. It is not we who do the great works in the world that bring love, peace and healing, but Jesus. He is the one we should feel grateful to.

Having a personal relationship with Jesus (or the Holy Spirit) prevents our identifying this self as the doer, and thus avoids the guilt over the separation from God. Many times apostles must serve as a "stand-in" for Jesus or the Holy Spirit, for those who do not know Them, yet experience Their love and peace through Their messengers. What is important is that the messengers *know* who the Source is, and for whom the gratitude is meant.

It is extremely tempting to see ourselves as teachers,

healers or spiritual leaders, all the more because many people would project that role upon us. The danger in seeing ourselves as the source of healing, rather than its instrument, is particularly insidious and destructive. It becomes merely another form of ego self-aggrandizement, which is a defense against facing up to what we truly believe about ourselves. Once this occurs, it becomes impossible not to form special relationships with those whose approval we need, since it will reinforce our defense of pretending we are something we are not. Without the confirmation and recognition of others, we would not believe our self-deception and would be thrust right back onto our guilt. In this way, then, others become important, not because we truly love them or seek to bring God's love into their frightened hearts, but because they make us feel better about ourselves. We have already seen how this merely reinforces our guilt, and our hatred of those who remind us of it.

We live in a society of hero-worshippers, where people are made into idols and placed on pedestals. This is but another form of the special relationship, where we seek in others what we have already projected onto them, hoping magically to overcome our own perceived lacks by identifying with them. The true God is never found, for we have sought outside ourselves for the One who can only be found within. We have already discussed the special love relationship the disciples had with Jesus and its devastating results. In our own day and age we have seen the great dangers of such a practice, where in their terror of being alone, people follow the charismatic egos of national leaders or the latest "spiritual teacher" to horrible consequences. Nazi Germany and the more recent disaster in Jonestown, Guiana, are two modern examples of such a mistake. However, this same mistake can more subtly occur when following a truly holy person where one substitutes an external god for the internal One.

Given this ego temptation, it is no accident that psychiatrists are said to have the highest suicide rate of any professional group. Mistakenly identifying themselves with the function of therapist or healer, they feel responsible for their patients' success or failure. If they improve, they feel an inflated sense of accomplishment and enhanced self-worth, which but ties them still further to the underlying belief of self-worthlessness and guilt over how they have used their patients. If a patient does not improve in the time or manner therapists require, they would feel a sense of failure, blaming themselves for the perceived lack of progress in the other. Either way, therefore, the therapist's own guilt is reinforced, with the ultimate expression of self-hatred being suicide.

In some form or another, all of us fall prey to this mistake of forgetting that we are not the Savior of the world, that we are not God. This has been a fairly common characteristic of many contemporary spiritualities, where our spiritual Self is identified with the Self of the Creator. The Course clarifies this: "Yet in creation you are not in reciprocal relation to God, since He created you but you did not create Him" (text, p. 104). And Jesus clarifies his scriptural statement of "I and my Father are one": " . . . there are two parts to the statement in recognition that the Father is greater" (text, p. 5).

To the ego, it is highly insulting to be told that we are not the ones who do things, that our job is merely to step back and let Jesus do the work. In the eyes of the world such an attitude is usually derided as weakness, indecision, or even psychosis, yet what could be more unreal than believing that we know what should be done for others, let alone carry out what should be done for others? What greater weakness can there be in the world than to cut ourselves off from the only source of strength that is present? Truly, of our ego selves we can do nothing. But of our true Self, which reflects the power of God, we can do everything —only we are not the agents of the doing. It is hardly humility but arrogance that pits our ego self against the power of God, and places this self in competition with Him. It is not only arrogant but insane, for we can only be the loser. Peace and happiness can never result from this fruitless endeavor.

There is a more subtle form that this arrogance takes, highly favored by the ego because it seems to be just the opposite: an expression of humility. This is the belief that accuses God of being mistaken in His choice on the grounds of incompetency. Jeremiah's classic response to God's call

—"Ah, Lord Yahweh; look, I do not know how to speak: I am a child!" (Jr 1:6) — echoes the response of practically every prophet God has called, and the response of each of us when we become aware of God's Will for us. This response seems to be an expression of personal humility, for we believe that we are unable to do the mighty work our mighty God would have us do; but on closer examination it, too, is merely arrogance, because it says to Him: "You have made a mistake; I could not possibly do what you are asking of me. I am not only unworthy, but inadequate to do Your Will. Please choose someone else." What we have really done, however, is arrogantly accuse Jesus or the Holy Spirit of not knowing Their business; that we know better than They do what should be done, and who should be the one to do it. Yet Jesus reminds us in the Course: "I am in charge of the Second Coming [plan of the Atonement], and my judgment, which is used only for protection, cannot be wrong because it never attacks. Yours may be so distorted that you believe I was mistaken in choosing you. I assure you this is a mistake of your ego. Do not mistake it for humility" (text pp. 58f). . . . "I do not choose God's channels wrongly. The Holy One shares my trust, and accepts my Atonement decisions because my will is never out of accord with His" (text, p. 62).

True humility is "to recognize and accept the fact that you do not know . . . [and] to recognize and accept the fact that He *does* know" (text, p. 308). The Course urges that we "be humble before Him, and yet great *in* Him" (text, p. 288), which is the point of Jesus' parable of "The Choice of Places at the Table" (Lk 14:7-11). When invited to a feast, Jesus instructs, "do not take your seat in the place of honor," but "make your way to the lowest place and sit there, so that, when your host comes, he may say, 'My friend, move up higher.' In that way, everyone with you at the table will see you honored, for everyone who exalts himself will be humbled, and the man who humbles himself will be exalted" (vv. 8, 10f). Jesus is calling us to renounce all self-righteous pretensions and be self-effacing before God. It is a call that we be truly humble, to come empty without defenses to God that He might fill us. As St. Paul stated: "We are only the earthenware jars that hold this treasure, to make it clear that such an overwhelming power comes from God and not from us" (2 Co 4:7).

Arrogance reflects the belief that the power comes from us, and thus we are the doers in the world. Clearly, if that were the case we could *not* do anything. But that is not what Jesus asks of us. In a beautiful passage from the Course he states: "For this alone I need; that you will hear the words I speak, and give them to the world. You are my voice, my eyes, my feet, my hands through which I save the world" (workbook, p. 322). He asks only that we let him save the world through us. Without our physical presence the world could not hear his words nor see the witnesses to his forgiving life. To say that we cannot do the work he has asked us to do is to deny him through our guilt and fear. This prevents his healing love from not only embracing the world, but from embracing ourselves as well. This is hardly humility, but the arrogance that always stems from fear and reinforces it: "To follow the Holy Spirit's guidance is to let yourself be absolved of guilt. . . . The imagined usurping of functions not your own is the basis of fear. . . . To return the function to the One to Whom it belongs is thus the escape from fear. And it is this that lets the memory of love return to you" (manual, p. 67).

True humility acknowledges the work and power of God through us, welcomes it in His name, and accepts our function of letting it through us. It recognizes that the world is "governed by a Power That is *in* them but not *of* them" (manual, p. 8). Undoing guilt through forgiveness allows us to accept God's loving Presence in our hearts, extending it to others who are still afraid and ridden with guilt. True humility does not say I cannot do it; but rather says, paraphrasing Mary, the mother of Jesus: "Let it be done *through* me according to your word" (Lk 1:38). Our forgiveness makes this statement possible.

"The Test For Truth"

One of the more frequently asked questions of *A Course in Miracles*, let alone any spiritual path, is how does one know whose voice we are listening to, the ego's or the Holy

Spirit's. It is all too clear that many times the ego sounds very much like the Voice for God, and we become convinced that our thoughts and actions are from the Holy Spirit when in reality they have resulted from our ego and our personal needs. How then can we know the difference, since our conscious goal would be only to follow the Holy Spirit's guidance?

Unfortunately, there is no iron-clad answer. If we could already hear God's Voice perfectly there would be no ego to contend with, and there would have been no need for the Holy Spirit or Jesus. We would already have returned home to God. It should, therefore, be no surprise that we are often confused about the source of help, since the ego *is* confusion, never truly knowing anything. Yet there is one rule that does hold, the guideline from the gospel: "You will be able to tell them by their fruits" (Mt 7:16). At the moment we are asking for help, it may be difficult to discern between the two voices, although over time we can become more proficient in our discernment. Yet, by the *results* of our decisions we can usually tell which voice has guided us. The fruits are twofold, and each must be present if it has indeed been the Holy Spirit we have heard.

The Course summarizes this twofold "test for truth":

> *You have one test, as sure as God, by which you recognize if what you learned is true. If you are wholly free of fear of any kind, and if all those who meet or even think of you share in your perfect peace, then you can be sure that you have learned God's lesson, and not your own. Unless all this is true, there are dark lessons in your mind that hurt and hinder you, and everyone around you (text, p. 276).*

If we have truly heard the Holy Spirit's Voice and are following His Will, we would experience nothing except His peace. Knowing He walked with us we would have nothing to fear, for His love would have already cast it out. We may be tempted to feel guilty or afraid, anxious about events or saddened by circumstances, but we could immediately refer these to Him and have them taken from us. His peace would naturally extend to others, and this is the test whereby we can know if we are truly following the Holy Spirit's guidance: those around us would be at peace, and this peace would reflect the peace in ourselves.

The second commandment that Jesus left us, that we should love our neighbors as ourselves, reflects the unity of God's love. If that love is absent from any place, then it cannot be of Heaven. If I am truly at peace, it must embrace all people, whether or not they are aware of it or choose to accept it. We have discussed how the light of peace can frequently mobilize the ego's darkness in another to mass against it, trying to attack what it perceives as threatening its existence. The life of Jesus provides a powerful example of how people's fear caused them to attack the peace they truly experienced in him. If the peace of his forgiveness were not so manifest, they would never have had to resort to such extreme forms of ego-protection.

The crucial question, however, should not really be "How do I know when I am hearing the Holy Spirit?" but "Why don't I do what He tells me to do so that I *can* hear His Voice better?" The shift in emphasis is important. Students of the Course, not to mention members of the various Pentecostal and Charismatic Christian churches, often become preoccupied with hearing the Holy Spirit, convinced that they are following His guidance in all they do. In reality, however, it is very often their own voice they are listening to, and the consequences are not always so Spirit-filled, for others or themselves. Because the Course places such emphasis, especially in the workbook, on hearing the Holy Spirit, it is easy to fall into this kind of mistake and fail to perceive the many cautions throughout the Course against this form of ego illusion as, for example, in the following statement: "Only very few can hear God's Voice [the Holy Spirit] at all" (manual, p. 30).

We live in a society of instant gratification, with little or no frustration tolerance. Thus, we also believe in instant salvation. The Course does tell us repeatedly how simple its salvation is, because of the consistency of the thought system it presents: "How simple is salvation! All it says is what was never true is not true now [the illusion of separation], and never will be. The impossible has not occurred, and can have no effects. And that is all. Can this be hard to learn by anyone who wants it to be true? Only unwillingness to learn it could make such an easy lesson difficult" (text, p. 600).

The Course, however, never really says it is easy to do, for our "unwillingness" to let go of our guilt is very great. As we have seen throughout this book, our deep attraction to remaining guilty makes forgiveness hard work. It requires dedication, persistence and discipline to practice our daily lessons of forgiveness. These lessons comprise more than just the 365 workbook exercises. Students of *A Course in Miracles* sometimes fall into the ego's trap of believing that at the close of the one year they will be instantly healed and one step away from Heaven. The workbook, however, warns against such magical hopes: "This course is a beginning, not an end" (workbook, p. 477). The purpose of the workbook is to "train your mind to think along the lines the text sets forth" (workbook, p. 1). Once we are able to dislodge our thinking from the ego, the purpose of this training, we must spend the rest of our lives reinforcing what we have learned, attempting to remember to apply its principles to *all* situations and relationships. It is this generalization of forgiveness, without exception, that constitutes the difficulty in hearing the Holy Spirit clearly and consistently.

Thus, if our focus remained on learning how to forgive, practicing this lesson in all our relationships, we would naturally hear God's Voice more and more clearly. When we are in a state of anxiety or tension, laden down with guilt, the Holy Spirit's Voice is inaudible. His "still, small voice" is drowned out by the ego's raucous shrieking. Our focus then should be on reducing the static, not straining to hear a Voice that has already been obscured. Such straining merely increases the tension and inner conflict, as we are pitting our desire to follow the Holy Spirit against our unconscious desire to flee from Him, the motivation behind all guilt and fear. The Bible urges us to "Pause a while and know that I am God" (Ps 46:10). When we can pause from our unforgiveness to change our mind, our inner peace allows us to ask with greater certainty. Forgiveness has removed the static and we can hear. By our love for one another that is born in our forgiveness, not only will others know we are Jesus' disciples — literally, for we will have learned from him — but so shall we.

Apostles of Light and Peace

Once disciples have chosen to identify with Jesus they become apostles, ready to bring his message to those who are without it. In fact, that is the essential mission of Jesus' followers: to "make disciples of all the nations . . . and teach them to observe all the commands I gave you" (Mt 28:19a, 20). In his prayer to the Father on behalf of his disciples, Jesus says: "As you sent me into the world, I have sent them into the world" (Jn 17:18).

As apostles we are sent into the world to bring Heaven's light which, through Jesus, we have seen and recognized. As he tells the disciples: "You are the light of the world. . . . your light must shine in the sight of men, so that, seeing your good works, they may give the praise to your Father in heaven" (Mt 5:14, 16). And later: "What I say to you in the dark, tell in the daylight; what you hear in whispers, proclaim from the housetops" (Mt 10:27). St. Paul echoes the same injunction to the Ephesians:

> *You were darkness once, but now you are light in the Lord; be like children of light, for the effects of the light are seen in complete goodness and right living and truth. Try to discover what the Lord wants of you, having nothing to do with the futile works of darkness but exposing them by contrast. The things which are done in secret are things that people are shamed even to speak of; but anything exposed by the light will be illuminated and anything illuminated turns into light (Ep 5:8-14).*

In the Course, Jesus writes:

> *In your [holy] relationship you have joined with me in bringing Heaven to the Son of God, who hid in darkness. You have been willing to bring the darkness to light, and this willingness has given strength to everyone who would remain in darkness. Those who would see will see. And they would*

join with me in carrying their light into the darkness, when the darkness in them is offered to the light, and is removed forever. . . . You who are now the bringers of salvation have the function of bringing light to darkness. . . . And from this light will the Great Rays extend back into darkness and forward into God, to shine away the past and so make room for His eternal Presence, in which everything is radiant in the light (text, p. 354).

As Jesus sends us out into the world we must learn not to become afraid, but to trust in the power and love of him who has sent us. Because of Heaven's protection, his apostles "can pick up snakes in their hands, and be unharmed should they drink deadly poison" (Mk 16:18). As the workbook lesson states: "I am under no laws but God's." The world holds many "laws" to be sacrosanct: the laws of medicine, nutrition, economics, immunization, etc. All teach: "Protect the body, and you will be saved. These are not laws, but madness" (workbook, p. 132), for they all pertain to the body, which to the ego is nothing but the instrument of the miscreative mind. "The body suffers just in order that the mind will fail to see it is the victim of itself . . . that it [the mind] attacks itself and wants to die. It is from this your 'laws' would save the body. It is for this you think you are a body" (workbook, p. 132). When we are totally centered on God, our minds restored to Him, no harm can befall us as we have withdrawn our investment in the body as a means of attacking or being attacked.

Ram Dass, a contemporary New Age leader, has described his experiences with his Indian guru who truly demonstrated that he was not under the body's laws. Calmly taking the LSD Ram Dass (then known as Richard Alpert) had concealed in his valise, the Indian master swallowed it without blinking an eye and experienced no effects whatsoever. *His* "trip" was only of God.

We must be cautious, however, not to assume a state of mind that we have not really achieved but would like to. Intent does not equal accomplishment. As the Course cautions: "Trust not your good intentions. They are not enough" (text p. 355). We must be clear within ourselves if we are truly guided to undertake something the world would judge as harmful, or whether it is our ego that is subtly trying to hurt us. In the prologue to John's gospel, it is said of Jesus that "to all who did accept him he gave power to become children of God" (Jn 1:12). Because he is with us always, we are assured of this power as long as we rely on him. We are not left comfortless, and Jesus has promised us that we would do even greater works than he did (Jn 14:12).

We demonstrate we are his apostles by putting into practice the word of God Jesus left with us, by loving our neighbor and putting our faith in our Father. This love, which we now have received from Jesus, he asks us to extend to everyone he brings to us, that we become "ambassadors for Christ" (2 Co 5:20). As he has loved us, so are we to love each other: "I commissioned you to go out and bear fruit, fruit that will last. . . . What I command you is to love one another" (Jn 15:16f). In the words of St. Paul: "We prove we are God's servants by our purity, knowledge, patience and kindness; by a spirit of holiness, by a love free from affectation" (2 Co 6:6).

Anything we ask in Jesus' name we will receive, for together with him we reflect the one Will of God. In Jesus' words: I tell you most solemnly, anything you ask for from the Father he will grant in my name. . . . Ask and you will receive, and so your joy will be complete" (Jn 16:23f). We have seen how our asking and receiving refers only to what is in our mind — peace or conflict, love or fear, forgiveness or guilt. If we ask for separation, that is what we receive; if we ask for restoration to our awareness of our oneness with all creation, that will be Jesus' gift to us, what he has patiently waited for us to accept. Indeed, this oneness with God and with himself is Jesus' final prayer for those who follow him: "Father, may they be one in us, as you are in me and I am in you, so that the world may believe it was you who sent me. . . . I have made your name known to them and will continue to make it known, so that the love with which you loved me may be in them, and so that I may be in them" (Jn 17:21,26).

It was said of Jesus that he was "to gather together in unity the scattered children of God" (Jn 11:52); and St Paul wrote: "For he is the peace between us, and has made the two into one and broken down the barrier which used to keep them apart . . . . This was to create one single New Man in himself out of the two of them and . . . to unite them both in a single Body and reconcile them with God" (Ep 2:14-16). Having accomplished that unity on the deepest level, by undoing the separation from God in his resurrection, Jesus now continues to work in his apostles throughout time, that all people come to accept the unity of God.

Separation is divisiveness, and divisiveness is war. Into this state of armed camps that *is* our world, Jesus sends his apostles. As is stated in the Course: "Into this hopeless and closed learning situation [the curriculum of the world], which teaches nothing but despair and death, God sends His teachers. And as they teach His lessons of joy and hope, their learning finally becomes complete" (manual, pp. 1f). These are the peacemakers who, like Jesus, walk midst war bringing peace, uniting the "one Body of Christ." We prove our love for Jesus, as did Peter, by feeding his lambs and his sheep (Jn 21:15-17). We prove it by "always wanting peace with all people, and the holiness without which no one can ever see the Lord" (Heb 12:14). Our prayer is for more apostles, as Jesus told his disciples: "The harvest is rich but the laborers are few, so ask the Lord of the harvest to send laborers to his harvest" (Mt 9:38). We express this prayer by our own peace, which leads others to the light of Christ that shines in us. Our situation today is that of Matthew 9:36, where Jesus felt sorry for the crowds "because they were harassed and dejected, like sheep without a shepherd."

All of us together make up the "one body of Christ," and each of us is essential to that body. As St. Paul explains the metaphor: "Just as each of our bodies has several parts and each part has a separate function, so all of us, in union with Christ, form one body, and as parts of it we belong to each other" (Rm 12:4-6). Each of us has different gifts, but the forms do not matter. As the Course states: "Everyone has a special part to play in the Atonement, but the message given to each one is always the same; *God's Son is guiltless.* Each one teaches the message differently, and learns it differently" (text, p. 262). St. Paul continues: "After all, what is Apollos [another apostle] and what is Paul? . . . I did the planting, Apollos did the watering, but God made things grow. Neither the planter nor the waterer matters: only God" (1 Co 3:5-7); and later in the same letter, Paul adds:

> *There is a variety of gifts but always the same Spirit; there are all sorts of service to be done, but always to the same Lord; working in all sorts of different ways in different people, it is the same God who is working in all of them. . . . it is precisely the parts of the body that seem to be the weakest which are the indispensable ones. . . . If one part is hurt, all parts are hurt with it. If one part is given special honor, all parts enjoy it (1 Co 12:4-6, 22, 26f).*

Each of us, therefore, is an integral part of the whole. As Paul tells the Ephesians: "You are part of a building that has the apostles and prophets for its foundations and Christ Jesus himself for its main cornerstone. As every structure is aligned with him, all grow into one holy temple in the Lord; and you too, in him, are being built into a house where God lives, in the Spirit" (Ep 2:20-22).

Jesus emphasizes the same point in the Course:

> *Teachers of innocence, each in his own way, have joined together, taking their part in the unified curriculum of the Atonement. There is no unity of learning goals apart from this. There is no conflict in this curriculum, which has one aim however it is taught. Each effort made on its behalf is offered for the single purpose of release from guilt. . . . The power of God Himself supports this teaching, and guarantees its limitless results.*
>
> *Join your own efforts to the power that cannot fail and must result in peace. No one can be untouched by teaching such as this. . . . The circle of Atonement has no end. And you will find ever-increasing confidence in your safe inclusion in the circle with everyone you bring within its safety and its perfect peace. . . . Within its holy*

> *circle is everyone whom God created as His Son. . . . Stand quietly within this circle, and attract all tortured minds to join with you in the safety of its peace and holiness. Abide with me within it, as teachers of Atonement, not of guilt.*
>
> *Blessed are you who teach with me. . . . I stand within the circle, calling you to peace. Teach peace with me, and stand with me on holy ground. . . . Come gladly to the holy circle, and look out in peace on all who think they are outside. Cast no one out, for here is what he seeks along with you. Come, let us join him in the holy place of peace which is for all of us, united as one within the Cause of peace (text, pp. 263f).*

We stand within this holy circle, building the house of God that St. Paul described to the Ephesians by loving as Jesus loved, setting aside all temptations to exclude certain persons or groups of persons from this love. The great temptation of the world is to decide that there are certain members of the family of God who belong outside the circle of Atonement, or who are more special and belong within it — opposite sides of the same error. Jesus sends us into the world, fulfilling certain functions, to teach a different lesson. On one level, the purpose of our work is obvious — to teach, to heal, to parent, to minister to people's needs in some way or another — and we must be faithful to this calling; but on a deeper level, another purpose is being fulfilled. We are sent to certain people not only to bring Jesus' message of forgiveness to them, but so that we may bring it to ourselves, and we will often be sent into situations that would tempt us to see people as other than our brothers and sisters. If, for example, our work takes us to the inner city, it is likely that not only would we identify with the poor, but this identification would be strengthened and solidified by identifying *against* the rich, or those who represent the "system" we believe is responsible for the pain and suffering of the community. If we teach suffering and neglected children, our work not only might reflect our sympathy and concern for them, but could easily turn to outrage at the parents or others who appear to have been so neglectful. If we seek to help free those who are oppressed, our dedication may well include anger and feelings of retribution towards the oppressor.

Given our ego states, such investment is unavoidable, but these same ego projections offer us the opportunity for becoming free of them. This is the principle of forgiveness as administered by the Holy Spirit. The work we are to do for Jesus is not only for the benefit of those we are sent to, but for our own as well. The process of healing is universal, and must embrace all those involved in it — the healed *and* the healer. In God's eyes there is no difference; He is not a respecter of persons.

In the letter to the Galatians, Paul contrasts the fruits of self-indulgence with the fruits of the Holy Spirit, the gifts He brings to those who choose to follow His guidance. These are the characteristics that can be found in all apostles: those who choose to follow the guidance of Jesus. In St. Paul's listing they are as follows: love, joy, peace, patience, kindness, goodness, trustfulness, gentleness and self-control (Ga 5:22).[1]

Having experienced the *love* of God, through forgiveness, we now step into the world to bring that same message to those to whom we are sent. Bringing this love to others, who could not but be filled with *joy* and *peace* through this great gift, which we receive as we extend it? If others reject the gift, or circumstances seem to move against this love, the apostles of Jesus wait *patiently*, assured of the ultimate success of their mission. Out of this patience, there is no need to impose our will on others, thereby freeing us to treat them with *kindness, goodness* and *gentleness*, always generous with the gift that is not ours but God's, regardless of the response of others. Our patience with our brothers and sisters is born of our faith, *trusting* that God's will is done on earth as in Heaven. As we continue on the path Jesus has set out before us, we remain constantly vigilant of our ego's

[1]*The Course's equivalent to these are the ten characteristics of a teacher of God, found in the manual for teachers: trust, honesty, tolerance, gentleness, joy, defenselessness, generosity, patience, faithfulness and open-mindedness (pp. 8-15). For a discussion of these, see my* Christian Psychology in "A Course in Miracles," *distributed by the Foundation for Inner Peace, Tiburon, CA 94920, p.35.*

desires, *controlling this personal self* so that the impersonal Self of Christ can truly be the light that leads us home.

In a world that has forgotten Him, Jesus needs us to be his apostles. To tired eyes grown weary of darkness, he asks us to bring His light, offering a vision of peace, joy and happiness in place of the pains and sorrows of the world of fear. He asks us to let him be visible in us, drawing others to himself as He draws us all to God. In this sense, as Jesus says in the Course: "I need you as much as you need me" (text, p.137). Jesus needs us to be his apostles of peace, or teachers of God, because only through us can be complete the saving work he undertook to begin in his own life. He needs our eyes to see the suffering in the world and yet see the light shining beyond it; he needs our ears to hear the calls for help of people frightened into responses of attack and violence; he needs our arms and feet to bring his hope and comfort to those who have forgotten him; he needs our voice to speak his message of salvation that all our sins have been forgiven. Most of all, he needs our willingness to become his messengers of love. As he brought God's forgiving word into the world, so are we to bring that same word to our world. Jesus asks only that we make his purpose our own, and in that union of our will with his, help unite the world in that single purpose of salvation: the forgiveness of our sin, which was the decision to remain separate from the Love that created us and which we are.

Through the unified perception of all people as children of God, we extend the love and oneness that we have experienced, thereby strengthening it in ourselves and in all the people of God. Thus, "the peace of God, which is so much greater than we can understand, will guard [our] hearts and [our] thoughts . . . "(Ph 4:7). Filled with Jesus' peace, we are sent to bring this peace to all who are without it. Within the Judaeo-Christian tradition, helping those in need has always been the key sign of the coming of God's kingdom; it is, in fact, the love that we show each other that will usher in the new Heaven and earth spoken of in scripture (Is 65:17; Rv 21:2), and will demonstrate to others the truth of Jesus' message of salvation (Jn 13:35). The Course's answer to this problem — accepting the Atonement for ourself —is a simple one, and echoes the basic message of inner conversion spoken of by the prophets and the gospel. Since we are not the healers of the world, the arbiters of divine justice, the correctors of mistakes, our only responsibility is to be as free as possible within ourselves to allow the One who *is* the Healer to work through us. To believe that any of us knows what is best for the world, let alone for ourselves, would be the height of arrogance. Jesus asks only that we let him be himself in us, so that he may bring himself to others through us.

Above all, we involve ourselves in plans for justice so that *we* may be healed of our belief in injustice. This is perhaps the most important point of all; for unless we see ourselves as part of the same process of healing and correction we are trying to bring about, we simply reinforce our belief in separation from God and from all humanity. As the Course says, "To perceive the healing of your brother as the healing of yourself is thus the way to remember God" (text, p. 203). There is no other way. The problem of the separation cannot be undone through a process that reinforces the very separation itself. And to keep one person outside the circle of healing is to exclude all the rest; for that one person becomes the projection of one's own guilt over the separation, and comes to symbolize the end of God's perfect creation.

Our one job, therefore, is to undo our own guilt which prevents us from being God's messengers here on earth. Whatever work we are directed to has as its focus not only the benefit it may bring to others, but the benefit it may bring to *us*. This is an integral part of God's plan for all of us. The work we do is the classroom in which we learn our own lessons of forgiveness. These always provide the chance to undo our belief in separation. When confronted by sickness, pain or suffering of any kind, there is One beside us who, tapping us gently on the shoulder, says: "There is another way of looking at this. Beyond the suffering and the fear there is a light that shines. See that light, and know that same light shines in you as well. Resist the temptation to see only darkness; in your efforts to comfort those who still identify with darkness, see past it to the light in others, asking to be joined once again. See that light shining in each and every person, so that they may all one day be reunited in the One Light your Father knows as Himself." The Course puts it this way: "Illusion recognized must disappear. Accept not suffering, and you remove the thought of suffering. Your blessing lies on everyone who suffers, when you choose to see all suffering as what it is" (workbook, p. 346).

Each of us is led to the group of people we can best teach and from whom we can best learn. There are no accidents in Heaven's plan for our salvation. Yet, though our particular ministry must of necessity be circumscribed, it is not meant to exclude others. In fact, if it does, and we see others as being in competition with us or even in opposition to us, then we are not learning the lesson of forgiveness we were meant to teach. This was illustrated in Jesus' own life, in which he reportedly dealt only with a relative few, and seemed to restrict his main ministry of the last three years, and that of his disciples, to the people of Israel. It was not until after his resurrection that Jesus sent his apostles to preach in all countries: "Go, therefore, make disciples of all the nations" (Mt 28:19a).

Every situation offers us this same opportunity to hear the Voice for forgiveness and truth speak to us in the very form we need to hear it, to practice forgiveness in the very way that may seem to be the most difficult. Let us identify with the Source of strength in us, not with our own weakness. In our going out to the needy, let us recognize that our own need for forgiveness is being held out to us. Let us not identify with the effect of the suffering, but with the one Cause that can undo our own little causes.

Let us pray with all people — poor and rich, oppressed and oppressor, murdered and murderer — that we may not wander into the temptation of separation, but will allow our Father to lead us out of it. Let us pray that we may share Jesus' perception of justice by sharing his identity in God, that we may not be tempted to exclude anyone from this identity. Let us not fear what seems to be a failure, but embrace the faith that knows that God's justice will prevail. As our own sins are forgiven and God's justice is allowed to reign in our hearts, this justice will radiate from our innocence, blessing all people with the love that true forgiveness makes free.

Let us pray for each other that each of us may do the small part that has been assigned to us, recognizing that in this part is found the Whole. Let us pray for forgiveness to become perfect in us so that it may become perfect in the world. This is the only role we have in God's plan for salvation, and it is to be accomplished in our hearts where it will become the reality it has always been. We are to live and walk in the world of separated people, but we are to walk with the perception of wholeness that comes from our belief in our own wholeness. When we have no longer placed thoughts of sin and guilt, of punishment and triumph, of separation and pain, between ourselves and the world we love, we shall succeed in the work we are to do in Jesus' name. Then we shall know that we are not apart from the world, nor is it apart from us.

PART IV: JESUS

INTRODUCTION

The preceding chapters discussed Jesus from a historical perspective, both from the importance of his teachings on forgiveness, and his own life two thousand years ago. His story does not stop there, however, for the resurrection did not complete his function. Jesus' risen life is as much present to us today as it was to the disciples who first experienced him in the period following his death. The present phase in Jesus' role as God's messenger is as the one who, having overcome death and sin, now reaches back to help us complete the same process of ego transcendence he completed: the offering of complete forgiveness which restores to our awareness our true identity in God. This is the Jesus who lives today and who, in recalling to mind the unbroken reality of the kingdom within us, remains our ever-present teacher.

This chapter is divided into three sections; in the first we consider the person in whom we are to place our faith and trust, answering the question: "Who is Jesus?" Next, we examine some of the obstacles to placing our trust in him, asking: "Why must we forgive Jesus?" Finally, we discuss what it means to believe in, and have a personal relationship with him, answering the question: "Do we need Jesus?"

Who Is Jesus?

The two major obstacles in knowing who Jesus is are the familiar errors of special love and hate relationships. The first of these we discuss in this section.

In special love relationships, we seek to idolize those we have chosen to be our special love partners, placing them on a pedestal. In so doing, we unconsciously elevate ourselves: how much better we must be if we are in association with one who is so special, and how much more special do we become when on the base of the pedestal is written the words: God's only begotten Son. In the language of traditional Christianity, Jesus was exclusively identified with Christ, the Second Person of the Trinity. He is God's only Son, while we are merely the adopted sons. St. Paul gave this teaching its clearest expression: ". . . when the appointed time came, God sent His Son, born of a woman, born a subject of the Law, to redeem the subjects of the Law and to enable us to be adopted as sons" (Ga 4:4), and "[God determined] that we should become his adopted sons, through Jesus Christ for his own kind purposes" (Ep 1:5).

By elevating Jesus to a position equal to God, Christians negated his singlemost contribution: that what he did we also could do. Denying his equality with us denies our using him as our model for learning. Having been born divine, Jesus has a "head start" or unfair advantage, as it were. The Course says:

> *The name of* Jesus *is the name of one who was a man but saw the fact of Christ [the symbol of forgiveness] in all his brothers and remembered God. So he became identified with Christ, a man no longer, but at one with God. . . . In his complete identification with the Christ — the perfect Son of God . . . —Jesus became what all of you must be. He led the way for you to follow him. He leads you back to God because he saw the road before him, and he followed it. . . . Is he the Christ? O yes, along with you (manual, p. 83).*

Jesus, thus, is the one who first completed his Atonement path. He began with us, believing in the reality of the separated world of the ego. Now, having learned his lessons perfectly and completely, he reaches back to help us walk forgiveness path, as he did. In the Course, he asks that we think of him as an elder brother, "entitled to respect for his greater experience, and obedience for his greater wisdom . . . to love because he is a brother, and to devotion . . . " (text, p. 5). But he does not ask for awe: "Equals should not be in awe of one another because awe implies inequality. It is therefore an inappropriate reaction to me" (text, p. 5). Emphasizing his equality with us, Jesus adds: "There is nothing about me that you cannot attain. I have nothing that does not come from God. The difference between us now is that I have nothing else" (text, p. 5).

Each of us comes into this world with two names: our

given name, as we are known in the body, and Christ, the name God gave us in creation. As the workbook lesson states: "The Name of God is my inheritance" (workbook, p. 336). By Jesus' transcending his ego identiy, he and Christ became one. In this sense he *is* the Christ, for he is no longer his ego. This is "a state which is only potential in [us]" (text, p.5). Thus we can say that we and Jesus are different in time, but not in eternity. In time, then, he says: "You stand below me and I stand below God. In the process of 'rising up,' I am higher because without me the distance between God and man would be too great for you to encompass. I bridge the distance as an elder brother to you on the one hand, and as a Son of God on the other. My devotion to my brothers has placed me in charge of the Sonship, which I render complete because I share it" (text p. 5).

Hans Kung, the controversial Catholic theologian, has nicely summarized this issue by stating that Jesus is the Son of God, "seated at the right hand of the Father," by *function*, not *nature*. In other words, Jesus became the Son of God, or Christ, by virtue of his having first completed his personal Atonement plan and helping us to do the same, but inherent in his nature is the Christ inherent in all of us.

How did this Christological error occur? It is sad to realize that the very guilt that Jesus came to undo ended up being the greatest obstacle to understanding his message and himself. We have already seen how the guilt of Jesus' early followers became reinforced during his life and death, and that this guilt was never undone. It led almost immediately to their misunderstandings of the crucifixion, discussed in Chapter 9, which merely strengthened the disciples' own guilt. The centuries of persecutions that followed were only one of these unfortunate consequences. Another was their Christological interpretions of Jesus. Their guilt not only demanded that they be punished, but also demanded that they be inferior. They could not be like Jesus because their guilt would not let them believe that they, too, were God's beloved Sons. Thus, one of the cornerstones of Jesus' message became lost, necessitating this reiteration in the Course as well as repetition in this book: "When you are afraid, be still and know that God is real, and you are His beloved Son in whom He is well pleased" (text, p. 49). The "best" the disciples could do was Paul's concept of adopted sons. Thus, the very separation that was Jesus' mission to undo became built into the perception of him who taught the unity of all children in the one God. In the words of the Orwellian nightmare world of *Animal Farm:* "All men are equal, but some are more equal than others." This belief in separation became perpetuated throughout Christian history in the projections onto others who were not seen to deserve God's kingdom, masking their unconscious belief that they did not deserve God's kingdom. Jesus thus became the special love object and all those who did not believe in him, as his followers did, became the special hate scapegoats. Under this massive cloud of specialness, the clear light of Jesus and his message became obscured.

On the special hate side of people's relationship with Jesus, we observe similar dynamics but in the opposite form. These we shall discuss in the following section on our need to forgive Jesus.

Why Must We Forgive Jesus?

Although the Course does not demand that we believe in Jesus (see following section), it does ask that we forgive him. Jesus states, for example, "I have great need of lilies, for the Son of God has not forgiven me" (text, p. 397). One does not usually think of the need to forgive Jesus, and for many people, especially Christians who have devoted their lives and hearts to him, forgiving Jesus would make no sense. Yet there is probably no more widespread and serious impediment to a spiritual aspirant of the Western world than the unforgiveness of the one who came to help us. Our understanding of the dynamics of the ego helps us to make sense of this otherwise incomprehensible situation. We can see that we actually have to forgive Jesus on *two* levels: for who he is *not* (the idols of specialness we have made of him), and on the deeper level, for who he truly is.

There has not been a more powerful symbol — of love and hate — in the Western world than Jesus. We have discussed the special love relationship with Jesus from the point of view of the disciples (Chapter 6) and of the Christian world (in the preceding section). In the former, we saw the disciples' need to project onto Jesus their own magical hopes for salvation (which two thousand years of disciples could also identify with — Jesus will do it for us), and their inevitable letdown when these hopes were not realized in the form they expected. In the latter, our need to have Jesus be special and different from everyone else led to idolizing him to the point of making him God.

In the foreword to this book, we commented briefly on the "bitter idols" that have been made of him. Our discussion of the misunderstandings of the crucifixion would explain the ego dynamics behind such projections, laying bare the reasons behind our special hate relationship with him. In this section we shall explore its forms in more depth.

It is not difficult to understand Jewish people's negative feelings toward Jesus. For Jews, Jesus has become synonymous with hatred and a symbol of two thousand years of persecution, rejection and murder. The long and tragic history of Christian anti-semitism (now being corrected in the post-Vatican II Catholic Church as well as Protestant ones), would certainly seem to justify this identification. It has even taken the extreme form of some Jews identifying Nazi Germany with Christianity, blaming Jesus for Hitler and the Holocaust. Clearly, attempts of many Christians to project guilt onto the Jews was a clear denial of the very message of love and forgiveness that Jesus taught and exemplified.

However, it is not only the Jewish people who have had difficulty with Jesus. For Christians, too, he has been a problematic figure. Perceived as the "Sacrificial Victim" whose death was demanded by God's plan of Atonement, Jesus became a symbol of sacrifice, suffering and death. Moreover, as the Christians' own guilt demanded scapegoats to attack, the resulting separations and divisions, too, became identified with the Will of God, with Jesus the rallying figure around whom such crusades and programs were carried out. One need only recall Constantine's vision of a cross, along with the words "In this sign you will conquer," as he set out to wage war against what he believed were the barbarians. The Prince of Peace had become the Prince of War.

If Christians believed, as we discussed in Parts II and III, that Jesus was asking them to sacrifice what they held dear so that they might find salvation, they would unconsciously resent the one who "told" them to do what they secretly did not want to do. As we have seen, changing one's behavior without also changing one's mind will never solve a problem or bring peace. Guilt remains associated with our thoughts, not our behavior alone. Thus, we can see how perfectly Christianity's relationship with Jesus fell into the specialness trap of the ego. Consciously feeling love and devotion to Jesus, Christians unconsciously would hate him for the life of sacrifice and pain they believed he was calling them to. His "suffering and dying body" on the cross symbolized the essence of salvation and their own guilt, pointing out their own failures to suffer likewise, the goal of every "good Christian." Centuries of magnificent art have resulted from this image of Jesus on the cross, on the one hand, inspiring thousands upon thousands of people; yet on the other, reinforcing the ego's view of salvation: atonement *with* sacrifice. Thus has guilt emerged triumphant upon the "cross of redemption."

This unconscious guilt is projected in many forms. The most obvious are the forms of persecution and attack we have already considered. As long as these continue, the conscious experiences would remain ones of special love for Jesus, the justification for a life of sacrifice, penance and division. This holds whether the object of projection is another, or one's own body through a life of sickness, suffering and, in its most extreme form, martyrdom. What emerges is the inner conflict the ego holds dear. On the conscious level we devote our life to Jesus, the symbol of God's love, while unconsciously holding on to feelings of guilt, pain and anger. This is the familiar paradigm we discussed under special love relationships, where the hate is split off, "protected" by the love that we believe is genuine. Thus, the basic guilt which is the root of all our problems is reinforced and perpetuated through continued projection, finding scapegoats — ourselves or others — to feed the guilt-attack cycle in which nothing can ever change.

There is another way that the ego can "resolve" its

conflict, if projection through scapegoating is unacceptable as a defense. We can deny our love and devotion to Jesus, thus minimizing the conflict between our hate and our love. Thus, the hidden life of sacrifice and projection no longer need conflict with following a teacher of mercy and forgiveness. We simply do not follow him at all. The forms of this defense vary greatly, including disbelieving that Jesus actually lived, denying his resurrection, or accepting his resurrection but dismissing his presence in the world today. Much of this negative feeling can be traced to the manner in which Jesus' name was invoked throughout centuries as means for justifying persecution and separation. We can observe a number of these reactions involving *A Course in Miracles*, where the specifically identifiable role of Jesus as author is denied. When this occurs, students of the Course are placed in a difficult position. On the one hand, they may swear by every word in it, taking it as their own spiritual path while, on the other hand, denying its source. In addition, if persons have experienced pain in their early experiences with Christianity, they will find the Christian terminology a problem as well as the first-person references of Jesus, needing to translate those particular words or concepts into more comfortable ones. Thus, the ego is subtly building conflict into their experience of the Course.

Trying to deny, ignore or rationalize these Christian elements is to deny one of the purposes *A Course in Miracles* serves: the forgiveness and reinterpretation of Christianity. One of the Course's aims can be seen as healing the divisions with Christianity, not to mention the enmity that has existed almost from the beginning between Christianity and Judaism, and other peoples of the world. Jesus came two thousand years ago to correct the errors inherent in Judaism, as well as to present his universal message to the world, hardly to inspire the birth of a *new* religion — "the one true faith" —by denying the validity of the old. Moreover, retranslating the Course's language and context protects the unforgiveness of Christianity and Jesus that has been projected. By not working through the unconscious feelings of hurt and anger that the Course may elicit, students are preventing themselves from experiencing the forgiveness that Jesus has asked us for.

We can understand the importance of forgiving Jesus on a deeper level: forgiving him for who he truly was and is, beyond the distortions of our special love and hate projections. We have already seen how to the ego the guiltless are guilty, for they deny the guilt that is the central concept in the ego's insane religion. Without guilt the ego's entire thought system crumbles, disappearing back into the nothingness from which it came. Since we all are egos, the part of us that still identifies with its thought system would find Jesus' forgiving presence absolutely intolerable. This is what the ego really holds against him. The images of guilt, sacrifice, and suffering it has made of him are but smoke screens that seek to veil the *true* source of our desiring to be separate from him: that he loves us. How scandalous Jesus' love is to the ego that is built on God's hatred! So we hate the one who has come to represent God for us because, as the Course states, the name of Jesus "stands for love that is not of this world. . . . .the shining symbol for the Word of God, so close to what it stands for that the little space between the two is lost" (manual, p. 55).

Because Jesus is so threatening to the ego, it must attack him and his message as viciously as it can, and the great distortions of Jesus' message throughout the centuries are witness to these attacks. A question may arise at this time: Did not Jesus know his death and resurrection would have the disastrous effects of being misunderstood by practically all people, including most of those judged to have been his closest disciples and friends? And if he did know, why did he choose to present his message in such a form? An answer suggests itself that would follow from the basic principles he sets forth in the Course.

Errors cannot be corrected while they are unseen. Only when they are brought into the light of forgiveness can they be let go. We have seen that the purpose of Jesus' life was to forgive sin. How could he accomplish this without bringing to people's consciousness their "secret sins and hidden hates?" What more effective way could there be than to present the perfect model of God's love and the invulnerability of His children? Jesus, thus, became the screen onto which our ego could project all of its darkness, offering us the opportunity of re-examining what the ego strove to hide from us.

The plan of the Atonement, which Jesus heads, called for this one radical act that brought out the "worst" in the egos of all who knew him, and all who were influenced by Christianity.[1] Practically no person could have known Jesus without having felt some form of guilt, hurt, anger, hopelessness or abandonment, believing that God let him or her down in a wake of broken promises. Whether on the side of special hate or special love, people would have been forced to look at the deepest regions of their egos. The flight from such confrontation has taken all the forms we have considered — from persecution and murder to seeming ignorance or indifference.

Perhaps we can best understand Jesus' purpose in terms of its long-range effects. It is useful to remember that his view of time is different from ours, for we are still immersed in its seeming reality. As he says in the Course, alluding to the unreality of time: "Yet what meaning can the words convey to those who count the hours still, and rise and work and go to sleep by them?" (workbook, p. 316). Standing at the end of time that borders eternity, Jesus waits patiently for the end of what he knows has never been. He does not explain this to us who could never understand, yet he asks that we trust his gentle guidance through the labyrinth of time as he leads us to where he stands, one step from Heaven and the instant when all God's children reunite, allowing our Father to take the "last step," leaning down and "raising [us] unto Himself" (text, p. 199).

What could not have been dealt with before now seems to be rising again in the surface in this age of psychology, where the unconscious dynamics of projection are commonly accepted and understood, and we can understand what earlier generations could not. In *A Course in Miracles*, Jesus presents an opportunity to re-examine the very ego issues that his life, death and resurrection presented to the world

[1]*We are speaking here, of course, only of the ego aspects; on the other side, Jesus also brought out the best in us: reminding us of who we are, and helping all people return to the home they never truly left.*

two thousand years ago. Not to forgive Jesus, or not even to recognize the need to forgive him or the religions that claim to have sprung from him is to deny the opportunity to forgive those parts of ourselves that still believe that truth can be crucified, and that we are responsible for it. We see here the very guilt over the separation that is inherent in each of us who walk this earth. Jesus brought it clearly before our eyes, and asks us now to forgive him that we may at last forgive ourselves for what never happened. "Choose once again," he calls to us, "Deny me not the little gift [of forgiveness] I ask, when in exchange I lay before your feet the peace of God, and power to bring this peace to everyone who wanders in the world . . . " (text, p. 621).

Do We Need Jesus?

In the first section of this part, we cited Kung's idea of Jesus being the Son of God according to function. It is precisely his function of being in charge of the process of Atonement that we need: "I am in charge of the Atonement. . . . My part in the Atonement is the cancelling out of all errors that you could not otherwise correct" (text, p. 6).

Yet this is a question easier to answer in the abstract than in the specific, for we are dealing with experience rather than intellectual thoughts. Who is Jesus for us, and why do we need him? Our only answer comes from an experience of his presence and his love. It is an experience born of faith and nourished by faith. It is an experience that requires no answer, as the experience itself is the answer.

Who is Jesus for us? He is the one who has come to us from God and has made his home in us. How do we know him? In our hearts and in our lives. Jesus is the beginning and the end of our journey, as he was for the ones who followed him two thousand years ago. He is the means as well, since it is he who guides and comforts us as we travel the spiritual path that leads to God. We may apply to Jesus the same words used by the Course in describing the Holy Spirit: "Our Love awaits us as we go to Him, and walks beside us showing us the way. He fails in nothing. He the end we seek, and He the means by which we go to Him" (workbook, p. 440). In the midst of the temptations and distractions of the world, it is Jesus who remains our steadfast light; his constant and steadfast love illuminates the otherwise darkened web we call our life; his meaning shines out midst the meaninglessness of our everyday lives, holding us fast to our purpose. A wonderful story illustrates this particular aspect of Jesus' life in us:

A man is near death and has a vision of standing upon a slight hill, overlooking a huge expanse of beach. Next to him stands Jesus, who shows him two sets of footprints that extend the entire length of the beach, explaining how he has walked with him throughout his life. The man is moved by Jesus' words, and then notices that there are some parts where only one set of footprints can be seen in the sand, and he recognizes that these reflected the difficult and painful periods of his life. Jumping to the ego conclusion of adding two and two and totalling five, he complains to Jesus: "But where were you when I needed you?" Gently Jesus explains that it was true that there was only one set of footprints during those periods of crisis, but then adds: "It was then that I carried you."

We can study Jesus' life and his words, practice the principles he left us, yet beyond them all remains the single experience of his love, gently carrying us along. This experience alone gives meaning to questions we may raise, and all answers we may receive. With him, all else shifts into focus; without him, our lives are chaos and beyond our ability to manage.

1. Is He the Only Teacher?

The gospel is not so much a message, but a person who is himself the message, and has remained so for two thousand years. If we wish to teach and learn this message, we can only do so through him. Our goal, as his apostles, is to be as like him as possible; that with Cardinal Newman we would pray: "Let them look up and see no longer me, but only Jesus." Thus do we ensure that his message will become our own. But is Jesus the only way to God, the only teacher we can follow?

The Course teaches that "Helpers are given you in

many forms, although upon the altar they are one. . . . They have names which differ for a time, for time needs symbols, being itself unreal. Their names are legion . . ." (manual, p. 83). Jesus is the name of one of God's helpers, the one who "was the first to complete his own part perfectly" (manual, p. 85). Certainly there could be others who have followed, including those who have already passed beyond "lower" ego states and can help those of us still stuck "below," all the while they are completing the little ground yet needed to be worked through.

Thus, the Course makes it clear that belief in Jesus is not required to pursue its goal of forgiveness: "It is possible to read his words and benefit from them without accepting him into your life" (manual, p. 84). It would surely be unfair of God to demand that people come to Him in a form that seemed unacceptable to them. Could a loving Father *but* provide help to His children in a manner they could accept and understand? Could He make belief in Jesus the prerequisite for salvation, limiting His Voice to a specific form, when only spirit is real and form illusory? Our Father calls all the world back to Him, and in doing so, reaches each of His children in the way that would be of greatest benefit. It is salvation's single message of forgiveness that is essential, not the distinctive form in which it comes.

We live in a world of many symbols, and no particular set can meet the needs of everyone. As we have seen, *A Course In Miracles* is only one form among "many thousands." Yet because it comes to us from Jesus it cannot be separated from him and remain what it is: "Ideas leave not their source." The Course states: " . . . we will not go beyond the names the course itself employs" (manual, p. 83), and thus we have confined our discussion in this book to these "names": *Jesus*, the manifestation of the *Holy Spirit*, Who is the Voice for *God*. "Is he God's only Helper?" the Course asks, and then answers: "No, indeed. For Christ takes many forms with different names until their oneness can be recognized. But Jesus is for you the bearer of Christ's single message of the Love of God. You need no other" (manual, p. 84). Elsewhere, the Course states:

> *This course has come from him [Jesus] because his words have reached you in a language you can love and understand. Are other teachers possible, to lead the way to those who speak in different tongues and appeal to different symbols? Certainly there are. . . . We need a many-faceted curriculum, not because of content differences, but because symbols must shift and change to suit the need. Jesus has come to answer yours. In him you find God's Answer. Do you, then, teach with him, for he is with you; he is always here (manual, p. 56).*

Thus, we may state that the Course's message of forgiveness can be learned independently of Jesus, but its source is based upon him. Although his message is universal, Jesus answered our call within a specific language and context, and has promised to be present if and when we asked for this help. As he states in the Course: "I will come in response to a single unequivocal call" (text, p. 56). This help is present even if we do not consciously believe in him; there are no egos in Heaven. It might even be said that Jesus' desire would be that we practice his message of salvation, learn to forgive and love one another, and leave the question of faith in him up to God. Whatever way we come to accept the Voice of our internal Teacher is welcome. We leave the manner in which we learn this message to the One who knows the difference between form and content, illusion and truth, the ego and God. As the Course emphasizes, its goal is experience not belief, since belief is an ego function; experience can only unify, while belief can often divide. It is only the *experience* of God's single Voice that is needed in practicing the Course's curriculum and learning its lessons, not a specific belief. For our present purposes, however, we shall accept Jesus' identity as that Voice and presence. It should be noted that in terms of *function* as internal Teacher, the Course uses Jesus and the Holy Spirit virtually interchangeably.

There is one qualification to this, however. If a person lacks belief in Jesus because of a special relationship with him, as we discussed above, it would be important that this ego defense against our true relationship with him be undone. Otherwise, resistance to the Course is inevitable and would of necessity interfere with learning it. The overcoming of this block, however, would still come through forgiveness in all our relationships. Jesus stands within them, awaiting our forgiveness of each other and of himself. As he states in the Course: "Be not separated from me, and let not the holy purpose of Atonement be lost to you in dreams of vengeance. Relationships in which such dreams are cherished have excluded me. Let me enter in the Name of God and bring you peace, that you may offer peace to me" (text, p. 333).

2. Jesus as Our Model

Taking Jesus as our model and teacher, our only question in any situation must be: What would Jesus do? This would not refer back to the historical Jesus of Nazareth, trying to model our actions on what is given to us in the gospels, for this would miss the whole point, mistaking form for content. The way Jesus lived on earth was to follow his Father's Will. Essential to this life were not the specific forms this entailed, but the principle of total abandonment of the ego's will to God's. *This* is what we seek to emulate. As Jesus said in the Sermon on the Mount, already quoted: "It is not those who say to me, 'Lord, Lord,' who will enter the kingdom of heaven, but the person who does the will of my Father in heaven" (Mt 7:21). Situations are different and circumstances change. Our responses need to be geared to the changing needs of the times in which we live. Thus, it is of little help to study what occurred at a time and place alien to our own. We cannot apply to a contemporary world the same standards of response that existed in a small Middle Eastern territory two thousand years ago, or the environs of the 16th century Spain of Sts. John of the Cross and Teresa of Avila, or that of a holy man from Tibet or India. Yet, we can apply the same *principle* of response: referring all decisions to the Holy Spirit's wisdom.

Thus our only function, as we have seen, is to be as free as possible within ourselves to hear Jesus or the Holy Spirit. In that way, we can always be sure that we are living according to his commandment that we love one another as he has loved us, and loves us still. Jesus is the model for our action; not so much for what he specifically did, but for the principles his life exemplified. These can be reduced to two basic ones: total faith in, and love for his Father; and the unfettered extension of his Father's love. This is the love that surpasses the world's understanding, for God's love embraces all people as equals and as one, overcoming any ego desire to project guilt and therefore exclude. This, as we have seen, is what forgiveness expresses, the overcoming of all barriers we have placed between ourselves and others. Thus, our responsibility as apostles, messengers of Jesus sent into the world, is not so much to proclaim his good news, but to *become* his good news. We are to have faith and trust in him, as he did in God, and to forgive others in his name, bringing to all the world his message of hope: Be at peace, for all your sins have been forgiven you.

Jesus has provided the perfect model of what our life could be, and stands before us as the example of what we can become. He is the ultimate proof that the light of Christ shines as radiantly as ever within us. In the inspiring words of Isaiah:

> *Arise, shine out, for your light has come, the glory of Yahweh is rising on you, though night still covers the earth and darkness the peoples. Above you Yahweh now rises and above you his glory appears. The nations come to your light and kings to your dawning brightness. Lift up your eyes and look around: all are assembling and coming toward you. . . . At this sight you will grow radiant, your heart throbbing and full. . . . No more will the sun give you daylight, nor moonlight shine on you, but Yahweh will be your everlasting light, your God will be your splendor. . . . and your days of mourning will be ended (Is 60:1-5, 19f).*

The Kabbalah, the body of Jewish mystical thought that flowered in the Middle Ages, teaches that at the beginning, the one great light that constituted God's creation shattered and split apart into thousands upon thousands of little fragments, sparks of light that became embedded within the separated forms of each living thing, each one seeming to have a separate existence. At the end of time, these sparks would reunite, returning to their original state of unity as one light.

Each of us as we walk this earth seems to be that separated spark, encased in our physical, ego selves. Jesus' ultimate message was that the powers of this world — the dark powers of death — had no hold over him, and so this light of God could not be extinguished in him or in us. He remains the shining symbol of what we are and shall always be. He is, in the phrase of Teilhard de Chardin, the "Omega Point" in which the unity of the world is already found, and towards which it is moving. As we join with him we manifest that light as well, and the darkness of the world is dispelled. The gospel of John teaches that the light of the resurrection is already shining in us and waits only for our acceptance of it. Jesus works with us now to make what has already been, and will be again, the only reality the present can offer us.

Our specific need for Jesus is obvious when we consider the one function we all share of forgiving our ego. We have already discussed the impossibility of becoming free of the quicksand that is our ego life without help from God. The gap between our separated selves — the ego and our true Self — is too great, remaining forever before our frightened eyes as the constant reminder of our sin. Jesus becomes this bridge, and in making a distinction between control and guidance he states in the Course (text, p. 25) that we should allow him to take *control* over everything that does not matter in our lives, turning our fears, anxieties and concerns over to him so that they may be removed from us (the three steps of forgiveness discussed in Part I). This then frees us to place what does matter under his *guidance*. By increasingly turning over to him all the ego interferences, we become freer and freer over time to hear no voice but his, which voice will then simply "guide our feet into the way of peace" (Lk 1:79). Without Jesus' control and guidance to correct our mistakes, we would be left to flounder on our own, unsure of whether we are following the direction of Heaven or of our ego, and without help from within it is certain we will flounder. However holy our desires and aspirations, we shall inevitably be following the dictates of the ego, expressing our own guilt and fear in thought and action and fulfilling the wishes of our ego-master on earth, rather than of our Father in Heaven.

We bring our guilt and fear as gifts to the altar of truth, where Jesus comes to us with his gifts of forgiveness and love. There they meet; and there only one remains. In the light of the truth Jesus brings to us from God, the darkness of the ego's world disappears. As Isaiah wrote: "Whoever walks in darkness, and has no light shining for him, let him trust in the name of Yahweh, let him lean on his God" (Is 50:10).

Jesus for us represents God's help, and it is our trust in him that enables us to find our true Self, being able once again to choose the strength of Heaven as our support and the light of truth as our guide. Without this help, sent to us from God, we would forever be stuck in the world of illusion we have called home, believing the separation from our Father to be real and forever beyond His healing and forgiving love. Jesus showed this is not so, and makes his home in us that we may make his home our own.

We cannot follow Jesus without this faith. The pressures of the world are too great and the power of our fear and guilt too overwhelming. Without our awareness of the strength Jesus gives us, we would not be able to continue. In him is our salvation already attained, for all our errors have been undone and wait but for our acceptance of their healing. He is the way, the truth and the life, and in taking his hand we are led to our one reality with him. To stand before the world and say, "This is my brother Jesus," is to acknowledge our oneness with him and in God.

We are told that faith is a gift of God. Yet how could it be that God's gifts are withheld from any of the children He loves? God's gift of Jesus, in whom are all the others found, has already been given to us. He but waits for us to accept them into our lives. In the gospels Jesus asks us not to be ashamed of him, for then he cannot help us. This is the real meaning of the otherwise threatening words in Luke: "For if anyone is ashamed of me and of my words, of him the Son of Man will be ashamed when he comes in his own glory and in the glory of the Father and the holy angels" (Lk 9:26). Our lack of faith in him results from our own fear and shame, not from Heaven's withholding.

As we have seen, Jesus stands at the door and knocks, waiting for our invitation to enter and abide with us: "Look, I am standing at the door, knocking. If one of you hears me calling and opens the door, I will come in to share his meal, side by side with him" (Rv 3:20). To speak of our unworthiness to have such a guest, to feel embarrassed by confessing our love and need for him, to experience fear of what his presence might mean, to deny the meaning that he *does* truly have for us — all these are but ego reactions reflecting our secret wish to remain separated from God, the only Source of life and joy this world contains for us.

To deny Jesus *is* to deny ourselves and our true identity in God. He asks only that we accept his love, not for his sake but for ours. In him we find God's answer to our prayer for life in a world of death. Through our love for Jesus, the world shines in light so radiant that we cannot help but rush to join with it. Rejoicing in Jesus our brother, we call all people brother and sister, loving them as we love him and as he loves us. He has told us that he is the vine and we are its branches (Jn 15:5). Cut off from him, we can literally do nothing but wither in the prison of fear; but joined with him, his strength becomes our own, and the fruits of our lives become the fruits of his kingdom.

Jesus calls to us that we accept his help. What peace is ours when at last we reach out for the hand that has never stopped reaching for ours! Imagine the joy in Heaven as our hands meet, for in that instant is the resurrection renewed and the world of fear and death once more transcended. In that same instant, the love of God is freed to embrace His children, drawing each of us back into His heart and to the oneness of His creation.

3. Our Gift to Jesus

As we learn Jesus' lesson of forgiveness, love and unity, he asks us to teach it to the world. He asks us now to bring it to others who "hear and hear again, but do not understand; see and see again, but do not perceive" (Is 6:9). He sends us out into the darkness of the world, not to preach the light, but to *be* the light. He exemplifies for us the perfect unity of his message with his life, the unity he wants us to exemplify as he did.

To speak his words of forgiveness without this same forgiveness expressed in our hearts would be to teach both forgiveness and unforgiveness as one; this conflict would then become our teaching message, and the one we would be learning as well. As the Course repeatedly emphasizes, as we teach so shall we learn. Jesus is there to teach his lesson to us in all the opportunities that our egos have provided. Joining us in them, he teaches us how look at all things as instruments of forgiveness, "healing . . . [our] perception of separation" (text, p. 41).

There is perhaps one last gift he would ask from us, though not for himself. This is the gift of gratitude. Our gratitude to Jesus is the expression of our gratitude to God for the gifts He has given us. It is born of the awareness that our Father has never left us, though in our deluded minds we believe we have left Him. The awareness of his presence and our gratitude for it, therefore, become another "way in which He [God] is remembered, for love cannot be far behind a grateful heart and thankful mind" (manual, p. 55).

Jesus led the way back to God. How could we not be grateful to him? He has asked from us only the gifts he wishes to bring to us. Our gratitude to him is the acceptance of these gifts of love. In Jesus we find the shining picture of who we truly are, the Christ whom God created one with Him. In Jesus we find not only the goal, but the loving hand that reaches back to lift us up to it. Our gratitude to him is reflected in our clasping his hand as his clasps ours, saying "Yes" to his plea on our behalf. In his clear and radiant eyes, we see the innocence our Father knows to be the light of all His children; and we give thanks we have not been left to wander uncertainly in a world dark with fear. In the midst of this ego hell, we hear Jesus call to us:

> *My brothers in salvation, do not fail to hear my voice and listen to my words. I ask for nothing but your own release. There is no place for hell within a world whose loveliness can yet be so intense and so inclusive it is but a step from there to Heaven. To your tired eyes I bring a vision of a different*

> *world, so new and clean and fresh you will forget the pain and sorrow that you saw before. Yet this a vision is which you must share with everyone you see, for otherwise you will behold it not. To give this gift is how to make it yours. And God ordained, in loving kindness, that it be for you (text, p. 621).*

When confronted by the dark despair buried deep within our hearts, seeing no way to be free from it, who would not be overwhelmed with gratitude to feel a comforting hand on the shoulder, a presence of gentle light, a reassuring word? When learning at last this light has a name, a certain identity, who would not be filled with tears at its sound, at its very taste upon one's lips when it is spoken? Who would not, upon discovering the personal love in the midst of the light, leave all darkness behind and fly to his open, welcoming arms?

Who would not, in joyous gratitude for his great gift of love and life and hope, do all he asked to bring this gift to others, so that all may share in it as one, letting the joyous "Thank You" resound in every instant salvation is offered to another and accepted in ourselves? Who would not, in all humility, love and gratitude, stand before him with empty hands and a lifted heart, and echo the words of every prophet since Abraham: "Here I am, Lord, I've come to do your will"?

EPILOGUE: TEACHING THE MESSAGE

The lesson Jesus came to teach was that pain, suffering and hurt, even unto death, are nothing but illusions of the ego. "The Prince of Peace was born to re-establish the condition of love by teaching that communication remains unbroken even if the body is destroyed" (text, p. 305). The greatest temptation of this world is to believe that one is a victim, unfairly treated by forces outside one's mind. Thus, Jesus asks us to take him as our "model for learning, since an extreme example is a particularly helpful learning device" (text, p. 84).

In the Course, Jesus says further:

> *The journey to the cross should be the last "useless journey." Do not dwell upon it, but dismiss it as accomplished. If you can accept it as your own last useless journey, you are also free to join my resurrection. . . . Do not make the pathetic error of "clinging to the old rugged cross." The only message of the crucifixion is that you can overcome the cross. Until then you are free to crucify yourself as often as you choose. This is not the Gospel I intended to offer you (text, p. 47).*

The crucifixion is the symbol of suffering, sacrifice and the death of innocence at the hands of sin. To feel victimized by the actions or decisions of others, or helpless in the face of "natural forces" or the forces of sickness, are all different names for the same mistake of believing that God is unjust and that we are His victims, deserving His punishment because of our sinfulness.

In the midst of this ego's insanity of sin, Jesus calls to speak a work of sanity. His forgiveness, given him by the Holy Spirit, is the gift he has given to us. "Hear me, my brothers, hear and join with me" (text, p. 621) in bringing this message of hope and peace to a world that long ago abandoned them. However, we cannot bring this message as long as we believe we are unfairly treated, innocent victims of a cruel and sinful world. *There is no world,* Jesus taught us, only a belief in it. Good and evil, victims and victimizers, life and death — all contrasts, differences and separation — disappeared in the shining light of his forgiveness. *There is no world,* proclaims this light, so how can an unreal world victimize? By learning and teaching this lesson to each other, we are released from the chains of guilt that made and sustain this world. The world *was* made as an attack on God, but since God did not recognize the attack the sin was forgiven, never having happened.

Completing his own Atonement path, Jesus is able now to help each of us do the same. He is the clearest model for making this decision to forgive — the condition for accepting God's kingdom — and Jesus' risen life is the witness to this statement we would hear in our prayers: "There can be no victims in a world where I am present." To identify as a victim denies his lesson and living presence within us. "Teach not that I died in vain," Jesus urges in the Course, "teach rather that I did not die by demonstrating that I live in you" (text, p. 193). He asks each of us, as his apostle in the world, to teach with him that he lives by identifying with the message of the resurrection, not the world's understanding of the crucifixion.

The road to hell is a long and wearying one, strewn with bodies that suffer at the hands of injustice. Forgiveness reverses this path instantly, reinterpreting injustice as a call for love, embracing all of us in this call and in its answer. Were it not for Jesus' perfect love, forgiveness would have been impossible. In his eyes no injustice *was* done, for only an ego can be unjustly treated. Repeating this quote from the Course, which would reflect the Course's principal ethic: "Where there is love, your brother must give it to you because of what it is. But where there is a call for love, you must give it because of what you are" (text, p. 275). Jesus was able to give it because he knew who he was and who his Father was. Because love was his only identity, that is what he taught. From such certainty, attack, defense and unforgiveness became unthinkable. *All* people were seen as one, and illusions of separateness were not accorded the power to destroy this oneness. Jesus' resurrection conclusively demonstrated that death has no hold over life. As the Course states, quoting from the *Bhagavad Gita:* "How can the immortal die?" (text, p. 375). Thus, nothing in the world

—no law, however sacrosanct it might seem — can interfere with the Will of God and make His children unlike to Him.

Jesus, therefore, asks us not to atone for sin through suffering — punishing others or ourselves — but rather asks that we atone through forgiveness as he did, correcting our misperceptions and thus healing the world's. It is the *belief* in our sinfulness that teaches us we are sinful. Jesus came to teach us we were simply mistaken: God's own image and likeness is invulnerable to the "sinful" forces of the world.

This, then, is Jesus' message to us all: to choose between sin and forgiveness, death and life, the ego and God. His life, death and resurrection hold this message clearly for us. The Course states it thus: "Teach only love, for that is what you are" (text, p. 87). It is the same choice Moses presented to the Children of Israel: "I set before you life or death, blessing or curse. Choose life, then, so that you and your descendents may live, in the love of . . . your God" (Dt 30:19). It now remains for us to choose to share in the peace and joy that is the eternal life Jesus offered us, and to teach with him the message of love the world has forgotten.

Now has a different dream come into the world: a dream of the Holy Spirit's justice in place of the ego's nightmare. Now can salvation's joyous song ring out through us from Him to all the world still enslaved by thoughts of sin. What died on the cross was the belief in the cross. What lives is the exultant cry of forgiveness, shouted in gladness by all who choose to live again with Jesus, that this call of love to love will nevermore be silenced. "Let this call live, my brothers and sisters," Jesus asks of us, "and let it live through your forgiveness of the world and of yourselves. Now we begin again, and what we have begun, God Himself has promised to complete."

APPENDIX

ABBREVIATIONS FOR SCRIPTURAL REFERENCES

OLD TESTAMENT

Gn .... Genesis
Ex .... Exodus
Lv .... Leviticus
Nb .... Numbers
Dt .... Deuteronomy
Ps .... Psalms
Ws .... Wisdom
Is .... Isaiah
Jr .... Jeremiah
Ezk .... Ezekiel
Ho .... Hosea
Jon .... Jonah
Mi .... Micah
Hab .... Habakkuk
Ml .... Malachi

NEW TESTAMENT

Mt .... Matthew
Mk .... Mark
Lk .... Luke
Jn .... John
Ac .... Acts
Rm .... Romans
1 Co .... 1 Corinthians
Ga .... Galatians
Ep .... Ephesians
Ph .... Philippians
Col .... Colossians
2 Th .... 2 Thessalonians
2 Tm .... 2 Timothy
Tt .... Titus
Heb .... Hebrews
Jm .... James
1 P .... 1 Peter
1 Jn .... 1 John
Rv .... Revelation

SCRIPTURAL INDEX

Old Testament

New Testament

SELECTED INCIDENTS, PARABLES, ETC.

Old Testament

New Testament

Parables